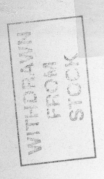

THE LITTLE LAND OF
CORNWALL

A.L. ROWSE

THE LITTLE LAND OF
CORNWALL

A.L. ROWSE

ALAN SUTTON
1986

ALAN SUTTON PUBLISHING
BRUNSWICK ROAD · GLOUCESTER

First Published 1986

Rowse, A.L.
    The little land of Cornwall.
    1. Cornwall—History
    I. Title
    942.3'7   DA670.C8

ISBN 0-86299-265-6

Cover picture: St Michael's Mount
by William Casley. Private Collection

Typesetting and origination by
Alan Sutton Publishing Limited
Photoset Goudy 11/12
Printed in Great Britain by
The Guernsey Press Company Limited
Guernsey, Channel Islands

To
Diana Colville of Penheale
for her love of Cornwall

Contents

Preface

I confess to some difficulty about my title: I should like to have called this book 'The Little Land' without having to qualify it. For 'the Little Land', just like that, is my private name for Cornwall, with its own strong individuality and character, history, tradition and folklore.

Today appearances are rather against us, with the swamping of Cornishry by the hordes of holiday makers, trippers, immigrants from England and Scotland, even from Ireland. So much so that we hear of 'Vanishing Cornwall'.

But that is just to look at the surfaces of things. It is the business of the historian and poet to look beneath the surface. Surfaces vanish, are evanescent. To the historian there is something continuous and permanent in the Cornwall of his knowledge and imagination. A little land of historic fact – as to the poet, of vision and consolation: places alive to the discerning mind in tune with their memories, even when in ruin or vanished in the appalling, over-trampled society we live in.

We can turn our backs on all that, as I do, withdraw as Celts are supposed to do into ourselves, into the living past which is history, or the lore which is the silted-up life of a people.

Here are the evidences.

I am glad of the opportunity to reprint the short history of my native parish of St. Austell, originally written to start a fund for the repair of the church. It has long been out of print and unobtainable, and I am often asked for it. I am happy to make it available for a larger public – as with other pieces, like that which explains the difference between the Duchy of Cornwall, and the County.

I make grateful acknowledgment to those periodicals, too varied to mention, in which some of these pieces originally appeared: now revised and brought up to date. Two new essays appear here for the first time: 'Place, Fowey, and the Treffrys', and 'Joseph Thomas Treffry: Industrial Leader.'

A.L.R.

The Seven Landscapes of Cornwall

The diversity of landscape within the little land of Cornwall – sticking out into the Atlantic like a foot, some seventy miles in length and not much more than twenty at most in breadth – is usually unrealised, except by those who know it intimately.

Cornwall is almost wholly surrounded by sea; even the frontier with England is mostly water – the whole length of the river Tamar. Most visitors coming into Cornwall come for the sake of the sea, the coast and the beaches; so they don't realise the variety and beauty of the landscape within. Especially if they come, as they mostly do, by A30 along the high spine of the county, across Bodmin Moor and Goss Moor, on through the bleak old mining country of Redruth and Camborne to the last uttermost peninsula, to Land's End.

Myself, a primitive inhabitant, indigenous and autochthonous, one of the natives, I reckon up more than half-a-dozen landscapes in Cornwall. Even if you think only in terms of cliff and coastal scenery, there are two or three. Addicts of North Cornwall will think first of the stupendous cliffs facing the Atlantic all the way down from Bude to Newquay. Some of these have a sheer drop of 700 feet into the sea – and how wonderful to look down on a summer's day from the churchyard of St. Gennys or above Crackington Haven to the heaving silence of blue far beneath. Still more, to confront the winter wind above Bedruthan Steps – sometimes I have been hardly able to stand against it: a wall of wind. The south coast scenery is much quieter; we have good cliffs and headlands here too, but of a more lyrical beauty, where the north coast is epic. And what about the sand-dune country, the towans of Perranporth and Hayle, and around the lovely Padstow estuary? We on the south have them too – Whitsand Bay, Pentewan, Marazion.

So here are three quite different coastal landscapes to enjoy.

I love the inland landscapes no less, possibly even more. Tamarside, for instance: all that unspoiled country of intricate river valleys running down from Launceston to Plymouth. Further south the tide comes right up those drowned valleys to Calstock or St. Germans, making lesser estuaries to explore, like the last and grandest of them all – the Hamoaze that divides Devon from Cornwall, Plymouth from Saltash. Here are the two great bridges – Brunel's 1859 railway bridge and the post-war road-bridge – to tell visitors that they are entering a different little land on its own.

Everywhere the river-valleys are exquisite, deep and winding – mostly on the south side: the Looe, the Fowey, the Fal and Helford. Stand in the churchyard of St. Winnow on the riverbank of the Fowey – the old grey church of the Saint behind you, complete with bench-ends, rood-screen, medieval heraldic window – and look across to the Arthurian woods of Lantyne and down river to the turn towards the open haven at Fowey, the tide running up the channel with a fresh breeze from the sea, invisible but making its presence felt. Or the secret places of the Fal – sequestered Lamorran, the flats of Ruan-lanihorne, an occasional heron flapping its great wing-spread, or the river-birds congregated at Ardevora Veor. Or, again, the trout-brown pools of the Lynher or upper Tamar at Trecarell or Poulson Bridge . . .

Those on the north – the Camel and the Hayle – have a different inflexion, barer and more sparse, with a paler, subtler colouring: those grey bent sedges, the willows like olive trees, grey-green, the tamarisk feathers over the wastes of sand.

My own secret love is for the edges of the moor: those parishes like Blisland or Northill where the bare moor tumbles down into good farming soil. An English friend of mine has pointed out to me how wonderfully the northern *massif* of Bodmin Moor looks, Rowtor and all, when you look back towards it south from St. Teath.

What a day in that country this summer! – a cloudless day in St. Kew parish, standing on an old prehistoric barrow whence I could see five church towers, the pinnacles of St. Endellion pricking up like ears above the horizon.

What about the corrugated lunar landscape of the St. Austell china-clay country – in the moonlight, under snow? I once saw an *aurora borealis* up there on a snowy day, by Hensbarrow, over a thousand feet up.

Or there is the last remote hilly Penwith peninsula – Zennor, Trencrom Hill, St. Buryan – so granitty and strange, almost sinister with its longstones and cromlechs and stone circles:

Home of the silent vanished races . . . to which we Cornish belong.

The Contribution of Cornwall and Cornishmen to Britain

It is an honour to be asked to give this lecture,[1] especially since I had the privilege of knowing George Johnstone in his later years. His friendship I greatly valued; but no less I admired him for the fortitude with which he confronted life, after an accident – very nearly fatal – had robbed him of the capacity of physical movement. He did not allow this to daunt him: he conducted his gardening operations from an electrical chair, and made himself one of the great horticulturists of his age, the creator of the beautiful garden of Trewithen. His splendid book on *The Asiatic Magnolia*, a work of art no less than of science, is a masterpiece of its kind.

George Johnstone was a man of gifts; though I cannot share his technical expertise. I can pay tribute from personal experience to his quality as a man. Courage, in face of what might have been overwhelming discouragement, constant and continued public spirit, personal kindness: these were the qualities that stood forth in him and enabled him to turn near-disaster into triumph – encouragement and inspiration for us all.

When the Cambridge historian, F.W. Maitland, came over to Oxford and chose to lecture on the town-fields of Cambridge, he apologised gracefully by saying, 'What fields has not Oxford made her own?'

1. The George Johnstone Lecture at Seale-Hayne College, at Newton Abbot, Devon.

4

Similarly, when a Cornishman comes up to Devon to speak about his native Cornwall, he recognises that it is a case of 'Friend, come up higher'. It was suggested that I might take as my subject the contribution of the West Country in general and deal with Devon along with Cornwall. There are several reasons against that course, one of them being that I am not competent to deal with Devon. Another is that they are really very diverse. Devon is a part of England; Cornwall is not, any more than Wales is.

The Cornish are a distinctive people, even according to the Oxford English Dictionary definition – a people characterised by common descent, language and history, anchored to their own territory. Anchored? – perhaps a better word would be the modern term 'geared'. For, though a faithful remnant has remained behind in Cornwall, keeping the lights in the windows burning, from all those little harbours and inlets the Cornish have been a keen people for emigrating – as much as the Scotch or Irish. And now the bulk of the Cornish people are overseas, dominantly in the United States, but also strongly represented in Australia, South Africa, Canada and New Zealand. Yet many of them are in a sense still 'geared' to Cornwall and refer to it as 'home' or 'back home'. A Harvard Cornishman told me that, of all the British stocks in the United States, the Cornish were the most addicted to going back to their native heath, if only on visits.

There is a horrid word in modern American historiography, 'filiopietistic' – I don't know what pedant invented it: it only means loyal, nothing worse, the loyalty of the native son. Devon is three times the size of Cornwall, and more than three times grander; but I hope you will not think it merely filiopietistic of me if I claim that the contribution of Cornwall to Britain and the world is not unworthy of comparison with Devon's. Of course we cannot bear a candle to Devon's blaze of illumination in the cultivated arts, particularly that of painting: Nicholas Hilliard of Exeter, first among Elizabethan painters; Turner, arguably the greatest of all English artists; Sir Joshua Reynolds, not to mention Northcote and others. And in literature we have no one to compare with your Coleridges. 'Q', Quiller-Couch, though he devoted himself to Cornwall, we really share with you: he was a Devonian, from the Newton Abbot area, on his mother's side.

So far as the arts are concerned the Cornish have not been a particularly cultivated people. But, it may not be generally realised, in sea-faring, in producing famous seamen, Cornwall can almost come up to Devon's record; and in everything to do with mining, mine-engineering, science and technology, we surpass.

Not with the Elizabethan seamen, however, whom the great Devon historian, James Anthony Froude, made his subject: we were still backward then, not yet fully emerged from our Celtic Middle Ages. But when you come to the 18th century, Admiral Hawke, son of a yeoman farmer of the parish of St. Clether, victor of Quiberon Bay that settled the hash of the French fleet during the Seven Years' War, was one of the three or four decisive figures in the nation's naval history. Admiral Boscawen, son of a famous if noble family, comes not far behind; so, too, Admiral Pellew of Penryn and the reduction of Algiers, who took his title from Exmouth and whose family moved up into quiet Devon pastures at Canonteign. Nor must we omit that much-maligned man, Bligh of the *Bounty*, whose only real failing was a lack of a sense of humour. There have been many others who have made their contributions to naval history – Killigrews, Trelawnys, Trelawny-Jago in the Arctic, Penroses, in our own time Bernard Rawlings, Admiral Vian, and gallant Robert Hichens of Falmouth, who developed the technique of fighting motor-gunboats.

Out of the remote Celtic past looms the figure of Arthur – popularly called King Arthur. We need not doubt that there was such a historic personage; but was he a Cornishman? You dared not deny that he was, or that he was still alive, in Cornwall in the Middle Ages: a visiting French cleric denied it in the church at Bodmin in the 12th century – and there was at once effusion of blood, and the church had, in the usual medieval manner, to be fumigated (as it were) and re-consecrated. One could always produce a riot in the medieval university of Paris – medieval universities were much given to student disturbances – by teasing the Bretons that Arthur wasn't still alive. All the Celtic peoples of Britain staked out a claim in Arthur; but, in some undeniable, if unfathomable, fashion the Arthurian story and its concomitants, Mark and Tristram and Iseult, are tethered to Cornwall. I do not know how much importance to attach to the collocation of names around the river Fowey – the Drustans-fili-Cunomori stone near Kilmarth, Castle Dore and Lantyne (the Lancien of the medieval French romances) – and the Fal, Malpas and Moresk (Maupas and Morois). But when I reflect that modern archaeology has revealed at Tintagel beneath the Norman castle a Celtic monastery of the Age of the Saints, and beneath that a prehistoric earthwork, I do not find it difficult to believe that something significant is attached to that impregnable fastness.

We owe the proliferation of the Arthur and Tristram stories in the literature and art of Europe to Geoffrey of Monmouth's *History of the Kings of Britain* – the most influential book ever to be written in Oxford. Taken altogether, the Arthurian myth has had a wider creative influence in European art and culture than perhaps any other, except the Christian myth itself. If we consider its reflections in English literature alone, from Malory to Spenser, or in Tennyson and Matthew Arnold,

Swinburne and Thomas Hardy, we see how inevitably men's imaginations have linked Arthur, King Mark and Tristan with Cornwall.

I pass over the Age of the Saints, which has left so many traces in place-names, church-dedications, holy wells and wayside crosses in Cornwall – with their extension into Devon too – for the saints mainly came to us from South Wales, and took Cornwall in their stride, on their way to wider mission-fields in Brittany. Cornwall does not seem to have been much given to producing saints. Certainly not such a saint as Devon's St. Boniface, one of the formative figures of Europe, who converted the Germans to Christianity – though he does not seem to have gone far enough, before he was martyred.

We come to good, firm, mineral ground with tin, which gave Cornwall its importance in European trade from prehistoric times. Then, in the Middle Ages, tin was essential to the making of pewter, and Cornwall was the chief and indispensable source of tin. The royal earldom, which was constituted by William the Conqueror for his half-brother, Robert of Mortain, after the Conquest, enjoyed royalties and coignage rights from Cornish tin. It was from these revenues – the surplus-value (to use a Marxist term) from impoverished Cornish tinners that Henry III's brother, Richard, was able to purchase his election as King of the Romans; i.e. a lot of money went into bribing the German electors to make him the successor as Holy Roman Emperor which he never became.

In 1337 Edward III erected out of the earldom the Duchy of Cornwall for the support of the sovereign's eldest son; confirmed by act of parliament, this is the peculiar institution as closely intertwined with Cornwall as an ivy tree on a beech – an institution which some people mistake for the county. The Duchy owns a great deal of property in Cornwall – increasingly more as the

8

local landowners fold up – but it owns more outside, most of Dartmoor for example, and a lot of land in South London.

We would not wish that proportion to increase, though it must be relatively less in modern circumstances than in the past. Charles Henderson used to think that it was owing to this outsize burden Cornwall had to support – rents, dues, royalties, coignage, officials – that the county had no indigenous peerage right through the Middle Ages and even up to the 17th century, unlike a normal county. There just wasn't room for good-sized trees to grow up. It is significant that the first Cornish peerage was founded on tin-dealing and trading, in the Roberts family of Truro – better known to us as Robartes. One of the charges in the impeachment of the Duke of Buckingham was that he had received £5,000 for the honour from the new peer. The answer came that he had been offered £10,000 for it before. These things have been bought and sold from the beginning. The Robartses were a very upright Puritan and Parliamentarian family. The second lord, a severe and self-righteous Presbyterian, was an able man, leader of the Parliamentarian cause in the West during the Civil War and, disappointed with the outcome in Cromwell's military dictatorship, became one of the architects of the Restoration of Charles II. The old lord's successful attempt to protect the virtue of his beautiful young wife from the attempts on it of Charles's brother, James – that 'known enemy of chastity' – makes amusing reading in Anthony Hamilton's naughty *Memoirs of the Restoration Court.*

When we were young, influenced perhaps by Q's tale *The Splendid Spur*, we were apt to take a 'romantic' view of the Civil War. Or to take sides, Cavalier or Parliamentarian, according to our prejudices, Church or Chapel. We can take a more adult view of it now, after the disillusioning events of our own appalling century:

we appreciate that a breakdown of government at the centre, as happened with the Stuarts, left the gate open for the usual collective foolery of human beings to be given its chance. We used to think of the 'heroic' events of the Civil War, of the 'heroism' indeed displayed by individuals on either side, poor fellows. But our final judgement on the Civil War, in this age inured to such displays of human folly, must be that of 'Hudibras' Butler:

> When civil fury first grew high
> And men fell out, they knew not why . . .
> And made them fight, like mad or drunk,
> For Dame Religion as for punk,
> Whose honesty they all durst swear for,
> Though not a man of them knew wherefore . . .

Cornwall made a valiant contribution to the conflict – if indeed it was worth making – raised a little army for the King that fought its way through the battles of Stratton, Lansdown, Roundway Down, till it was decimated (in the literal sense of the word) at the siege of Bristol, lost most of its leaders and its effectiveness as a fighting force. That was in 1643. In 1644 two armies entered Cornwall, the Parliamentarian under Essex, which surrendered to the King's. All this had no effect on the outcome of the war, which was decided elsewhere, at Marston Moor and Naseby. After that Cromwell's victorious army entered Cornwall and the Royalist cause was beaten. Three armies in as many years! The little land was eaten up, besides being exhausted by its efforts. I am sure it has not been realised what a terrible experience the Civil War was for the Cornish people, how much they suffered and endured and paid out – certainly for the conflicts and convictions of their betters, and all to no effect. It ended in the military dictatorship of Cromwell, which nobody intended, certainly not himself.

When Cromwell died and this hiatus came to an end, the two sections of the upper classes, whose conflict had made the war, came together to patch things up and make a moderate settlement, which could have been had twenty years before. In this sensible, unidealistic settlement the West Country was well represented. Indeed the person who chiefly brought it about was a Devonshireman, General Monk – whom the cynical restored monarch was able to salute as 'Father of his Country'; while in the negotiations that brought about the restoration of King and Parliament, Monk's cousin, Sir John Grenville, played a useful part. The old Parliamentarian Lord Robartes became a prominent figure in the government of the restored monarchy, as Lord Lieutenant of Ireland, Lord Privy Seal and Lord President of the Council. The motto of the settlement was 'Never Again'! The aristocracy resumed its natural right to govern at the centre; in the country the natural alliance of squire and parson kept the lower classes in order – right up to the social revolution of our time. Now it is all over. But, when arrived at, it provided a stable foundation upon which the nation could thrive and accomplish great things, forge both a trading empire and an industrial revolution which changed the face of the world.

It is in this last that Cornwall made its most significant contribution – evidences of which are scattered all over the outside world today. It is difficult for us to visualise Cornwall, a favourite resort area of the welfare-state masses, as a hub of the Industrial Revolution, smoke pouring from hundreds of chimneys of mines, foundries, and eventually china-clay pits. But so it was; Cornwall's heyday was the age of steam, and intimately bound up with its development. Many of us here will remember its last phase, as I do in the china-clay area.

It began early in the 18th century with Newcomen's primitive steam-engine developed at Dartmouth. This enabled the mines to be worked more deeply, pumping the water out. The decisive step was taken by James Watt, the Scotsman, whose engine used steam as force: this was the basis of the famous Cornish beam-engine which, constantly improved in design and performance, was in use principally in mines, but also for pumping in waterworks, canals, etc. all over the world in the age of steam. The largest and most famous of these engines is a national monument in Holland: constructed by the historic foundry of Harvey's at Hayle,[2] it was used to drain the Haarlem Meer – now proudly exhibited in its Gothic engine-house outside Haarlem.

The development of the Cornish beam-engine went along with the development of the mines and the technique of mining: reacting on each other, each rendered the other possible. The second quarter of the 19th century, 1825–1850, was an intensely competitive period in raising the performance of the engines, i.e. the amount of water raised for coal consumed. A whole generation of engineers – Hornblowers, Trevithicks, Arthur Woolf, Sims, Taylor – devoted themselves to improving the 'duty' – intense competition prevailed among the engineers, as with other people over horse-racing, excitement among the men as today over football-matches. By 1850 the Cornish beam-engine had reached its peak of perfection. 'By 1850 Cornishmen had more experience of deep mining, and with it deep-pumping, than the rest of the world together.'[3] The result was that Cornish engines and Cornish engineers to work them were in request all round the world.

This was a consequence of the immense development of the mining in the first half of the 19th century. There always had been tin, but during this period copper took precedence. From 1800 to the 1830s Cornwall produced

2. v. E. Vale, *The Harveys of Hayle.*
3. D.B. Barton, *The Cornish Beam Engine*, 252.

two-thirds of the world's copper; in the 1850s it still produced one-quarter. In the middle of the 1860s copper-mining collapsed; tin continued for some decades, gradually declining. At the peak there were some 650 beam-engines at work, with another 60 in West Devon. The collapse of mining meant the export of many of these engines to other parts of Britain or abroad, along with the thousands of miners leaving Cornwall every decade from the 1830s, to build up the mining wealth and expertise of the United States and Canada, Australia and South Africa. This flow of emigration has had marked effects in the peopling of those countries, a distinctive contribution in building them up, observable today.

It is the earlier creative period, before and after 1800, that is most fascinating to look back upon, when everything was being hammered out and forged, engineering problems were tackled and worked out, steam-locomotion brought to birth, Trevithick's first steam-locomotive run up Camborne Hill, Humphry Davy making his first experiments with gases and elements. This is the age of Richard Trevithick and Humphry Davy, of Davies Gilbert, President of the Royal Society, and John Opie of the Royal Academy; the heyday of the remarkable Williams family, with their business ability in several generations, of entrepreneurs and patrons of enterprise, like Francis Basset, Sir Christopher Hawkins, Sir Charles Lemon, the scientific (and Quaker) Foxes. A little later there was the no less remarkable work of the Vivian family in the industrial development of Swansea – a complex of activities deserving a whole volume in itself. This was also the age that sent Henry Martyn abroad on his missionary and linguistic exploits in India, forerunner of the Colensos in Natal and New Zealand.

Davies Gilbert's career is a portent of the future. Born Davies Giddy, the son of a tin-dealing curate at the charming old farm of Tredrea in St. Erth, he made no important inventions himself, though he did apply his mathematical knowledge to aid in solving the engineering problems of his *protégés*. In the end he became a scientific adviser to the government; refusing the confinement, and the frustrations, of office he was able to become a sort of unofficial Minister of Technology. He advised government on a whole range of technical questions from agriculture to currency, on building trunk roads and harbours, the harnessing of steam-power to industry, food supplies for the increasing population, poor laws to help in periods of trade-depression and unemployment, the building of bridges such as the famous Menai Suspension Bridge – in such matters this country then led the world. To how many politicians is it given to live such useful, creative lives?[4]

I detect a tendency among some recent writers on the Industrial Revolution in Cornwall to decry the work of Richard Trevithick as inventor – and certainly he was his own worst enemy, with more than the usual defects of the Celtic temperament. Of his many individual inventions I am incompetent to speak, having no mechanical bent whatever. But Mr. Rolt, who has, tells us that Trevithick's 'genius did not stop with the development of the high-pressure engine. Trevithick patented the use of iron tanks in ships and an iron floating dock, he built a steam tug-boat, a steam winch, a dredger, and a steam agricultural cultivator.'[5] It is by a pleasant historical propriety that Trevithick's little portable steam-engine for agricultural use was purchased by Sir Christopher Hawkins – Mr. G.H. Johnstone's family predecessor at Trewithen – and set to thresh corn. This was the first practical agricultural steam-engine: it worked well for many years at Trewithen and earned its

4. Cf. A.C. Todd's biography of him, *Beyond the Blaze*.
5. L.T.C. Rolt, *The Cornish Giant. The Story of Richard Trevithick*, 112.

historic place now in the Science Museum. No one can take away from him his fundamental achievement, that he was the inventor of the steam-locomotive, the first person to make a steam-engine to move and haul – therefore, the initiator of the Railway Age. It was, perhaps, characteristic that it was left to the application and industry of a North Countryman, the combination of engineering genius with business ability, to reap the profits and the fame.

What are we to say of Sir Humphry Davy? – *the* Cornishman of genius *par excellence*, first of us all, if I were asked to name one. We all know that, when presented with the problem of fire-damp in mines causing the deaths of hundreds of miners, he solved the problem by inventing his safety-lamp, refusing a penny-piece for it. We know that he was the first to demonstrate that sodium and potassium were elements, and also the constitution of chlorine and oxymuriatic acid, besides his investigation of carburetted hydrogen and other gases. He certainly advanced chemistry along the whole front, was a proponent of the application of chemicals to agriculture, and among those taking the lead in the investigation of electricity. There were not wanting unkind friends who said that his greatest discovery was his apprentice, Michael Faraday. In addition to all his discoveries, inventions, experiments, Davy's career was something of a portent: he was the principal propagandist for science. It is true that Davy had to be first in everything he did – but why shouldn't he be? Nothing great is ever accomplished without a man having a good opinion of himself.

Perhaps we may sum up in the words of a contemporary scientist, Sir Harold Hartley: 'Davy's genius lay in chemistry, and his incursions into other subjects were less fruitful. He was the brilliant pioneer of electrochemistry; he exposed the myth of oxygen as the constituent of all acids; he foresaw the grouping of the elements in families; he discovered the principle of the safety lamp - on those his fame will rest . . . His romantic genius made an enduring mark. We can leave him with the epitaph Berzelius wrote. When, after Davy's death, he had tied up the slender bundle of their broken correspondence, he wrote upon it: "the greatest chemist of his time".[6]

I had almost omitted to mention the special contribution of my own area of Cornwall – the unique china-clay industry. We owe the original discovery of china-clay to a Devonian, Cookworthy; but there are no big figures in the history of the industry. We owe its development to a number of canny small men on the spot, yeomen-farmers, tradespeople of the St. Austell district.

What are we to say of the political contribution of Cornwall to the life of the nation?

Most people of education will think first of the 'rotten boroughs' in which we abounded. Up to the Reform Bill of 1832 Cornwall returned 44 members to Parliament as against 45 for the whole of Scotland. This gave the county an undue political importance; but in those days it was interests that were represented, not heads – for what they are worth. Under that unreformed old system able brains were able to get into Parliament at a much earlier age, before they were exhausted – men like the younger Pitt and Fox in their early twenties.

Thus it was that there sat for Cornish seats such people as Sir Francis Drake and Sir Walter Ralegh; Sir Edward Coke, greatest of Common lawyers, and Gibbon, greatest of our historians; John Hampden on one side, Edward Hyde, Lord Clarendon, on the other; among seamen, Admirals Hawke, Rodney, Exmouth, St. Vincent; among soldiers, Wellington before he became a duke. And this is to say nothing of our own

6. Sir H. Hartley, *Humphry Davy*, 148–9.

home products: Sir Richard Grenville of the *Revenge*, Trelawnys, Godolphins, Edgcumbes, Eliots, Boscawens, Carews.

Among these Lord Treasurer Godolphin attained the highest eminence – Queen Anne's Prime Minister during Marlborough's victorious war against Louis XIV, and his closest friend and colleague. Godolphin was really an administrator by nature; he hated party-politics and the arts of publicity and propaganda. The result is that he is the most underrated of Prime Ministers: he held things together for nine years during a long European war, in the midst of which he piloted through the Act of Union with Scotland. This was an achievement of historic importance: the fact that he was a Cornishman may have helped – I doubt if he had the usual English superiority-complex about other peoples within the British Isles, peoples who were here before them.

I have sometimes wondered if there is not a doctrinaire streak among our indigenous politicians. Perhaps this comes from overemphasising the importance of Sir John Eliot, the Parliamentary leader against Charles I – the Whigs of the 18th century and the Liberals of the 19th made a cult of him, martyr to liberty, and all that. The historian attaches less importance to speechifying in Parliament, and more to government, government in the long-term interests of the country – which is what politicians are *for*, if they knew it.

A doctrinaire streak also appears in those more constructive Radicals, Sir William Molesworth, Secretary of State for the Colonies, a chief promoter of the colonisation of Australia and New Zealand, and Charles Buller, principal author of the Durham Report, and thus of the Constitution of Canada. Both these men would have made a bigger mark in history, had they not died young. Leonard Courtney, Lord Courtney of Penwith, conscientious objector to the Boer War, was another doctrinaire who might have gone further but for his doctrinairism. The same might be said of two eminent Liberal M.P.s for Cornish seats in our time, Sir Francis Acland and Isaac Foot – but they were both Devonians.

I have said enough to bear out my original contention that the chief contribution of the Cornish has been in technology and science, mining and seamanship, not in literature and the arts. Yet, curiously enough, a medieval Cornishman, John of Trevisa, is of signal importance in the history of the English language: he was primarily a translator, but his translations helped to shape the form that the language would take in the following centuries. No doubt his linguistic gifts, his genius as a translator, reflected the fact that a 14th century Cornishman would be bilingual.

It is provoking that though the little land, like the Duke of Wellington, has been much exposed to authors, we have only a half share in the more famous names, in the Brontës, in the poets Matthew Arnold and Keats. Even Hawker of Morwenstow, whose poetry is wholly devoted to Cornwall, was a Plymouthian born. Samuel Foote, the 18th century dramatist, and even Q., as I have said, we share with Devon. Though the beauty of the landscape has provided inspiration for whole schools of painters, few of them have been natives: besides Opie, the Bone family of Truro, miniature and enamel painters, Christopher Wood partly, Peter Lanyon and Alfred Wallis. Altogether it is not a great deal – where Devon is incomparable (except only for Suffolk).

There has been a far larger and more significant outpouring overseas. Since I have devoted a book to *The Cornish in America*, I will not duplicate what I have to say there on their idiosyncratic contribution to building up the greatest of modern nations – merely underline that the bulk of the Cornish people are in the United States. In spite of the concentration on mining, their contribution there covers a wide spectrum, from the Quaker founder of West Jersey, Edward Billing, and governors of states, to those eminent families of Pennsylvania, Penroses and Rawles, and a remarkable leader of the American Socialist Party, John Spargo. If only a Cornishman had achieved the Presidency, as so many Scots have done, people would have been more aware of our existence.

In Canada there was the wonderful work of Grenfell of Labrador, doctor and saint – as much of a saint as Henry Martyn in India. Or in India the unique contribution of General Sleeman, who suppressed Thuggee, a dreadful pest of Indian society – they were ritual robbers and murderers – for 500 years. In Central Africa another Grenfell was at work, George Grenfell, intrepid missionary and explorer of the Congo. In Australia we can claim the first of Australian soldiers in Field Marshal Blamey, and today a Prime Minister in Bob Hawke, Cornish on both sides, where his predecessor, Sir Robert Menzies was Cornish on his mother's, a Sampson. In New Zealand similarly with the poet Alan Curnow, and the first of New Zealand naturalists in William Colenso. He was a cousin of Bishop Colenso, famous alike for his epoch-making Higher Criticism of the Bible, as missionary in Natal, and for his defence of the natives against the depredations of the whites. With that gallant Christian gentleman, in my view another saint, we come to a native of my own parish: it is time to call a halt.

But I think I have submitted enough evidence to justify my title – that the contribution of the Cornish is a distinctive one and, conversely, evidence of their claim to be a distinctive people, interesting alike to the historian, the scientist and sociologist.

Borlase's Cornwall

Leicester University has made itself the prime centre for regional, county and local history, under a succession of professors devoted to the subject. Their leading figure, Professor Jack Simmons, has inspired an extensive project of republishing a series of the finest *Classical Country Histories*.

Borlase's *Cornwall* has been given two admirable Introductions, one by Peter Pool on the Man and his Work, the other by Charles Thomas on him as Archaeologist and Field Worker.[1] Borlase merits his place not only as a classic of Cornish scholarship, but high up in the antiquarian succession of his time. He may have been prompted by the contemporary *réclame* of Stukeley; but Borlase never fell for the fantastic theorising that ruined Stukeley's later work, though himself devoting a section of his book to the Druids. In this matter Borlase was constantly trying to think through to the anthropological and religious purpose of the prehistoric monuments that surrounded him – using all the evidence available from classical literary sources as well as from the Old Testament.

This was good comparative method, often revealing in its results and lighting up standing stones, barrows, caers, cromlechs, quoits, urn-burials, and their uses for us. In reading Borlase one feels that the 18th-century

1. W. Borlase: *Antiquities Historical and Monumental of the County of Cornwall*. With a new Introduction by P.A.S. Pool and Charles Thomas.

clergyman had a point as against more rationalist and denuding archaeologists of the next century. He is closer in spirit to the modern archaeologist who derives insights into our earlier societies from evidence from Masai or Australian aborigines.

Even with regard to Borlase's Druids, we may profit from a contemporary view emphasising the ritual significance that these monuments must have had for the people who made and used them. Lady Fox writes in her *South-West England*: 'it is now axiomatic that a barrow is not just a heap of earth or stones covering a burial, but the result of a series of ritual acts and constructions by a community'. Borlase glimpsed that; it is interesting to see to what an extent he and Lady Fox follow a similar method and plan of treatment in their books at the interval of two centuries. Actually it was almost two hundred years before Borlase's book had a successor, in a complete survey of the Cornish field, in Hencken's *The Archaeology of Cornwall and Scilly* (1932).

William Borlase was well situated by circumstances for his life's work, and ideally constituted for it by his interests and habits of mind. Born in 1696 of a family of old Cornish gentry within a few miles of Land's End, he was from the first surrounded by these striking prehistoric objects with which West Cornwall is more crowded – still more numerous then – than any part of the island. After the usual spell at Exeter College, Oxford, he settled down on the shores of Mount's Bay as rector of Ludgvan, to this adding his native parish of St. Just later. His letters give a delightful picture of his life there: 'there is no part of England that abounds so much in the necessaries and at the same time has so many of the elegancies of life as that of Mount's Bay. The gentry, most of whom are our near relations, are of a free frolicking disposition. In the summer time we meet (some ten or a dozen) at a bowling green; there we have built a little pleasure-house and there we dine – after dinner, at bowls, and by so frequently meeting together we are like so many brothers of one family, so united, and so glad to see one the other.'

In fact, Borlase was a conscientious parson and a hard-working man, as his published work and the far larger mass of his unpublished work show. The one heavy drawback to his station was his remoteness from libraries and from intercourse with people of similar intellectual interests. He maintained a large and varied correspondence – that with Stukeley (published in *Cornish Archaeology*, vol. v) was brief – and a number of the Cornish gentry and clergy were interested enough in these matters.

Particularly two of the St. Aubyn baronets of the Mount. The first of these Sir Johns received Sir Robert Walpole's tribute, 'everybody has his price, except the little Cornish baronet'. The second was Borlase's pupil, to whom he dedicated his book: 'I seldom added anything without communicating it to your late excellent father, who – curious as he was in most parts of knowledge and particularly fond of this his native county, received double pleasure from everything remarkable in art, nature, and antiquity, which it was found to contain'. Local patriotism was the inspiration. All the same, Borlase ploughed a lonely furrow. He found it difficult to get books. This reminds us of another point apt to be overlooked – how much easier it is for us with all the aids at our elbow, how much more difficult it was for them in their day to accomplish their work.

Borlase never allowed himself to be discouraged – his mental energy and interests, the inspiration of his life, were too great for that. He told Stukeley 'that share of curiosity which I had imbibed during the time of my education was grown too strong for me, when I settled, to be easily got rid of. My turn was to antiquity . . . and we had a great variety of monuments here which were of the most remote antiquity.' He found himself frequently examining them, taking measurements and notes; but he did not begin to publish until he was well on in his fifties, and then by the encouragement of two Deans of Exeter, Lyttelton and Milles, both Presidents of the Society of Antiquaries. (Professor Thomas is a little apologetic for awarding Borlase the style of antiquary rather than archaeologist – quite unnecessarily: the former is the more venerable title, in both senses of the word.) Borlase was particularly well qualified for an archaeologist, from his equal knowledge of, and good grounding in, geology and mineralogy (he was also a good meteorologist.) In 1750 he was made a Fellow of the Royal Society for his treatise on 'Spar and Sparry Productions, called Cornish Diamonds'; this was the first of thirteen papers contributed to the *Transactions.*

In 1754 Borlase published his *Antiquities*; it went into a second edition in 1769, from which the present is reproduced. In 1756 appeared his *Observations on the Ancient and Present State of the Islands of Scilly*, a pretty quarto containing the results of a fortnight's intensive field-work, along with his reading. One more obstacle to work may be recorded, like that encountered earlier by Edward Lhuyd in his penetration of primitive suspicious Celtic areas. Borlase and his curate were excavating a covered gallery – probably a fogou – on St. Mary's, when a furious storm broke; the islanders would not allow them to resume excavation, for it had provoked the fury of the giants in their graves.

In 1758 there followed Borlase's second big folio, *The Natural History of Cornwall*, covering a very wide field, though with the accent on geology and minerals. These Borlase was collecting all his life; many specimens were sent abroad, to receive encomiums from *savants* like Linnaeus; others decorated Pope's grotto at Twickenham. A residue of fossils was presented to the Ashmolean at Oxford, and at the age of seventy – not yet a fossil himself – his old university made Borlase an honorary Doctor. The old boy was still working at his *Private Thoughts of the Creation and the Deluge*, an attempt to reconcile the facts of a lifetime of observation with the authority of Moses. He had planned a full-scale Parochial History of Cornwall, for which his Memoranda remain, along with his genealogical and armorial collection, his Description of Ludgvan, his Field Note Books, which are yet to be published, and of course his delightful Correspondence, which I would rather have than anything. We much hope for a Life and Letters of this admirable man, by Mr. Pool – quite as good a subject as William Stukeley, if not better. When Borlase died in 1772, what a life's work altogether he had accomplished!

Professor Thomas describes him as a great antiquary, for 'he was among the first to practise systematic field-work, in the sense of the planned first-hand recording of visible antiquities, area by area'. Borlase insisted on the importance of acccurate recording, particularly of measuring – for neglecting which he chides Toland. Hencken hardly appreciated this quality in him forty years ago; but Thomas records that Borlase's notes were so exact that they led him to the rediscovery of St. Ia's lost well and cross at Camborne. Borlase's 'linear observation allows one to make with absolute confidence several similar identifications where monuments have since been moved, or altered, or destroyed'.

Here is a prime utility of his book and field-notes today, when so many objects have disappeared since his time. In the parish of Constantine the tallest of megaliths had recently been broken up: it was over 20 feet high, and made 24 gateposts. When passing a place still called Longstone, in St. Mabyn, I always think of the vanished stone there, which was over 17 feet. To make the road to Charlestown at least one barrow on St. Austell Downs was obliterated in the late 18th century. Borlase noted that the plan-an-guary, or playing place, at St. Just had lately been disfigured by 'injudicious repairs'. The fortified camp of Chegwidden vean in Sancreed, with its fogou or *souterrain*, has gone. The process of destruction in our time has been speeded up, like everything else, with our marvellous equipment for it.

When one thinks of earlier centuries, with less encumbrance all round, how much greater power upon the imagination these prehistoric objects must have had, often dominating the skyline as the tumulus upon Hensbarrow used to do around St. Austell. Borlase sometimes recorded the folklore surrounding these objects. The Men-an-Tol, at Madron, means the stone with the hole: people crawled through the hole for various complaints, children with rickets; local people now call it the Crickstone, good for that Cornish complaint 'crick' in the back. Lovers resorting to it placed crossed pins upon it, to work their desires. One recalls a theme of Estyn Evans' admirable book, *Irish Heritage:* the continuing creativeness of folklore (cf. R.A.F. gremlins, etc.) Borlase notes the Midsummer bonfires (bone-fires) regular in Cornwall in his day, and some snake-lore.

Borlase wrote of the folklore veneration of rocks as of stone-monuments: it was the ritual significance, not merely the material object that held his attention. He realised that early peoples worship standing stones, and collected evidence of their libations not only from the Old Testament and the classics, but from the contemporary Shetlands. Although this came under the heading of Druidism, Borlase knew its purpose; a respectable 18th century clergyman could hardly go into the phallic nature of these cults – that was left to a remarkable anthropologist, Payne Knight, to explore. (Lady Fox has two plates of a Celtic fertility figurine, from South Devon.) The plates in Borlase, of rocks etc., are sometimes a little fantasticated in accordance with rococo taste; but the plans and measured drawings are indispensable, for so many stones have disappeared since, or a monument fallen.

Of magnificent Lanyon Quoit, with its huge capstone of 19 feet resting on three uprights, Borlase tells us that in his time it was so high that a man could sit horseback beneath it. In 1815 it fell (a tremor from Waterloo?), but though reconstructed the stones had been broken, the height lowered. Borlase annotated his account of logan, or rocking stones, from Pliny. The Puritan governor of Pendennis during the Commonwealth threw down the top stone of the fine Logan in Sithney – Borlase got the account from the mss. of Scawen, an earlier antiquary. One sees the Puritan objection to other people's 'superstitions' at work – no idea that their own were equally so; the Cavalier and Tory mind was much more propitious to the study of antiquities, as Alan Everitt has observed in his study of Civil War Kent.

Borlase appreciated that ancient peoples had the powers of removing vast weights of rocks. He was himself convinced that rock-basins were artificial, made by human hands; this is in keeping with his views as to their uses. If Borlase was wrong here, he has had his revenge on later theorists. A Victorian astronomer was able to deduce from the position of the two stones in line with the Men-an-Tol that all was arranged for observation of sunrise, sun-worship, etc. Borlase's drawing shows that they were not in line in the 18th century, but formed a triangle, and this was corroborated by Charles Henderson in our time from an estate map of 1778.

Borlase was strong on the resemblances in idolatrous cults among different peoples, and was alert to the occurrence of human sacrifice. This finds corroboration in Lady Fox's comment on the mound at Kingswear, with at its centre 'a small hole tight-packed with the burnt bones of a child of ten; the primary ritual act implied here is a sacrifice'. When one looks at the evolutionary record, one reflects that (some) humans have come a long way; all the same, what brutes we are, and what brutes we pursue! The evidences are all round us today.

One finds so many respects in which Borlase's instinct, trained by his lifelong habits of observation, seems to have been right. He was perhaps wrong about fogous – the function of which is still in dispute – he thought that their purpose was storage of goods; it seems more likely that they were for ritual uses. He was apparently right about cliff-castles (I write in sight of one, on the Black Head at Trenarren.) Borlase held that they were not refuges for landsmen but landing points for immigrants by sea. Again he was correct in assuming that there were more Roman roads and tracks in Cornwall than 19th century archaeology was willing to recognise. Borlase went up into the church tower – the nearest the 18th century could get to air-photography – to view the country and roads around Stratton, the name of which shows that it was on a street, i.e. a Roman road.

The excavation of Nanstallon camp near Bodmin, by Lady Fox and Professor W. Ravenhill (cf. *Britannia*, III, 56 foll.), has very much illuminated the character of the Roman interest in Cornwall – a backward area, it was mostly marginal. Again Borlase was not wide of the mark. He appreciated that Roman and Romanized buildings were rectangular, as against the curvilinear instinct of the Celts. He notes that collections of coins were apt to turn up along the banks of harbours, and related them to the tin trade. Quite recently a large hoard turned up at Carvossa (the fort with walls), in Probus: excavation revealed a rectangular Roman camp, conveniently placed for transport by the Fal. When we come to the post-Roman period, and the monuments with Latin or Ogam inscriptions, Borlase is corroborated by Lady Fox in pointing out that the majority of the names are Celtic – after the withdrawal of Rome the old Celtic way of life resumed its course in the South West. It was a back-water, the less disturbed because of its material poverty. Hence the South-West pursued an independent line, with a cultural idiosyncrasy of its own, its closest racial affinities with Brittany. This is corroborated in turn by the British migration, so that Roman Armorica became Brittany, the land of the Britons, and by the coming to and fro of the Saints by the seaways along the Atlantic littoral. Turn the map round, and one sees what a unity the western world possessed across

That dolphin-torn, that gong-tormented sea.

Following his excellent logical scheme, which coincided to some extent with the chronological, Borlase ended with the Norman castles. To this he appended, 'for the amusement of the curious', a fanciful List of British rulers from the legendary Brutus, which links him more with Geoffrey of Monmouth than with Lady Fox or Professor Thomas. This is followed by his collections for a Cornish-English vocabulary, of which, though no authority, I derive a favourable impression. Here Borlase was much helped by scholars in the language, like Edward Lluyd and John Keigwin, William Gwavas and Thomas Tonkin, and from Scawen's ms. of *Mount Calvary* with 'a verbal English translation, no small hope for a beginner'.

There is a revival of all this in Cornwall today, with an altogether more informed appreciation of what Borlase accomplished, with little aid, in his day. Professor Thomas tells us that there are plans to publish works of Borlase such as his description of St. Michael's Mount, besides the Field Notes. An Institute of Cornish Studies has been founded under Charles Thomas's leadership, himself the inspirer of *Cornish Archaeology*, altogether more technical and scholastic than dear Borlase. In him Borlase finds his successor, well equipped to carry on the work.

Richard Polwhele as Historian

The Reverend Richard Polwhele, most prolific and miscellaneous of Cornish writers, was a fairly well known figure in his time. Since he was born 6 January 1760 and died in 1838, his long life spanned the reigns of George III, George IV and William IV, and the American and French Revolutions with their accompanying crises and wars. He died in the first year of Queen Victoria's reign, prelude to the blissful century of security and progress won for us by Trafalgar and Waterloo. Something of all this is reflected in this patriotic Cornishman's *History of Cornwall*.

He came from an ancient family of indigenous small gentry, going back to the early Middle Ages, who took their name from their place near Truro, at the northernmost outpost of St Clement's parish, in the church of which he is buried. Born at Truro, while the old family house was under repair, much of his life pivoted upon our remote little capital – or he would have received the more generous recognition his industrious life and multifarious work deserved. He received a good education at Truro Grammar School, which many Cornishmen of note attended. Thence he went to Christ Church, Oxford, which he left unwisely without a degree for a too precocious marriage with a Truro girl; and, when she died, he quickly married again, a Devonshire lass, so that he encumbered himself with a mass of children.

He was no less precocious and philoprogenitive in a literary way, beginning at seventeen by publishing the

Odes to the celebrated Mrs. Catherine Macaulay, which he had 'publickly read to a polite and brilliant audience assembled at Alfred House, Bath'. His next effort was published there too while still a schoolboy; upon which an unkind reviewer – in the way these creatures have – suggested that the Headmaster should have stopped its publication. Nothing, however could stop Polwhele from proliferation. In this same year 1778, at eighteen, he published an Ode to the unfortunate General Burgoyne of the surrender at Saratoga. A few years later there followed *The Follies of Oxford, or cursory sketches on a university education from an Undergraduate to his friend in the country.* Like most such undergraduate efforts this was rather unappreciative of the university opportunities he had neglected.

So he never rose far in the Church, not even to a canonry at Exeter, let alone the deanery his work and application, not to mention his orthodoxy, merited. His *History of Devonshire* came out in parts from 1793 onwards; before completing it in 1806 he had begun publishing his *History of Cornwall*, also in parts from 1803 onwards to 1806. The bibliography of these publications is rather complicated, and for those who like such things, interesting – myself, I am always more interested in the contents of books.

We need say little more about Polwhele's numerous publications, most of them in verse. *The Influence of Local Attachment* received some notice and had some success, running into three editions. Polwhele's prose works are more interesting than his verse, we can still read them for the information they contain. Perhaps the best of them are the autobiographical *Traditions and Recollections* of 1826, and the *Biographical Sketches in Cornwall* of 1831. Polwhele, who seems to have published everything he could lay hands on, did not afflict us with many of his sermons; but he did publish his correspondence with Sir Walter Scott, Davies Gilbert,

President of the Royal Society, Francis Douce, Keeper of Manuscripts at the British Museum, and others who shared his scholarly and antiquarian interests.

He received no recognition from Church or State, and singularly little in the way of preferment. He subsisted most of his life on curacies and then the exiguous vicarages of Manaccan (1794–1821) and St. Anthony-in-Meneage (1809–1821). Not until he was a man of sixty-one did he acquire the better living of Newlyn East (1821–1838). As a Polwhele, a small squire in his own right, he had some means of his own, which he spent on rebuilding or improving the vicarages where he resided, and in the end on planting up the paternal estate of Polwhele to which he retired for his last decade.

His *History of Cornwall*, perhaps unexpectedly, is a remarkably different book from his *History of Devonshire*, not only from difference in subject but in the character of the work. The book about Devon is a county history comparable with that of other county histories in that respect-worthy, indeed distinguished, tradition. But Cornwall is not just another English county: it is a little land on its own, with its own character, its own Celtic language along with its two dialects of English, its astonishing richness in prehistoric antiquities and archaeological remains, its fugitive literature in old Cornish, its own customs and folklore, its people with their recognisable individuality, its roll-call of eminent men, and the history which it has shared with the English.

It all adds up to something very different from Devon, and Polwhele has tried to put it all in, everything he had collected about Cornwall. He never learned to cut and slim and shape up his work; thus this book is more comprehensive and miscellaneous, more of a gallimaufry. One reads in it selectively for the information it contains – one never knows what will turn up next.

Other differences strike the attentive reader. In Devon Polwhele got help and encouragement from the improving gentry around Exeter; one sees the evidence in the numerous plates displaying their elegant new mansions and well laid out parks. Something of the same movement was going on contemporaneously in Cornwall, but on a smaller scale. The most significant thing here at the time was the Industrial Revolution – in mining and the development of steam-power Cornwall was leading the world. This was the area to which the energies of the leading Cornishmen – three generations of the great mining entrepreneurs of the Williams family, Sir Francis Basset, Davies Gilbert, Sir Humphry Davy and later Joseph Austen Treffry. There is something, but not much, of this in Polwhele's *Cornwall*. His mind was firmly turned to the past – not a bad thing for an historian – and he received little support or encouragement from his fellow-Cornishmen.

In his sequestered vicarage near the Lizard, where he wrote his book, he was more isolated than before. He had a few clerical friends among the antiquaries with whom to compare notes, like the Reverend John Whittaker, rector of Ruan-lanihorne (1777–1808), for whom Polwhele had a perhaps exaggerated respect as a Fellow of the Society of Antiquaries. But Whittaker was as isolated in his remote parsonage at Ruan-lanihorne as Polwhele in his. Then Polwhele was a friend of the celebrated General Simcoe, who had a gallant career in the American war (severely wounded at Brandywine), was the first Governor of Upper Canada and came home to command for a time at Plymouth. These contacts did not amount to much; Polwhele ploughed on on his own – he had all the more time for writing, and nothing like enough criticism of his work. He conscientiously collected all the material he could, penetrating into various family archives – some of which have been dispersed, others not made available to scholars even today. He consulted manuscripts at Prideaux Place and Pencarrow, and the Tonkin material at Tehidy of the Bassets, though some Borlase material was denied to him by the Lawrences at Launceston. (Thomas Tonkin of Trevaunance at St. Agnes was an admirable antiquary, but he was one of those who could never bring his learning to a point and produce it: *unus ex istibus*).

On the other hand, where Polwhele regretted the absence of a biographical dictionary in his *Devon* (we have Prince's *Worthies of Devon*), in his *Cornwall* we are given many biographies and much information about people, sometimes hard to come by: another thing specific to Cornwall – we have a good deal of information about the language. Polwhele did not know it, nor did anybody else at the time – except old Dolly Pentreath who spoke it. Much progress has been made in its study in our time, and perhaps we may say that it has been placed on a firm linguistic foundation. Polwhele, however, gives us valuable information about those who had known the old language, Keigwin, Gwavas, and others. Above all, he gives us the fascinating correspondence about this and other antiquarian matters between Tonkin and Edward Lhuyd, the Welsh scholar at Oxford, who was one of the best Celtic students there have ever been.

Lhuyd was Keeper of the Ashmolean at Oxford, and travelled extensively in the Celtic countries – Ireland, Scotland, Wales, Cornwall and Brittany – collecting fossils and materials for his *Archaeologia Britannica*, the first volume of which was published at Oxford in 1707. Shortly after, in 1709, Lhuyd died, and his work was never completed. Many manuscripts and letters of this admirable antiquary remain: he would make a better subject for a biography than many that receive that attention.

We learn that when Lhuyd and his Welsh companions were down here at the end of William III's reign,

travelling on foot with knapsacks, they were apprehended as thieves and taken before a J.P. A later
antiquary, who became a respectable bishop of Oxford,
was caught in the act of drawing plans, and taken up for
a spy. So, later, was the celebrated Bligh of the *Bounty*,
while surveying Helford; so, too, even in our time,
during the late war, a rather conspicuous emissary of
MI5, who continued to display as a professor at Oxford,
was similarly questioned in that area. Such is our
exposed position on the coast in time of war – and the
suspicion which is a natural trait with us.

Edward Lhuyd was a natural scientist as well as a
philologist, and was as interested in Cornish folklore,
charms and amulets and magical stones, as he was in
fossils and simples. We see how full of excitements life
was for the old illiterate country folk – it is like that
depicted in Hardy's novels, its place with the people
today taken by the intellectual excitements of Bingo.
Lhuyd provided material for the revision of Camden's
Britannia by Bishop Gibson – to whom Tonkin
propounded his proposals in a long letter which
Polwhele gives us. This impetus for antiquarian research
came from a distinguished group of scholars at Queen's
College, which is why, I suppose, the famous Oxford
Almanac of the year of the Jacobite Rising of '45
represents William Trevanion, 'the last, I believe, of the
old Trevanions', being carried off from Exeter to
Queen's. The Trevanions were Jacobites, and this last of
the old male line would be, like so many West Coun-
trymen, up at Exeter College.[1]

One never knows what may turn up in Polwhele's
Cornwall, he was very knowledgable about folklore, as
became a parson overlooking his parishioners or riding
about the countryside visiting county folk. We learn that

1. Foreword to Polwhele's *History of Cornwall*, republished by
   Kohler and Coombes at Dorking, 1977.

mistletoe was plentiful at Tetcott of the Arscotts on the Devon border. There follow conjectures about the Druids, though he was not so sold on them as was Borlase, from whom Polwhele was evidently anxious to distinguish himself. We learn that the Cornish would not eat hare – a good deal of Elizabethan lore exists about poor Wat; the best apple-tree in the orchard was sprinkled with cider at Christmas – a relic of sympathetic magic, I suppose. The voice of a drowned person was heard shortly after by the shore or river where he was lost. We still light bonfires on high places at Midsummer, but do we realise that they were originally bone-fires?

The Lizard once had its Maytime Furry dance as Helston still has. The Bodmin Riding has gone out, with its procession to the site of the Priory, where there had been a holy well – discouraged and eventually stopped up by the Gilberts in residence. 'In many parts of Cornwall', says Polwhele in the voice of a Georgian cleric, 'the vulgar may still be said to worship brooks and wells. [Perhaps as good as, and certainly more salubrious than, Bingo worship.] From those streams and wells put into agitation after a ritual manner our forefathers pretended to foretell future events. This mode of divination (which is recorded by Plutarch in his life of Caesar) has been transmitted from age to age in Cornwall; and still exists among the vulgar, who resort to some well of celebrity at particular seasons and there observe the bubbles that rise and the state of the water on their throwing in pins and pebbles, and thence read their future destiny'. Polwhele then gives us a list of the most efficacious, or at least favoured, wells, beginning with the impressive one at Madron, where I have myself duly observed the rites. I wish someone would restore the thatched roof of the chapel and the Saint's altar.

On the scholarly side it would please Polwhele that modern research has vindicated his view that the

Romans were better acquainted with Cornwall than has been generally thought. Borlase had traced the course of a Roman road east of Stratton, and Polwhele held that the causeway west of Stratton, headed towards Camelford, was 'sufficient to show that the Romans had a way in the north of Cornwall'. The recent excavation of the considerable Roman camp at Nanstallon has borne him out.

And may he not have been right about something far better known and more controversial? Great interest today – from as far afield as Switzerland – is taken in the so-called Tristan stone along the road from Castle Dore into Fowey. Pundits today may have been too ready to read the inscription as referring to Tristan, for in the 18th century it was clearer to read, and Polwhele reads it as Cirusius and wonders whether the name may not be preserved in the neighbouring Pol-kerris. No archaeologist myself, I prefer the safer highways of recorded history, but, at the risk of raising a hornets' nest, to me it seems at least as likely.

I feel on securer ground once I have emerged from the Middle Ages, let alone the Dark Ages, and am charmed by the Georgian mason's account of his repairs to the familiar Robartes monument now in Truro Cathedral. 'To putting one new foot to Mr. John Robarts – mending the other; putting seven new buttons to his coat, and a new string to his breeches' knees. To two new feet to his wife Philippa – mending her eyes, and putting a nosegay in her hand. To two new hands, and a new nose, to the Captain. To two new hands, and mending the nose of his wife – repairing her eyes, and putting a new cuff to her gown. To making and fixing two new wings on Time's shoulders, and making a new great toe, mending the handle of his scythe, and putting a new blade to it'. What this fine monument, from the Southwark workshops which provided Shakespeare's at Stratford, must have looked like before its repairs! – perhaps from Civil War damage, more likely later.

On that subject Polwhele gives us interesting information, as on so many. 'Sir John Killigrew, with his own hands, set fire to his noble mansion at Arwennack that the rebels laying siege to Pendennis might find no shelter there'. What a loss that was from the odious Civil War, an Elizabethan house comparable to Godolphin or Trerice or Penheale! Polwhele tells us that Colonel Lewis Tremayne, who was in Pendennis Castle throughout the siege, 'made almost a miraculous escape by swimming over from one of the blockhouses to Trefusis Point through all the enemy's fire.' Nor does Polwhele fail to mention the large losses his own family suffered, along with others, from the penal impositions of the victorious Parliamentarians (like their descendants, the bureaucratic and parasitic tax-hounds of today).

It is hardly surprising that Polwhele had a strong line in his own day against the revolutionaries of the French Revolution. Nor was it to be expected that he would have much liking for Dissenters. He has a description, for once, of Dr. Johnson's acquaintance, the Reverend Zachary Mudge, who was 'educated in an academy of Dissenters but afterwards conformed to the Church of England. He preached a sermon in St. Peter's church, Exeter, which gave offence to people of various denominations, particularly to the Dissenters; for, considering him as an apostate from their Society, they were little inclined to admire either his learning or his eloquence. This, and his other sermons convey, in my opinion, no very favourable idea of his abilities as a preacher. They are very abstruse and consequently ill adapted to the pulpit: they are metaphysical essays'. There follow some dismissive lines in verse, always at the tip of Polwhele's pen.

He reached the headlines with his controversy over Methodism with Dr. Hawker, the Evangelical vicar of

Charles Church, Plymouth, better known today as the father of the poet Robert Stephen Hawker of Morwenstow.

Polwhele was not solely an antiquarian, *littérateur*, biographer, he has much information for the social historian, the kind of thing to the fore today. Along with the pedigrees of old families, lists of sheriffs, county officials, epitaphs, inscriptions, what not, he has a considerable section on population, with tables of vital statistics, abstracts for each parish throughout the county giving details of employment, whether in agriculture or trade, manufacture, handicraft, etc.; with the number of houses inhabited or uninhabited. This alone makes him a useful source for historians and economists. Then we have a long chapter on disease, longevity and medicine. Immensely industrious, he did his best to research into all the sources of information available to him, unprinted as well as in print – and these were not easy to come by in his day. Thus we come upon unexpected information, such as the way the estates of the Recusant Tregians came into the hands of Lord Chamberlain Hunsdon, patron of Shakespeare's Company, whose mistress Emilia Bassano was the Dark Lady of the Sonnets.[2]

Geographically, Polwhele is no less useful. He gives us information about prehistoric camps and 'castles', barrows and fogous, some of which have been subsequently obliterated; and about earlier archaeological finds, some of which have been lost. One did not know, for example, that there had been a plan-an-gwary, or playing place – a kind of amphitheatre for performance of the medieval miracle-plays – at Redruth, like that at Perranporth or at St. Just, of which he gives us a fine plate.

As I have said, he does not seem to have had the support in Cornwall which he had received in Devon,

2. For him, see my *The Byrons and Trevanions*.

and so we have few plates of country houses with their owners' improvements and parks. In their place we have romantic views of the valley of the Fowey seen through an arch of ruined Restormel Castle, of Fowey harbour or Falmouth bay with Pendennis and St. Mawes in the distance. Polwhele employed the admirable water-colourist, James Bourne, for these; other drawings he owed to Captain Tremenheere, of whose work I possess a small collection. John Rogers of Penrose paid for a very large folding view of Mount's Bay, with Marazion and St. Michael's Mount. The Vyvyans of Trelowarren and the St. Aubyns gave Polwhele some support; in conse-quence, we have a large number of plates of St. Aubyn monuments in Crowan church, some of which have since disappeared.

We see what an extraordinary amount of miscellaneous information, of some appeal to various kinds of readers, may be extracted from Polwhele's abounding gallimaufry.

The Duchy

The Duchy of Cornwall is a peculiar and fascinating institution, with a constitutional status and characteristics all its own, of which few people are aware. We must first clear our of the way the popular confusion between the Duchy and the county of Cornwall. They are two entirely separate entities, utterly differing in character. The one is an ordinary county, as it might be Devonshire or Dorset; whereas the Duchy is an institution, an aggregation of estates vested in the eldest son of the Sovereign (or, in the absence of a son, lying dormant in the Crown). It has been based from time immemorial upon extensive lands in Cornwall and outside, and has existed as a duchy, save for the interregnum of the Commonwealth period, since 1337.

The habit of referring to the 'Duchy' when people mean the county of Cornwall is due to one of Q.'s early books, *The Delectable Duchy*, the title of which caught on and has become popular over the last forty years. When my name was entered in the register on becoming a Fellow of All Souls, I was entered as having been born in the 'Duchy' of Cornwall. It was intended as a compliment and taken as such, without protest; but it was inaccurate.

The Duchy, in the exact sense, goes back direct as an institution to the reign of Edward III, who created it in 1337 for the support of his eldest son, the Black Prince; and indirectly to the Norman earldom of Cornwall, and beyond that to the conquests of the House of Wessex upon Cornish soil. Two of the Duchy castles, Launceston and Trematon, were at places with names ending in "ton", indicating Saxon settlement; their positions guarded entries into or exits from Cornwall across the Tamar – the one in the north, the other in the south.

Saxon settlement does not seem to have gone a great way deeper into Cornwall, except around Bude; but it was a conquered country when the Saxons themselves were conquered by William of Normandy. He made his half-brother, Robert of Mortain, Earl of Cornwall, who immediately began constructing mottes and earthworks at Launceston and Trematon, the strategic keys of the county. Something of the status of conquest remained on under the earldom and into the Duchy. The lands of both earldom and Duchy were chiefly in the eastern half of the county; while villeinage went on on the Duchy manors in Cornwall longer than anywhere else in the country. I have come across numbers of manumissions of bondmen upon these manors right throughout the sixteenth century, in the reigns of Henry VII, Mary, and Elizabeth; it was not until the reign of James I that all were finally freed. The surname 'Bond', not uncommon in Cornwall, goes back to the time when they were unfree in status, villeins tied to the land, at the will of their lord – in this case the Duchy.[1] These manumissions were made mostly upon the manor of Stokeclimsland, the largest of the Duchy manors, still the chief agricultural centre of the Duchy in Cornwall.

Of the Norman Earls of Cornwall, the most famous was Richard, King of the Romans, brother of Henry III, and the most important person in the kingdom, after the King. He was a crusader and went to Palestine in 1240. He returned to England to become a prominent figure in internal politics – his brother was in difficulties with the

---

1. By 1500 a family of Bond had become armigerous, at the manor of Earth, by Saltash; but this was because they were conventionary tenants of that Duchy manor by bond: they were not bondmen.

baronial opposition led by Simon de Montfort – and later became a personage of European renown. For he used his wealth as Earl of Cornwall, especially from the dues on tin, to bring about his election as Holy Roman Emperor. He was elected by the majority of the electors; but, in spite of his coronation at Aix-la-Chapelle, he never could secure obedience to his rule of more than the immediate Rhineland. Defeated by the intrigues of German politics, when his money ran out he returned to this country and the resources of his earldom.

In the last years of his life he turned his attention to Cornwall, strengthening his position there by gaining possession of Tintagel and Trematon Castles, and getting the last of the Cardinhams to hand over Restormel Castle and the town of Lostwithiel. From this time Lostwithiel became the chief administrative centre of the earldom in Cornwall, as it subsequently remained for centuries for the Duchy. Richard's son, Edmund Earl of Cornwall, 1272–99, built between the church and the river there a fine range of buildings to house the administrative offices, which became known as the 'Duchy Palace'. Here was the Shire Hall, in which the county court met, the exchequer of the earldom, later of the Duchy, the Coignage Hall (for Lostwithiel was one of the stannary towns for the coignage of tin),[2] and the gaol for the Cornish stannaries, which continued in use as late as the eighteenth century for prisoners brought before the stannary courts. The exterior of the Shire Hall still exists, somewhat Victorianised, with buttresses and fragments of buildings and a medieval archway leading to the quayside, over worn stones up which trundled the consignments and cargoes from abroad, linens from Brittany, wine from Gascony. Since those

2. This word refers to the coign, or corner, of the blocks of tin, which were the dues of the Duchy, stamped as its property: a valuable source of revenue.

days the river Fowey has changed its course a little: then the Duchy Palace fronted conveniently right on the river, which would have been deeper for vessels, before the silting up of centuries.

Restormel Castle, some way out of the town, high up on a hill above the valley of the Fowey, the river rippling down between the oaks and glades of fern, has been more fortunate. After an uneventful history – though it woke to life once again in the Civil War, when it was taken in turn by Parliament and the King – it has now fallen into the careful hands of the Office of Works. Stripped of ivy and with walls made firm and secure, the round shell of the keep stands well up on its hill, where one may see it among the trees on the right hand as the train nears Lostwithiel.

The earldom as organised by Richard and Edmund was substantially what constituted the Duchy later. There was an intervening period after Edmund's death in 1299, when Piers Gaveston, Edward II's favourite, became earl, and after he came to a sticky end John of Eltham, the King's second son. Upon his death Edward III decided to use the vacant earldom as a means of support for his eldest son, who had not yet been created Prince of Wales. The original charter by which it was created, March 17th, 11 Edward III, differentiates the dukedom from the principality of Wales; for whereas the title of Prince of Wales is conferred by special investiture by the monarch, the eldest son of the reigning sovereign is born Duke of Cornwall. The Duchy Auditor who wrote an account of the Duchy in 1609 for Henry, Prince of Wales, James I's elder son, says: 'The King's first begotten and eldest sons are as touching livery to be made unto them of the Duchy, accounted of full and perfect age, that is to say, of twenty-one years on the very day of their birth, so as even then in right, they ought to have livery thereof'. The Duchy is therefore a shifting possession from the Crown to the Duke and back to the Crown, for when the Duke dies or ascends the throne the Duchy reverts to the Sovereign. During the dormancy of the dukedom the King functions 'as he was Duke', according to the formula.

A further peculiarity of the Duchy is that, since it was constituted by royal charter expressly forbidding the alienation of its lands, the Duke is unable to sever lands from it except with the consent of Parliament. When lands were so severed, as in the case of Henry VIII's annexation of the honour of Wallingford and Knaresborough and other lands to the Crown – previously belonging to the Duchy – a number of other manors were annexed in its place, mainly within Cornwall. These were more conveniently administered as part of the Duchy since they lay in the West.

This process increased the number of manors of which the Duchy was comprised to some seventy-eight by the time of the Civil War, instead of the thirty-five with which it had been originally endowed. They fell into several classes. There were, first, the seventeen 'Antiqua Maneria' in Cornwall, which had formed part of the earldom; secondly, there were the 'Forinseca Maneria' outside the county, which were included by Edward III in his grant; and, thirdly, the 'Annexata Maneria', both inside Cornwall and without, which had been incorporated subsequently by Act of Parliament. The original nucleus in Cornwall were the manors of Stokeclimsland, Rillaton, Helston-in-Trigg, Liskeard, Tybesta, Tywarnhaile, Talskedy, Penmayne, Calstock, Trematon, Restormel, Penkneth, Penlyne, Tewington, Helston-in-Kerrier, Tintagel, and Moresk. Upon these there existed a special conventionary form of tenure, from seven-year to seven-year, right up to the middle of the last century. The lands of the Duchy outside Cornwall were no less extensive than they were within, including an equal number of manors in various counties and, as it still does, the honour of Bradninch in

Devonshire, all that high country between the rivers Exe and Culm, between Tiverton and Cullompton. In London the manor of Kennington, upon which the Black Prince resided, must be the most remunerative of all the Duchy's sources of income.

This being its constitution, the history of the dukedom has been one of dormancy in the Crown almost as much as of separate and independent existence under the Duke. The Black Prince, whose father, Edward III, lived to such an exceptional age, enjoyed the Duchy for close on forty years; but with his son, Richard II, who had no children, the Duchy lay dormant in the Crown. Under Henry IV, the later Henry V – Shakespeare's Prince Hal – was Duke; then for the forty years from 1413 to 1453 the Duchy was again in the possession of the Crown, and there were lapses again in the fifteenth century.

With the death of Prince Arthur, Henry VII's elder son, in 1502, a new problem arose: did the King's surviving son and heir succeed to the Duchy under the charter? Sir John Doddridge, whose book on the Principality of Wales and the Duchy of Cornwall was published in 1630, says that the intention of the charter was 'first that none should be Dukes of Cornwall but such as were eldest sons and heirs apparent to the Crown; and that when there was any fail of such person, then the said dignity should remain in suspense, until such son and heir apparent were extant'. But the lawyers interpreted the phrase the King's 'eldest son' in the original charter to mean his eldest surviving son; so that Henry, subsequently Henry VIII, was enabled to succeed to his brother's Duchy, as he did later to his wife. The precedent was followed in 1612, upon the death of Prince Henry, when his younger brother Charles succeeded.

The Crown was in possession of the Duchy for long periods in the sixteenth century: under Henry VIII from

1509 till 1537, when his son Edward was born, and throughout the whole reigns of Edward, Mary, and Elizabeth – i.e. from 1547 to 1603. In the seventeenth century there were similar periods: under Charles I, from 1625 to 1630, when his eldest son was born; under the Commonwealth, when the Duchy ceased for a time to exist and its manors were sold. It was restored under Charles II, but there was no son to inherit the dukedom from 1649 right up to the death of Queen Anne in 1714, except for the brief and fugitive appearance of James II's infant son upon the public scene in 1688.

The Hanoverians, being a prolific stock, did their duty by the Duchy more regularly. The later George II was Duke from 1714 to 1727, then Frederick Prince of Wales from 1727 to 1751. There followed upon his death an interval until the later George IV was born in 1762. Again the Crown was in possession from 1820 to 1841, when the Prince who became Edward VII was born. From then up to the accession of Edward VIII there has been a Duke of Cornwall, the longest continuous stretch in its history. With Edward VIII's accession the Duchy fell once more to the Crown, until the accession of Elizabeth II, with a son, Prince Charles, to become Duke. The remarkable feature of the dukedom historically, it will be observed, is its discontinuity, as compared with the virtually unbroken continuity of the Duchy.

Of the long line of its Dukes, few have been in a position to make acquaintance with, or take personal interest in, their Duchy. The first Duke, the Black Prince himself, owing to his length of tenure, was in a position to do so. According to Charles Henderson, when the Black Prince came to man's estate and was renowned as a warrior all over Christendom, he paid more than one visit to his Duchy. Restormel was his chief halting-place. . . . In May 1354, the Duchy Council wrote to John de Kendal, the receiver of

Cornwall, ordering him to repair the castles in Cornwall, and especially the 'conduit' in the castle of Restormel, as quickly as possible. In August following, the Prince himself came down to Cornwall, with a gallant company of knights whose names are immortalised in the pages of Froissart. Here the Prince remained from August 20th to about September 4th.

This was eight years after the Prince's first youthful campaign, which had culminated at Crécy, where he led the van and won fame as the Black Prince, from his armour. He was twenty-four on this first visit to the West – just before he was appointed lieutenant of Gascony, whence he made his marauding campaigns over the south of France, ending up with the famous victory at Poitiers, where he took the King of France prisoner.

Nine years after his first visit to the Duchy he paid another, at Eastertide 1363, to Restormel. He had been created Prince of Aquitaine and Gascony the year before, and was about to go abroad to take up his charge, which consumed the remaining good years of his life in ceaseless war in the south of France and upon the borders of Spain. He came home, wasted with disease, in 1371, but came no more to his Duchy. The Duchy went on as an administrative unit; it had been strongly organised and its officers did not fail. During all these years they kept their books duly; there remains to us the register dealing with the Prince's affairs in Cornwall known as the *White Book of Cornwall*, published by H.M. Stationery Office as part of the *Black Prince's Register*.

From it we learn how the Prince's affairs in Cornwall were managed – how his revenues arose, the rents, fines, and profits of all kinds from his lands, the moneys arising from his stannary rights, the coignage of tin, the profits of his courts and the innumerable small change of feudal tenure, the issues from wreck upon his manors on the coast. Then we have all the outgoings – payments to the Duchy's full complement of officers from the steward, sheriff, and receiver, the havenor who dealt with customs at the ports, the 'Prince's batchelor and keeper of his game', down to his keepers, bailiffs and chaplains. All the multifarious purposes, charitable and devotional or purely customary, of a noble feudatory we find provided for: a chaplain to sing masses for the souls of the Prince's ancestors in the chapel of the castle at Trematon, another to sing for the souls of former Earls of Cornwall in the hermitage dedicated to the Holy Trinity in the park of Restormel. This stood by the river-bank below the castle on the site of 'Trinity' – the present Georgian-Gothic farmhouse – within earshot of the river rushing by outside. Oaks were to be given from the Duchy parks to the Dominican Friars of Truro to build their church, to the Prior of Tywardreath, or to the parishioners of Stokeclimsland to repair their church; a grant of a tun of wine to a chaplain; or to a canon of Exeter going to keep his residence there the gift of 'twelve does from this season of grease[3] to be taken from the Prince's parks'.

The deer-parks were an essential part in the economy of the Duchy. When it was constituted there were seven: Kerrybullock (now Stokeclimsland), with 150 deer; Liskeard Old Park, with 200; Lanteglos and Helsbury, with 180; Trematon, with 42; Launceston, with 15; and Restormel, with 300. One must imagine all that landscape as one deer-park, the river Fowey rippling through it. After the Black Prince, the castles tended to fall into disrepair and there was less point in maintaining the deer-parks. With the movement for enclosure that grew strong in the sixteenth century, Henry VIII decided to dispark the Duchy parks and turn them more profitably into pasture. It is the site of Kerrybullock Park, in the parish of Stokeclimsland, that the large Duchy farm now occupies.

3. i.e. when the deer were fat.

The Duchy continued to be administered upon the lines laid down under the Black Prince. Politicians and royal favourites came and went at remote Westminster; dynasties changed; civil war and battles raged upon English soil. Still the administration of the Duchy went on, the most permanent feature in the landscape of society in Cornwall, the diurnal routine of its tenants living close to the soil, unchanging, or changing slowly only with the slow tides of the ages. One gets the impression of an institution essentially conservative, one that neither relaxed its rights nor vexed its tenantry with new impositions; the fines it took upon leases remained stable over long periods. Custom and tradition, the bedrock of human history.

The drastic social changes of the Reformation, however, took effect, and the Duchy emerged with a larger concentration of its lands in the West. Henry VIII detached the honours of Wallingford and St Valery, and in exchange granted the Cornish estates of the Earls of Devon, which fell to the Crown by the attainder of the Marquis of Exeter, some fifteen manors in all, and fifteen more Cornish manors belonging to the dissolved priories of Launceston and Tywardreath. This meant a considerable extension of Duchy lands into mid-Cornwall, though the main concentration still remained in the east of the county. In the far west, the farm of the Scilly Isles now became for the first time Duchy property. In the last years of Elizabeth, with the constant drain of the long war with Spain and the campaigns in the Netherlands and Ireland, she found it necessary to sell eighteen of these newly-annexed manors. But it was held on James I's accession that the sale was illegal under the charter of the Duchy and they were recovered.

It used to be thought that the great increase which the Tudors made in the parliamentary representation of Cornwall was intended to strengthen royal influence upon Parliament by the return of so many members –

forty-four in all – from a county where the Duchy had such an extensive influence. We now know that that was not the case: it was the pressure of the rising gentry – particularly marked in the West Country with increasing sea-power and trade and now in the front-line of oceanic enterprise – that led them to require seats in Parliament. The places allotted seats were convenient, many but villages that occasioned no trouble. In Elizabeth's reign the Puritan leaders Peter and Paul Wentworth, the initiators of parliamentary opposition, sat for Cornish boroughs; while in the reign of Charles I, at election after election, the Duchy failed to get its candidates returned against the local influence of Sir John Eliot, William Coryton, and such Parliamentarian families as the Robartses, Rouses of Halton, Bullers, and Trefusises.

With the outbreak of the Civil War the Duchy reached a new peak of importance; for upon its administrative system and its revenues, Charles I had to rely for the sinews of his cause in the West. This phase of the Duchy's existence has been described by Mary Coate in her *Cornwall in the Civil War*. In 1645, at the decisive downward turn of his fortunes, Charles I took the decision to grant livery of the Duchy to the young Prince of Wales, then fifteen, and to send him into the West with a Council attendant upon him, to govern in his name. Hyde was the chief member of the Prince's Council, and for a year he laboured hard to screw up resources and to stay the decline of the royalist forces. He was successful only in the first; the production of tin was much increased and shipped across to France and Holland to buy munitions. But nothing could stave off the military defeat; the Prince's Council was riddled with dissensions, and in March 1646 young Charles embarked at Falmouth for Scilly and later for France.

In these years Cornwall was being drained by both sides; after the immense sacrifices the county had made, both of manpower for the King – the Cornish army raised by Sir Bevil Grenville, which achieved such feats in the campaign of 1643, was bled white – and of its resources by both King and Parliament, Cornwall accepted the Parliamentarian victory submissively enough. It had been a disadvantage for Cornwall to have been forced into invidious prominence by its association with the Duchy. However, the latter paid for the part it had played in the struggle. It was sold up by the victorious Parliament, its organisation dissolved. When Charles II came back to his throne all had to be reconstituted.

The old foundations, the old routine, however, were there; it remained only to follow out their lines. The Duchy was revived, officers appointed; at the head of them all was John Grenville, Earl of Bath, Sir Bevil's son, who as a lad of sixteen, when his father was killed at Lansdown, was lifted on his horse to take his place and encourage the dispirited Cornish foot. In 1661 he was made High Steward of the Duchy, Lord Warden of the Stannaries, Rider and Master of Dartmoor Forest, offices which went with the Duchy, and later Lord Lieutenant of Cornwall. The age-long customs of the Duchy temporarily disturbed, then continued under temporary owners. renewed their ancient routine; the manor courts were held in the King's name, the Lord Warden came down in person to preside at the Parliament of the Stannaries; the tin trade flourished; money went up for Charles to support his mistresses at Whitehall.

There remains only to notice the stannaries, from which the Duchy had early drawn some part of its revenues. With increasing return from the mines this source of revenue was expanding and, after the Restoration, the economic factor of the stannaries became still more important. Theirs is a history distinct from, though subordinate to, the Duchy; it has been treated in full in G.R. Lewis' *The Stannaries*. The popular view of what the stannaries were is even less clear than as to the

Duchy: they were areas of jurisdiction covering not only the tin mines, but the whole of the tin industry and affairs arising out of it. They formed a peculiar jurisdiction springing from the royal prerogative in the working of metals. As such they were not subject to common law; after many disputes on the point, the leading case of Trewinnard in the reign of Elizabeth decided that there was no appeal from the stannary courts to the ordinary courts of law. They had their own system of courts with an ultimate appeal to the Council of the Prince as Duke of Cornwall. The last relic of the ancient stannary courts remained until as late as 1896, when the court of the Vice-Warden of the Stannaries was abolished.[4]

When the Duchy was created in 1337 the stannaries of Cornwall and Devon were incorporated into it; from that time the Duke took the place of the King in receiving their revenues and regulating their affairs. His Council formed the fountainhead of all stannary administration. He appointed the Lord Warden to act as his representative in governing the stannaries, naming their officers, summoning the tinners' parliaments, assenting to their legislation, promulgating new laws and enactments for their regulation. As a peculiar jurisdiction with its own rights, the stannaries mustered their own men for service in times of danger. In the years before and after the Spanish Armada we find frequent complaints from the deputy-lieutenants of Cornwall against the stannaries on the ground of the overlapping of jurisdictions and the consequent inability of the deputy-lieutenants to make complete returns of men for the musters. Sir Walter Ralegh's position as Lord Warden was sufficient to maintain the independence of the stannaries from the ordinary local administration,

---

4. H.A.L. Fisher's father was the last Vice-Warden, virtually a sinecure.

and co-ordination of the two was usually provided for by the appointment of the Lord Warden as lord lieutenant of the county. With the immense development of the mining industry in the eighteenth century the revenues from the stannary must have become an increasing part of the revenues of the Duchy.

We may sum up what the economic effect of the Duchy has been upon Cornwall through the centuries. It meant a constant drain of wealth from a county which was, except for its minerals, poor in resources. Charles Henderson used to think this the reason why so few large estates were formed in Cornwall, and why there were no Cornish peerages right up until the 17th century. Richard Carew of Antony, who wrote his *Survey of Cornwall* towards the end of Elizabeth's reign, comments upon there being no Cornish peerage in his time, no one in Cornwall of however ancient a family, whom the Queen might call cousin.

Under the Hanoverian dynasty the Duchy ambled on according to its old-established order; though I do not know that any of the first four Georges paid any personal visits to their Duchy. All sovereigns from Victoria onwards have done so. Edward VII as Prince of Wales visited his Cornish estates on several occasions. The revenues which accumulated during his minority enabled him to buy Sandringham, as they enabled Edward VIII when Duke to buy Fort Belvedere. Perhaps it was in consequence of this, or simply out of sentiment, that the Duchy of Cornwall flag was always flown at Fort Belvedere.

Looking back over the long story of the Duchy many images come to mind – the centuries-old buildings going back to Edmund Earl of Cornwall, by the quayside at Lostwithiel, lapped by the tidal waters of the river Fowey; the house at Trematon within the old walls of the castle where Sir Richard Grenville, grandfather of the hero, took refuge in the time of the Prayer Book

Rebellion of 1549, the castle to which Drake took the treasure which he brought home from his Voyage round the World, the grey walls looking down upon the broad waters of the Hamoaze; or Launceston Castle, with the ruined shell of its keep; or Tintagel, grim, barbaric upon its desolate headland, the inspiration of so much poetry and legend.

St. Austell: Church, Town, Parish

Church

Exterior

St. Austell church is memorable among even the finest of West Country churches for the remarkable sculpture upon its tower and outside walls. In its conception, design, and in the figures themselves, we can see the stamp of the imagination, the skill in execution, of a long-dead master craftsman, unknown and unnamed. So strong is its idiosyncrasy that I recognise that same hand in the gargoyles upon the tower of Lanlivery, and again at St. Enoder. But the sculpture at St. Austell, especially the composition upon the western face of the tower, was his masterpiece.

St. Austell belongs to that finest class of church-towers, the Somerset type, that extends in a band all the way across the West Country from Cornwall to Oxford. We have to imagine *corps* of West Country craftsmen journeying about from their centres in Somerset and Devon, in the decades before and after 1500, not long before the Reformation, to accomplish such excellent structures as Linkinhorne and Fowey church-towers and, noblest in its general design, Probus. The glory of St. Austell is in its sculpture.

When the church was dedicated by Bishop Bronescombe, 9 October 1259 – on that autumn day in the reign of king Henry III, the new bishop of Exeter journeying back from a long and strenuous programme of dedicating churches and getting things in order in his diocese – the church was named in honour of the Trinity. It is this conception that is carried out in stone in the group of figures on the western face of the tower: three tiers, three figures in the lowest, two in the second, leading to the representation of the Trinity – God the Father with the crucified Son between his knees, and there may have been originally the dove of the Spirit – at the top.

This topmost group is given emphasis as usual by its larger scale and richness of embellishment. There is majesty in the face of the Father, hands raised in blessing over the Son extended upon his cross, the head drooping to one side; underneath in a fold of linen held by two angels are the faithful departed awaiting judgment. *Justorum animae sunt in manu Dei.*

The second group is in clear contrast. In place of the majesty of God the Father, we have the tenderness and joy of the Annunciation. The Virgin raises her hands in that gesture familiar to us from so many medieval pictures; the naïveté of expression that is a bond of communication between her and the angel Gabriel, across the vase with the lilies.

The lowest tier has for its central figure the risen Lord, one hand raised in blessing, the other holding the cross of the Resurrection. This niche is again given enrichment, subordinate figures, elaborate canopy, incrusted carving. The other two figures, one on either side, are probably St. Mewan and St. Austell, the saintly couple to whom we owe the origin of the church, going back to the early Celtic days after the Roman Empire had withdrawn from Britain, the age of the Saints. The figure on the left of our Lord is vested as a bishop or mitred abbot; the figure on the right is of a lower rank, he is a pilgrim or hermit, yet he has the place of honour. This would be right for the patron saint; the tradition of the parish in the Middle Ages was that he was a younger disciple of the more important St. Mewan, founder of the abbey of St. Méen in Brittany.

We know very little else about them. After all, it is not to be expected that we should know much about these shadowy figures from so remote an antiquity, fourteen hundred years ago, to whom nevertheless we owe the evangelising of this area, to whose close friendship in life we certainly owe the proximity of the dedications of the two parishes, St. Mewan and St. Austell.

There has been a curious reversal between the status of their two parishes and the two men in life. St. Austell became the much larger and more important parish; the growth of a town made it a fairly well known name, the development of mining and of the china clay industry carried its name across the world. But in the age of the Saints, when sea-communications made more of a unity of the western Celtic lands, and the early evangelists journeyed freely across the intervening channels from South Wales or Ireland to Cornwall and on to Brittany, St. Mewan had an important career there as founder of churches and of his abbey, where he had the devotion of the younger St. Austell. They would have evangelised together here and sanctified the wells beside which they lived. These Celtic missionaries were not recognised as saints by Rome, so that when Bishop Bronescombe came to dedicate the church seven hundred years ago – midway in the history of Christianity in this place – he probably chose the Trinity dedication as the feast day falling nearest that of the old Celtic saint, so as not to disturb the age-long custom of the people.

The other three faces of this second stage have the twelve apostles, four on each side, each of them originally identifiable by his symbol: St. Peter with his key, St. John the Divine, young and beardless, holding the chalice, St. Thomas with his carpenter's square, and so on. The topmost stage has the most elaborately carved stonework, in accordance with the usual design of Somerset towers, carrying the eye heavenward – no less than ten bands of carved stones of different patterns, diaper and quatrefoil and spaced shields. This stage springs from grotesque animals at the corners, leaping antlered stags, with full-faced lions at the coigns supporting coats of arms – in these forceful creatures of the imagination one sees the characteristic humour of that unknown medieval sculptor. The tower ends with a row of these creatures along the cornice at the base of the battlements, on each face, while the corner turrets throw up their fine pinnacles free and clear into the sky.

The tower is a masterpiece. People of our parish nearly four hundred years ago had reason to be proud of it when the scaffolding was taken away and the structure first stood revealed in the rich cream colour of Pentewan stone, quarried out of the cliff by the sea within the parish, which has now in the course of the centuries taken on more varied blooms of honey-colour, ochre and green, splashes of purple along with plain gold of the western sun.

People should step aside from the busy street and devote half-an-hour to studying through field-glasses one of the sights most worth seeing in Cornwall.

That is not the full tale of our sculptor's achievements, for along the façades of both aisles, north and south, are evidences of his hand – especially the south side, which gets the sun and the beat of the weather. This is decorated by a series of shields displaying emblems of the faith, and is punctuated by a good two-storey porch with a priest's chamber above the entrance. Over the arch is another admirable composition in stone: the pelican in her piety with outspread wings over her nest feeding her brood of young with the blood from her breast: emblem of the Church, with medieval lettering above, INRI and KY CH, Kyrios Christos, Christ the Lord.

The gateway below has elaborate late tracery, almost Renaissance, it is so rounded in its lines – the arch springing from a sculpted angel on either side. When J.P. St. Aubyn, who did much to spoil the interior of many churches, including ours, 'restored' the church – one can always recognise his handiwork by the pitch-pine pews, and iron scraper outside the door – he hacked off the angels' faces to insert the hinges of his iron gate.

The shields along the south side, some fourteen in number, tell the story of the Passion. Several of them have the instruments of the Passion, with a discerning eye for pattern, looking properly heraldic. The seventh, for example, has the centurion's spear and the spear with the sponge of hyssop at the end diagonally crossed, with the hammer and three great nails in the four quarters. The tenth represents the descent from the cross and has the ladder down the middle, with a pair of pincers on either side. The eleventh has the sealed and chambered tomb. The twelfth represents the harrowing of Hell – Christ's descent into Hell to preach to the spirits there; the thirteenth the Resurrection, with the stone rolled away, halberds and ensign of the soldiers, the cross in the centre in triumph, all disposed with geometrical precision. The fourteenth is the most complex and describes the Ascension, with the sun, moon and stars and amid them Christ's feet beneath his robe disappearing into heaven. Another shield has the Veronica theme: the imprint of Christ upon the napkin with which she wiped his face in the travail of bearing the cross. We see so much of the myth that nourished the faith of medieval folk, all set out in speaking stone.

The church looks its finest from this south side, from almost any position down below in Church Street: one looks up and sees its shapely pile high upon its mound, under the wheeling shadow of the tower, grey skies of winter, or blue of spring and autumn with a cloud floating like a plume above it; or strangely white with black shadows in cold moonlight, gleaming like snow upon the roofs.

The north side has little sunlight, except the late light of summer evenings; it has much less weathering, so that one can see better the carved cornice, of varied design, and the grotesques – gargoyles of comic aspect, grinning monsters – one in particular like a petrified camel-head with lascivious lips – that appealed to the medieval sense of humour.

Here is a Bible in stone: the beliefs and teachings, the events and stories of the Church displayed for all to see. The medievals, who were mostly unlettered peasants, learned through the eye. In modern times, with the new emphasis on visual education and enjoyment, are we coming back to it?

All this relates to the nave and aisles as they were rebuilt in the late fifteenth century. This saw the culmination of medieval church building in the West Country; if you want to see a complete example, look at Bodmin parish church, the grandest of its type. Here at St. Austell the rebuilding went no further than nave and aisles; it did not include the chancel and St. Michael's chapel.

Why did it stop short?

Well, St. Michael's chantry chapel was a separate foundation, with its own endowment that was extra-parochial – the rectorial tithes of St. Clether. Perhaps funds ran short; the parish had done itself proud on the tower and all the sculpture. It was only a country parish, though a large one; and Bodmin, which was a corporate borough, though it did with difficulty complete its church, did not rebuild the tower.

Such works of architecture were a heavy burden on the resources of the peasant communities that raised them. Those people were poor folk, but they did not consume all that they produced on trivial objects of consumption; they thought that they were building for eternity.

From a coat of arms of the Courtenays high up on the tower it would appear that the work was nearing completion when Peter Courtenay was bishop of Exeter from 1478 to 1487. After that a time of trouble set in for Cornwall, with the reaction of the Cornish people against the encroaching Tudor state that led to two rebellions in the year 1497. The Cornish were heavily punished – financially; and that also may have had a part in calling building operations to a close.

So they contented themselves with joining up with the chancel of the old church, on a smaller scale, of the 13th and 14th centuries, and on a slightly different axis. The eastern end of the church, chancel and its aisles, belong to that which was dedicated by Bishop Bronescombe seven hundred years ago.

To appreciate that, the most ancient part of the building, we must go inside.

Interior

We enter by the south porch, the way the parish has done through the centuries, for then we have a good perspective of the best feature of the interior – the nave arcades of five bays of creamy white moor-stone, and the wagon-roofs in their original state, timbers with the soft patina of ages upon them, colour upon the carved bosses showing through. It is good to have these roofs complete and in their proper form, with the compartments ceiled. In so many Cornish churches the plaster ceilings have been stripped away to reveal the rafters – like stripping off the flesh to reveal the skeleton. Not so here. On the other hand, the last century and this have interfered in other respects – Victorian pews, inferior stained glass make a disappointing interior after the fine exterior.

If we want to realise what the interior should look like, and once did, we should visit a Cornish church complete with rood-screen, like Lanreath or Blisland; or with carved bench-ends intact as at Talland, Altarnun or St. Winnow by the river Fowey. Here at St. Austell the rood-stairs remain within their turret at the junction of north aisle with chancel – but no rood-screen. What was left of the bench-ends was placed under the tower where they are invisible. They should be brought out again into the light of day.

How rich the effect must have been when the nave was filled with them, instead of J.P. St. Aubyn's pitch-pine! For they are of good design, each a double panel with quatrefoil at the bottom, tracery at the top and varying *motifs* in the middle. Some of these are again of the Passion, reflecting those on the stone shields outside, the instruments, pickaxes, shovels, pincers, spear, or of emblems like the five wounds, pierced hands, sacred feet and heart. Others have a crowned M for the Virgin Mary, or IHS, or a St. Andrew's cross, which points to the connection of the church with St. Andrew's priory at Tywardreath at the other end of the bay.

This vanished monastery owned the rectories, i.e. the greater tithes, of a number of parishes round about – these formed its endowment. Those of St. Austell were given to the priory for its support in the twelfth century by the Cardinham family, Tywardreath's founders. With the Reformation these rectorial tithes were thrown on the market, and ultimately came into the possession of the Tremaynes of Heligan and the Rashleigh family. Actually the vicarial tithes, i.e. the tithes on lesser agricultural produce, hay, cattle, fish, honey etc., were rather more valuable at St. Austell, since the parish was not primarily corn-bearing. These went to the upkeep of the vicar and, since the parish was a large one, the living was in old days a fairly good one, as livings went.

Upon other bench-ends one still recognises coats of arms. One is that of the Prince of Wales in its original form, the three feathers displayed separately. The bench-ends were probably made in the early sixteenth century, so this would refer to one of the Tudor princes, Prince Arthur or Henry, later Henry VIII. A bench-end that always attracted my attention as a choir-boy depicts a fox in a surplice, preaching from a pulpit to a credulous woman in contemporary costume kneeling below. A favourite theme with medieval folk.

Moving east into the chancel we are in the midst of what remains of the earlier church Bishop Bronescombe saw. The round pier and the low pointed arches of the south arcade are of the thirteenth century, nearly three hundred years earlier than the nave. So too with the north arcade, which has an octagonal pier of complex design, one that comes to us from Devon churches, perhaps by sea. The stone too is different: it is of a beautiful grey-green, from the Catacluse quarry in the cliffs by Padstow.

About 1300 a St. Austell man named Philip, who became Archdeacon of Winchester, founded the chantry chapel of St. Michael, to sing masses for his soul and those of his parents. When that chapel was built on the Early English style was just developing into the Decorated – as one can see from the tracery of the windows. This necessitated raising the roof of the chancel and inserting the east window, to keep pace with Master Philip's foundation.

The chantry chapel was a tall building, with an interesting east window of its own: three lights and over them, a multifoliate window like a six-petalled flower. Archdeacon Philip did his native parish proud. He purchased the rectory and advowson of St. Clether, i.e. the greater tithes there and the presentation to the living, for the support of his chantry; later he added a house and some thirty acres of land in Menacuddle. So that henceforward until the Reformation there was sufficient maintenance for a priest to officiate in the chapel, and to aid the vicar at mass on feast days and holy days.

It often fell to the chantry priests to teach the children of the parish, and most of what education there was we owed to the Church. From then on followed a regular succession of chantry priests. At the Reformation the chantries were dissolved, and their property came to the Crown, that is, was nationalised. The property of St. Michael's chantry came into the hands of Sir Thomas Pomeroy, a Devonshireman who cut a poor figure in the Prayer Book Rebellion of 1549. No doubt the education of St. Austell children suffered somewhat.

The one object that remains over from the earlier church is the font; people were apt to be conservative about changing that. In design it belongs to the type of the larger Bodmin font: that set the model for the churches in our neighbourhood. Ours is simpler, yet with a fine exfoliation of beasts on three sides and the tree of life on the fourth sculpted round the bowl, with the tops of the four columns carved into heads of an hieratic simplicity.

Looking down upon it is the best glass window in the church. This is a Kempe window of the second generation of the firm, actually by Walter Tower, Kempe's successor. A follower of the Pre-Raphaelites, Kempe revived the medieval tradition in stained glass and recaptured something of medieval religious feeling. This one is of the Old Testament kings, in cool blues, pale gold and silvery surface, with the firm's sign of the wheat-sheaf and tower within on the left-hand side.

We should acquire the habit of reading the monuments and their inscriptions like an open book – as indeed they are, for upon them one finds something of the history of the place. The most attractive is a Georgian monument of white marble with black urn on top, standing squarely by the priest's door in the south aisle. It is to the memory of the last Sawles of Penrice in the male line: Joseph, who died in 1737, and his son

John, who died in 1783. Mary Sawle, John's sister, 'the only surviving person of the family', erected the monument. She herself died, also unmarried, in 1803, leaving Penrice to a cousin, Joseph Graves, the son of Admiral John Graves who had married a Sawle. The Graveses were a naval family who figured a good deal in the naval wars of the eighteenth century; of Ulster origin they anchored in Devon and ran to several admirals and an Irish peerage. This fortunate sprig to whom Penrice came blossomed out in the fulness of time into a baronetcy under the name of Sir Joseph Sawle Graves Sawle.

In the Middle Ages St. Austell does not seem to have had any outstanding family – unlike Fowey with its Treffrys, or Trevanions and Bodrugans at neighbouring Caerhays and Bodrugan, let alone Grenvilles or Arundells. It was a parish of peasants, miners and fishermen, the place of leading landowner taken by the Duchy of Cornwall, with its large manor of Tewington (or Towan), and with the priory of Tywardreath coming second. Not until the later seventeenth century did the Sawles, formerly of Towan, achieve a certain priority among the families in the parish.

This reading of our history is confirmed by the monuments that fill the walls of St. Michael's chapel, of good types, decent design and interesting to read. Beneath was the family vault.

The first of these monuments is of the reign of George I: a tall ledger-slab of white marble with grey surround, decorative nulling, urn at the top and coloured coat-of-arms at the foot. At the other end of this wall is the Regency monument to the Admiral Graves who married the Sawle heiress: a Grecian lady mourns over a tomb with a recumbent anchor. The Admiral is described as

> Religious, just and brave, feared only God,
> Death struck the blow, resigned he kissed the rod.

> Honour and honesty in life adorned,
> Merit he noticed, knavery he scorned,
> To humble worth a friend! – to rogues a thorn!

I feel sure he was: this imperfectly rhymed sentiment generally describes the Georgian magistrate.

The next tablet to be put up, a pleasant Grecian affair, was 'erected by Joseph Sawle Sawle'. One sees that he was in some doubt what to call himself until he ultimately blossomed forth as Sir Joseph Sawle Graves Sawle. He is commemorated by a Victorian Gothic tablet over the south entrance.

His son, a Sir Charles, married a Welsh girl who was the inspiration of a famous poem, 'Rose Aylmer':

> Ah, what avails the sceptred race!
> Ah, what the form divine!
> What every virtue, every grace!
> Rose Aylmer, all were thine.
>
> Rose Aylmer, whom these wakeful eyes
> May weep, but never see,
> A night of memories and of sighs
> I consecrate to thee.

So wrote Walter Savage Landor of the young Rose Paynter of Pembrokeshire; it is commemorated in the name of her elder son, Sir Francis Aylmer Graves Sawle. Here is his memorial too, along with that of his brother, another Rear Admiral, the last baronet, with whom the male line of the family came to an end. For his only son, a lieutenant in the Coldstream Guards, was killed in the battle of Ypres on All Souls day, 1914. His monument is here also, along with those of his parents and a sister – good modern workmanship and lettering – rather touching: the end of the family.

Among other memorials is one to the sister of Ralph Allen of Prior Park, a celebrated figure in the eighteenth

century, born at St. Blazey, made an immense fortune as
Postmaster. He attained celebrity in literature as the
original of Squire Allworthy in Fielding's *Tom Jones*.
Ralph Allen's mother was a St. Austell woman. In the
north aisle is a tablet to an eminent business man of the
nineteenth century – Charles Geach. His career belied
his ill-omened name, which in Cornish means 'thief '. A
clerk in the Bank of England, he became one of the
founders of the bank from which the Midland Bank is
descended. Becoming a railway contractor, he made a
fortune as an iron manufacturer, and was a leading figure
in the industrial development of Birmingham, of which
he became mayor in 1847. Member of Parliament for
Coventry, only forty-six when he died, he would have
made a bigger name in industry and politics if he had
lived out his span.

After these come two of the three St. Austell men to
have won a place in the *Dictionary of National Biography*.
By the south door is a tablet to worthy Samuel Drew,
Methodist – shoemaker – metaphysician. The son of a
poor farm-labourer and tin-streamer, he was entirely
self-taught. At the height of the French Revolution he
published one of the many replies to Tom Paine's *Age of
Reason*, in the interest of orthodoxy; and this, coming
from a man of the people, gained him favourable
attention. He next answered back the prolific
clergyman, Richard Polwhele, on the subject of Methodism. From that he progressed to his indigestible, and
unintelligible, *Essay on the Immateriality and Immortality
of the Soul*, and *On the Identity and Resurrection of the
Human Body*. Later on he won a prize with an *Essay on
the Being and Attributes of the Deity*. I have not found
these works readable, but the remote university of
Aberdeen awarded him an honorary degree for them.
Along with Malachy Hitchins, Drew next tackled the
more intelligible subject of the History of Cornwall; but
this bankrupted the publisher. Samuel Drew, no genius,

was a good man who raised himself out of the life of his parish into the notice of the nation.

The second was a much more remarkable man, Bishop Colenso, a very controversial figure in his own time, whose life and career have a living importance for us today. Of the two crucial subjects around which his life revolved – the 'higher criticism' of the Bible, and relations with the native races of Africa – the second is a critical issue for our own time. Colenso took a progressive leader's part in both, and, though not an aggressive man but a straight Christian gentleman, was involved in storms of controversy all his life. In his lifetime he was excommunicated by his brother-bishops in South Africa, upheld by the secular law-courts, coarsely reviled by the orthodox, caricatured by the press. He was in fact a Modernist; it hardly needs saying that on both issues he was right. But a singular tactlessness of fate dogged him, added to his own innate honesty and truthfulness. He seems to have taken Luther's *Ich kann nichts anders* for his motto. Even when we come to the window dedicated to his memory by his 'fellow-townsmen and friends' – it does not mention that he was Bishop of Natal – the words chosen, with curious obtuseness, to illustrate the scene of Christ before the High Priest are, 'He hath spoken blasphemy'. Poor Bishop Colenso had no luck; nevertheless he was a great man and is an historic name.

He was born at Pondhu in 1814, the year before Waterloo; his father losing his money, he had the usual difficulties in getting himself educated. Supporting himself as a sizar at Cambridge, he became a distinguished mathematician. Elected a Fellow of St. John's, he took orders but made money by his mathematical text-books. Choosing always the hard way, he went out to South Africa as Bishop of Natal. From the first he made a deep impression on the Africans; he learned the Zulu language, compiled a grammar and dictionary of it, and proceeded to translate the earlier books of the Old Testament and the New Testament into it.

In the course of his work he came up against conundrums and contradictions, absurdities about the animals in the ark etc., which affronted the good sense of his Zulu converts. Applying himself to straightening this out, he found himself in line with the modern German movement in the textual criticism of the Bible. In all this he became, from his eyrie in Natal, the outstanding English figure. The first volume of his *Critical Examination of the Pentateuch* raised an uproar; himself somewhat surprised, but fearless and unflinching, he went on to the end.

Similarly with regard to native policy. He regarded the Zulus as his children; they had absolute confidence in him – Sobantu, as they called him, the 'father of the people'. He made himself their spokesman to the government at home, their defender in all their troubles. At the back of their troubles was the constant pressure of the white settlers upon their land and means of subsistence, the restlessness and pressure of the militant Zulu kingdom. When trouble came to a head in the ill-treatment of a chief, Langalibalele, it was Colenso who came to his defence; in 1879 when the Zulu war broke out, he denounced it and the whole course of policy leading to it. Four years later, in 1883, the bishop died, worn out with a lifetime of struggle. He was a true father-in-God to the Africans; I hope his life and example will be remembered by them in the day of their release. A happy omen is that the centenary of his death was observed in his cathedral at Pietermaritzburg and in Durban by the Anglican clergy of Natal, among whom the blacks figured largely.

St. Austell has done well to call the first of its working-class housing sites, built after the first war, after the name of this most famous son.

This brings us to the last and saddest monuments in the church, the memorials to the men who gave their lives in the two great wars of our time – on the west wall of the north aisle; these were men, some of whom we have all known and with whom we grew up.

The Old Town

St. Austell is a church-town, as we say in Cornwall, and its whole character is given by that fact. It is not an ancient town, still less a corporate borough like Bodmin or Launceston, Truro, Liskeard or Fowey; and so it has not much history compared with those. It is comparable with Camborne or Redruth, or earlier with St. Stephen's or St. Columb: a collection of houses, a few small streets around the church, the natural meeting place for the parish, which later acquired for itself a market. The modern growth of St. Austell into one of the bigger Cornish towns is mainly due to its being the hub of the china-clay industry and has largely taken place in this century.

All this is reflected in the look of the place, and its buildings, to a discerning eye.

Geography seems to have dictated the site of the settlement, for it is at the natural meeting place of three valleys, Bodmin, Gover and Pentewan, – which come together at the western end of the town. From here it extends up along the southward slope where the tracks come down from the high moorland, now the china-clay area, and where it meets the coastal plain around the bay. The valleys were wooded, the slopes and the plain had fertile soil, there was a little river, the Vinnick, (i.e. Weedy) no lack of wells and water: evidently a good site for an early settlement.

The old part of the town around the church is little changed from Victorian times, and has some attractive features. We notice, first, the pretty curves of the narrow streets: the half-moon crescent of Church Street skirting the mounded churchyard, the serpentine twist of Fore Street with two curves in it, giving glimpses of the western face of the church-tower at the end. The older houses and roofs group themselves pleasantly, especially as one comes round the corner of Church Street to catch sight of the Old Manor-house at the neck of North Street.

Starting at the eastern end of the churchyard, we look up High Cross Street noticing on the left two good Victorian bank buildings, scholarly Italianate inflexion, now uglified by printed signs. Further up on the right the modern Post Office, grey granite and slate roofs, is of good design. But at the bottom, dominating this area is a large Edwardian red-brick office building, with grotesque minarets and roof-scape. This was a masterpiece of Silvanus Trevail, a noted Cornish architect of his day – actually President of the R.I.B.A. – who committed suicide in a railway-train in the early nineteen hundreds. (Defenestration from his redbrick horror would have been more the thing.)

Across the way, a salutary contrast, is the White Hart hotel, a pleasant late Georgian house of granite, built by a remarkable man, Charles Rashleigh of Duporth.[1] It was at Oxford that I learned that the dining-room of the White Hart had possessed a beautiful eighteenth-century land-scape wall-paper, now, fortunately, in the Victoria and Albert Museum. That room, once so distinguished, still has its Georgian chimney-piece and Venetian window, along with a large Edward Lear landscape and a painting by a Pre-Raphaelite follower, a fine Augustus John of a claypit and a characteristic Paul Nash: improbable finds to come upon in the dining-room of a country town hotel.

1.   His story is told in the narrative poem, 'Duporth', in my *A Life: Collected Poems*.

This eastern area between White Hart and Red Bank used to be known as the Bull Ring – from the days, no doubt, when bulls were baited here – there was a tradition to that effect in the last century. Canon Joseph Hammond reports the tradition that a lady of the neighbourhood had her stand for viewing the sport upon the churchyard wall. Or perhaps the bulls were tethered here for market? I have myself come upon an early documentary reference to the 'playing-place' in St. Austell. Many towns had their place where the traditional miracle-plays, or later the Mummers' play, were performed. Perhaps this was the place.

To appreciate Church Street mount the steps of the churchyard and walk along the path: one then can see how agreeable the upper storeys of these Regency and early Victorian buildings are. No style of building is more suited to Cornwall than plain stucco surfaces with colour washes. The building above the modern Co-operative ground floor is a good specimen: pale grey colour turned out with primrose yellow paint, original small panes to the windows: nothing could be nicer. Next to it is an attractive curiosity: a country version of a small Renaissance palazzo, with a plaque to J. Robins 1865: he deserves commemoration for his enterprise.[2]

Turn the corner and one is looking up towards the Old Manor house of about 1700. In the seventeenth century manor-courts were held there, so I suppose this must have been the manor-house of the big manor of Tewington, the most important secular organisation in the parish in the Middle Ages: it owned a great deal of land within it, and belonged to the Duchy of Cornwall. There was no other landowner to compare with it – some of the best old names in the parish, Hexts and Higmans, were its conventionary tenants. The Sawles were its

2. Since writing this it has been destroyed, for a nondescript piece of concrete. Victorians had better taste.

stewards, and after the tremendous upset of the Civil War and the sales of Crown and Duchy lands, they emerged as the possessors of a good deal of what had belonged to it – Towan itself, for instance, King's Wood in Pentewan valley, which speaks for itself, and property in the town – along with others, Rashleigh, Hawkins and Tremaynes. I do not know how this Duchy manor came to be broken up or why it was not resumed by the Duchy along with all its other lands at the Restoration. Somehow the Sawles came well out of the Civil War.

Just here, built into the corner of the house opposite the Queen's Head, is or used to be the Mengu stone, which probably means the boundary stone. In early times stones of this kind were important as landmarks, as we note in Anglo-Saxon charters. This small dark stone, unnoticed today, was for centuries a landmark: it marked the meeting point of the three manors, Tewington, Trenance and Treverbyn. All kinds of folk-custom and folklore came to be attached to it – the tradition of a witch having been burned there, the impounding of cattle, and even into our time the reading of public proclamations and notices at that spot.

Opposite the church is the best building in the town, after the church itself – the Market House and Town Hall, built in 1844. I do not know the architect, evidently a good scholar of the Italian Renaissance style; I detect the same hand in the fine town hall [now City Hall] at Truro. The building has as fine an interior as its exterior, with a vaulted granite entrance like the crypt of a Norman cathedral; up a few steps to a noble market-hall, with splendid roof of a complex timber structure – a masterly monument to the workmanship of those days. To reach this one goes up a stone staircase to an upper section that used to be used for public meetings – my father heard the young Winston Churchill speak there in his Liberal days.

No building worthy to be compared to this combined Market House and Town Hall has been put up in St. Austell since that was built in the early Victorian age.

St. Austell used to be governed in earlier centuries by the twelve men of its leading inhabitants. I suspect that this developed from the twelve men of the homage of the dominant manor of Tewington, and that earlier government was simply manorial, with manor courts, etc. In 1661, at the time of the Restoration – what was restored was the governing class with monarchy and Church, and society was settled on that basis – the tolls from the Friday market and the annual fairs were granted to Oliver Sawle and Henry Carlyon in trust for the poor of the parish, who were the chief burden upon public expense. The parish possessed the assize of bread and ale, that is, the right to fix their prices and exact fines for breaches of them; and that also comes down from the custom of the manor.

At the foot of Menacuddle hill started an institution of which St. Austell has reason to be proud, Walter Hicks's brewery. I cannot personally witness to the excellence of its beer – better testimony comes from all over Cornwall. But the heavy, sweet, soporific odour of hops and malt from the brewery up the hill is a constant reminder of my schooldays. We owe a great debt to the St. Austell Brewery for its visual appeal too; wherever one goes about in Cornwall, one can recognise its inns by the good taste in colour-wash and paint, decent lettering in black and gold, admirably painted inn-signs. For a generation now St. Austell Brewery has set this good example, been a patron of the arts – to its managers we owe the pictures in the White Hart and occasional exhibitions of paintings.

From the Market steps we get a view of the sinuosities of Fore Street, with bright colour-wash of many of the fronts. The north side of the street is older, an attractive huddle of small irregular houses going back to the eighteenth and even seventeenth century. I can remember the Caroline porch of the Tremayne house in the middle of this stretch. It is surprising how little the old town has changed above the ground floor with its twentieth century frontages – more interesting to keep the eyes upward. However, the Fore Street that appears in the old Georgian print of it is recognisable still.

And so around the last curve into the Bodmin Road, off which lies the Wesleyan chapel, a good plain building of beautifully mottled Pentewan stone; inside, a memorial tablet to Dr. Adam Clarke, most distinguished of the early ministers. Not far along is the Roman-looking railway viaduct, which in 1898 took the place of the more exciting timber trestle–bridge of the original Cornwall Railway. Under the arch spanning the road we look up the Bodmin valley that leads into the heart of the china-clay country. And down on the lefthand side is the holy well, Menacuddle[3] well, with its tiny medieval chapel still covering it, the source and origin of the place, beside which the Saint ministered way back in the age of the Saints.

Retracing our steps to the west end of the town we are at the top of the dauntingly steep West Hill. This was the original road the coaches went down on the way to Truro, until the Truro Road was made later. At the bottom was the old St. Austell Foundry, which played an important part when our industry was mining, before the days of china-clay. I relish the view down that declivity – like looking into a ravine, with the villas embowered among dark greenery climbing up the other slope.[4]

The best general view of the town is from that opposite slope up the Truro Road: it takes in the grand viaduct spanning the valley, while the grey roofs mount

3. Menacuddle means rock well; this describes it, the well among the rocks, a romantic rhododendrony spot.
4. Less spectacular now since the narrow entrance to it has been widened and houses prised away.

up to the church-tower presiding over the clutter like a hen above its brood. From one or two vantage-points one can see the old town girdled with gardens, though it hasn't the Regency terraces of Truro, Falmouth or Penzance. The best it has to offer is the pretty early nineteenth century group of gabled stucco houses off the Truro Road, with the rhododendrons that set all this corner ablaze with colour in the Spring.

Beneath the high fortress-like wall of the station is the Friends' Meeting house, honey-coloured stone with a vein of rose-pink in it, secluded in its garden. Opposite is the green enclosure which I have celebrated in 'The Old Cemetery at St. Austell':

> Cypresses, oaks, ilexes and yews
> Compose the sober scene with sombre hues;
> The narrow path runs down the southward slope
> Among the graves, where our forefathers sleep
> In the sure and certain hope of resurrection:
> Head to foot they lie, looking to the east
>
> Whence cometh their salvation – or so at least
> They thought in former, simpler days. No such
> Certainty now: all that we know is that they
> Are asleep hard by where they lived their useful
> lives;
> Here they still are together, husbands and wives,
> Fathers and children: in death they are not lost.[5]

Historical associations

When John Leland, the King's antiquary, rode round Cornwall in the reign of Henry VIII, jotting down notes of what he saw in the years of the Dissolution of the

5. in *A Life: Collected Poems*. Since writing it the headstones have been tidied away back to wall, the place turned into a tiny park of no particular interest.

monasteries, he had not much to say about St. Austell. 'To Pentewan, a sandy bay whither the fisher boats repair for succour. Here issueth out a pretty river that cometh from St. Austell, about two miles and a half. And there is a bridge of stone of the name of the town. This river runneth under the west side of the hill that the tower of St. Austell standeth on. At St. Austell is nothing notable but the parish church . . . And in the cliffs between the Black Head and Tywardreath bay is a certain cave wherein appeareth things like images gilded. From Dodman Foreland to Tywardreath[6] the country somewhat barren of grass and corn, and replenished with tin works, with veins in the sea-cliffs of copper.'

There was then nothing to be said of a town, as there was of Tywardreath where there was a monastic house to be described or Fowey which was a well known port with a history. The country round St. Austell was not very fertile or much cultivated – mostly open downs with streaming for tin going on, isolated farms or hamlets in the waste. The great work of reclamation of the waste got going in the eighteenth century, especially with the enclosure movement.

Most of the surplus wealth in those days got skimmed off by the Duchy manor to support the Prince of Wales or the monarch. When Tywardreath priory was dissolved its small manor in St. Austell, Trenance Prior, was annexed to the Duchy.

St. Austell was too unimportant to receive mention in the Civil War, but shortly afterwards a group of early Quakers here became the central focus of Cornish Quakerism. Loveday Hambly of Tregangeeves, a widow of good family, was converted by George Fox and, being a woman of strong character and some substance,

6. Dodman means turfed rock; Tywardreath, the house (i.e. monastic house) on the sands, celebrated in Daphne du Maurier's *The House on the Strand*.

gathered round her a number of similarly infected people, including Thomas Lower, her nephew and heir. Another was Thomas Salthouse, a wool-dealer; then Anne Upcott, the 'priest's' daughter – actually daughter of the Puritan minister intruded as vicar by the Parliament-arians. They all went through a lot of trouble for their obstreporous opinions. Salthouse and Anne Upcott made the best of it by marrying.

Under Cromwell and Charles II alike they were in and out of prison for refusal to pay tithes, or taxes to maintain soldiers, or for repair of the church. They refused to contribute to 'the Pope's old decayed mass-house', as they described the poor parish church. Love-day Hambly was well enough off to make Tregangeeves a rallying place, entertaining George Fox there and holding meetings in the house. It was 'long time famous for hospitality and good works', and a faithful remnant continued in the town up to our time.

When we come to the sprightly Celia Fiennes, riding through England on a side-saddle just before 1700 – very venturesome of her in those days of highwaymen and what not – she has more to tell us. At Par she ferried across the inlet that then ran up as far as St. Blazey at high tide; at low tide it could be forded across at the sandy spit, now Spit beach. 'Thence I went over the heath [note, uncultivated downs] to St. Austell, which is a little market town where I lay; but their houses are like barns up to the top of the house, [that is, unceiled up to the roof]. Here was a pretty good dining room, and within it [i.e. inside] a chamber, and very neat country women. My landlady brought me one of the West Country tarts . . . it's an apple pie with a custard all on the top. It's the most acceptable entertainment that could be made me. They scald their cream and milk and so it's a sort of clotted cream, as we call it. I was much pleased with my supper, though not with the custom of the country, which is a universal smoking, both men,

women and children have all their pipes of tobacco in
their mouths and so sit round the fire smoking, which
was not delightful to me when I went down to talk with
my landlady for information of any matter and customs
amongst them. I must say they are as comely sort of
women as I have seen anywhere, though in ordinary
dress, good black eyes and crafty enough and very neat.
Half a mile from hence they blow their tin, which I went
to see'.

Half a century later we have the evidence of John
Wesley, who became a regular visitor. In the summer of
1755 he preached at five in the morning 'to more than
our room could contain'. Two years later he stayed over
Sunday and went to church. 'The whole church service
was performed by a clergyman above ninety years of age.
His name is Stephen Hugo. He has been vicar of St.
Austell between sixty and seventy years. O, what might
a man full of faith and zeal have done for God in such a
course of time!' Poor old parson Hugo; I dare say he had
done his best, but that was not up to the expectations of
a Wesley. Nevertheless, he found that we were 'an
exceeding civil people' – unlike the people of Falmouth
and St. Ives who gave him a rough reception.

In course of time St. Austell provided one of the most
steadfast of his societies. From the first he had devoted
disciples here: Richard Vercoe held preaching and prayer
meetings in his house, and Wesley used to stay with Mr.
Flamank, of an ancient family, in Fore Street and preach
from the steps of his house. By 1769 Wesley was
preaching in the Lower Street to 'a very numerous and
very serious congregation'. Next year, 'I stood at the
head of the street in St. Austell, and enforced on a large
and quiet congregation, "Thou shalt worship the Lord
thy God, and Him only shalt thou serve".'

By 1776 – the year of the Declaration of
Independence of the American Colonies, of which
Wesley by no means approved – the society at St.

Austell had a meeting house, for 'the rain drove us into the house at St. Austell where, I think, some of the stout-hearted trembled'. By 1787 the Methodists were moving to a new house, on a site given by Mr. Flamank, now part of the Baptist chapel on West Hill. 'We went on through a swiftly improving country to St. Austell and preached in the new house, though not quite finished, to a crowded audience, who seemed all sensible that God was there. The old house was well filled at five in the morning'.

On his last visit, in August 1789 – just a month after the fall of the Bastille announced the French Revolution, still more to Wesley's distaste – now an old man of eighty-six he rose at 2.30 in the morning, walked to the boat at Devonport and took his chaise on the other side. Travelling through Liskeard, where he stopped for tea at 7.30 – Wesley was as much of a tea-addict as Dr. Johnson – and Lostwithiel, where he stopped for an hour's talk with the faithful, 'we easily reached our friends at St. Austell by dinner-time'. That was at two; after a brief rest, 'I knew not where to preach, the street being so dirty and the preaching-house so small. At length we determined to squeeze as many as we could into the preaching-house, and truly God was there' – i.e., he preached a successful sermon. At six he was within doors for supper and prayer, to bed at nine. Next morning he was up at five for prayer, writing and tea; at 7.15 he took his chaise for Truro.

Wesley's observation of the improvement in the country is corroborated by another acute observer, who was almost as much of a traveller, William Cobbett. Cobbett was touring Cornwall some twenty years later, in 1808, and he noted that there was as good corn-growing land between Grampound and St. Austell as any he had seen. This was the result of enclosure and the tremendous work of draining, rotating crops, planting trees, carried forward by the improving landlords of the eighteenth century. They were at work everywhere; the results of their labours are to be observed still wherever the landscape looks cared for.

Wesley's later journeys, as an old man, were made in his chaise, his visits to St. Austell rendered much easier by the construction of the new turnpike that followed the southern route from Devonport to Truro, passing through St. Austell. Hitherto, the through road had been the old one running along the spine of the county across Goss Moor, (A.30). The new road placed St. Austell from 1760 on the map. The topographer Lysons notes that since the time that Carew wrote his *Survey of Cornwall*, in which St. Austell makes no appearance, now 'from its vicinity to the great mine of Polgooth, and from its having become a great thoroughfare on the road from Plymouth to the Land's End, St. Austell has grown from a mere village to be a considerable town'.

Most people connect this first phase in the rise of the town with the prosperity of Polgooth[7] mine, on the top of the hill that dominates the western prospect. Still the shell of its ruined engine-house makes a characteristic and romantic silhouette against the sunset. This mine was at its apogee in these last years of the eighteenth century. In that decade it yielded some £18,000 a year in profits to the proprietors. Lipscomb, who was here in 1799, says that 'the profits are immense, the labour of getting out the ore being so inconsiderable. More business is now transacted at St. Austell than at either of the other [Stannary] towns.' Polgooth mine brought a good deal of work and business to the little town. During the war with Napoleon it suffered a recession, but picked up with the peace and produced quantities of copper from 1815 to 1834 when Cornwall was the Copper Kingdom of the world, producing more copper than all the rest of the world together.

This was the brief period when St. Austell was a

7. Polgooth means goose-pool.

Coinage town, from 1833 to 1838, for the stamping of tin and taking of toll for the Duchy, like the ancient Coinage towns, Liskeard, Lostwithiel, Truro and Helston. This mining activity on the western side of the town was reflected in the blowing houses there. When Stockdale was here on his sketching excursion in the 1820s, he saw 'three very spacious blowing houses. In two of them cylinders are adopted instead of the common-formed bellows, and this mode of operation is considered preferable to the other.' The town's only manufacture was in coarse woollens, 'yet its commerce in various branches is very considerable, and its inhabitants are in general remarked for being an industrious thriving people'.

Though Polgooth mine came effectively to an end about 1840, its place was taken by the rise of the mines in the eastern half of the parish and by the gradual development of the china-clay trade throughout the nineteenth century. The next stage in the town's development may be marked by the opening of the through railway in 1859. The railway became even more important to Cornwall than to most counties; for, with the decline of mining, the transport of early garden produce, flowers, fish and, increasingly, tourists came to take its place. The Great Western Railway created the 'Cornish Riviera', and made Cornwall's modern fame and fortune.

At length the age-long institutions of the place, part country parish, part defunct manor, were brought up to date. First, the parish of over 10,000 acres, one of the largest in Cornwall, was reduced in size by having Treverbyn taken out of it in 1846, and Charlestown in 1847. These were new ecclesiastical parishes. The ancient parish retained its civil unity under the new Local Board established in 1864, until thirty years later when an Urban district was carved out of it to administer the town; while the rest of the parish was thrown in with other parishes to form a Rural District Council. In this century, with the crazy urban growth characteristic of it, we watch the urban caterpillars gradually eating up the rural cabbage and absorbing it into their system. In the early 1900s there was still a strong independent feeling in the villages and an equally vigorous resistance to absorption in the town. That has come to an end now; suburbia has won.

The modern age has brought public institutions – most important, the schools. A diocesan return from our deanery of Powder in 1665, states that there was 'never a free school within this deanery'. That there was no school in the parish through the centuries must have had an important effect on the inhabitants; we probably owe to it that St. Austell produced so few men who made any mark in the life of the nation. Contrast the record of the old Grammar School at Truro, and the number of remarkable Cornishmen who passed through it.[8] The first elementary school to come into existence under the Act of 1870 opened in the Church Sunday School building in South Street. This was followed in course of time by a girdle of elementary schools around the old parish. It was not until 1908 that the greatest lack was remedied – in pursuance of the Act of 1902, perhaps the grandest measure of social progress in this century – with the building of a grammar school on a good site near the brewery.

Now new schools are springing up everywhere, perhaps over-compensating the wants, the straitened ways, of the past.

Parish

Social Structure

The parish of St. Austell is of particular interest from several points of view. It is fascinating geologically as

8. v. R.E. Davidson, *Truro Cathedral Grammar School.*

well as archaeologically, it is as idiosyncratic socially as it is from the visual point of view. Its exceptional variety is visible on its face: dominated by the granite mass of Hensbarrow in the north, it extends from the lunar landscape of the clay-district – like a Paul Nash, a Sutherland or a Piper, if nature is to imitate art – southwards to the shapely bay with its coloured cliffs and headlands, the white beaches and small harbours. The land is creased by valleys, crested and wooded like Pentewan, sequestered like the Gover valley, with their own beauty even when industrialised and broken into by villages and clayworks like the Bodmin valley.[9] I respond to the nostalgic appeal of the old mining country, overgrown and forlorn, like the slopes and twisting lanes of Polgooth, the country round Crinnis, the waste of Boscoppa,[10] or even the mineralised marshes of Par Moor or Pentewan, several times up and down under the sea. It would be difficult to find any parish in Cornwall to surpass it in variety of interest – perhaps rather unique, when one considers the combination of china-clay landscape, with its mountainous burrows and chasms with a bay as beautiful as any in Cornwall.

A marked difference exists between what used to be called the Higher Quarters and the lower-lying districts converging upon the town. The difference stands out in physical make-up and history, in social character and composition as well as religious inflexion, even the looks and ways of the people. In earlier centuries right up to the china-clay era of the nineteenth century the northern half of the parish, mostly moors, high up and exposed country, was thinly inhabited. It was typical Celtic country of scattered holdings cultivating a bit of the waste around them, gradually breaking in the soil,

9.   Pentewan, the head of the sands; Gover, stream; Bodmin, the dwelling of the monks. Hensbarrow means the old barrow.
10. i.e. the dwelling place of some ancient Celt, 'Coppa'.

small patches marked by stone walls gradually creeping up the hillside. These small farmers also streamed for tin in the bottoms – all the higher ground is pock-marked with their workings; and these were the same people who first took to working the china-clay, in much the same manner and with the same equipment. A hardy folk, independent and self-reliant, rough and rude, full of character. Quite unsubmissive, they grew, with china-clay, into democratic communities, all the same social level, egalitarian, their social and cultural life centring upon their Methodist chapels which they ran themselves.

All through the centuries there was no old family of gentry up there – the Rescorlas were just good yeoman stock – not a single manor-house, and that speaks for itself. Most of the land in the Higher Quarter belonged to the manor of Treverbyn, part of the possessions of the Courtenay Earls of Devon, the rest to the Duchy manor of Tewington. What surplus wealth there was – rentals, tolls of tin and other minerals – went mostly 'up the country' to support those grandees.

For their religious needs Higher Quarters people had only a little chapelry at Treverbyn and, for the rest marrying, baptising, burying – had to come all the way down to the parish church at St. Austell. It stands to reason that it was impossible for a parson, one man on his nag, to minister to such an enormous parish. In the eighteenth century the living was even held in plurality with St. Blazey, the vicar and a curate to deal with both. Wesley's appeal in Cornwall was largely to the growing mining communities which the Church could not cope with anyway. So it was natural that as these china-clay villages grew they should revolve round their Methodist chapels. Even here an interesting distinction is to be observed. Where, in the town and lower-lying part of the parish, Wesleyan Methodism was strong, along with the older Dissenting sects, Congregationalists and

Baptists, in the Higher Quarters the more radical branches of Methodism flourished, Primitive and United Methodists. The difference was social: these last were more democratic and egalitarian, really working class.

The social structure and lay-out of the southern half of the parish stands in some contrast. Though we had no grand aristocratic family, no Grenvilles or Godolphins – and in that way the parish was more independent-spirited and individualistic than the usual English parish would be – yet St. Austell had its small gentry, some recently emerged from yeoman stock. Their houses, nothing very grand, remain about the place as visible evidences of the historical and social facts.

Though the Sawles, moving up from yeoman-farmers at Towan to Penrice in the seventeenth century, achieved priority, two families who rooted themselves were older, the Hexts and the Coodes. The Hexts are a medieval family going back in Devon to the fourteenth century, or even earlier. They came into Cornwall in the reign of Elizabeth, and to Trenarren[11] a generation later in 1618. This exquisite, sheltered valley, like a V-shaped ravine looking south towards the Black Head and the sea, was a paradisal, though not particularly profitable, place to settle. It had belonged to the monks of Tywardreath across the bay. The little gabled manor-house stood on the site of the present farm-house. In 1810 the Hexts moved uphill to build their Georgian house – actually begun in 1805, the year of Trafalgar – of grey stone mottled with lime and lavender, in a situation which could not be bettered. The family devoted themselves to the professions and the services, earlier the law, later chiefly the army. Through the generations one finds them as J.P.s, churchwardens, overseers of the poor; from the seventeenth century to the restoration of 1870 they had their own pew in church.

11. Trenarren means the hamlet of arable land.

The Coodes also go back to the fourteenth century, though they did not come into the parish until the end of the eighteenth, with Edward Coode, a county official, Clerk of the Peace and treasurer of Cornwall. His son succeeded him in those offices, and in the nineteenth century this branch of a prolific family made a more considerable contribution to the life of the town – as lawyers, bankers, in local government – than any other. We can follow them round in their houses that remain. Their late Georgian Moor Cottage, white stucco embowered in rhododendrons, lies back from the road behind the little bridge at Tregorrick.[12] their old town-house at the foot of East Hill became china-clay offices; and the various villas into which they blossomed around the town in the expansive Victorian age, now mostly offices too. This family also had a good record of service to the state, particularly in India and the Indian army, right up to the end of that unique and exceptionally civilised episode in history, the British Raj.

Older houses, or fragments of them, remain to attest the transitory passage of other families in the more squirearchical part of the parish. At Polruddon,[13] on the cliff above Pentewan, John Polruddon built himself a fine house in early Tudor days. It was unwise of him to expose his prosperity so vulnerably, for one fine night a Breton boat came in and carried him off into captivity. John Polruddon was never heard of again, and that was the end of his family; the mullions from his windows may be seen built into the pleasant Regency terrace at Pentewan.

At Trevissick – the place of the cornfield – looking down another southward gully to the sea, is a delightful

12. Tregorrick means the hamlet of the little weir, i.e. on the St. Austell river, the Cober, meaning stream.
13. Polruddon, pronounced Polreddon, means pool of the stream. The story is celebrated in an excellent ballad by Charles Causley.

old house built by the Moyles, to whom succeeded the Slades: big Jacobean hall-kitchen at the back, symmetrical Queen Anne front with pretty staircase within, old cob-walled fruit-garden, arched gateway with arms of Moyle and the rebus of a mule, with the date 1631. Menagwins (white rocks) was the home of the Scobells, and over its classic doorcase is the date 1675. This family produced the third – first in order of time – of the St. Austell men to win a place in the *Dictionary of National Biography*. This was Henry Scobell, constitutional lawyer, who emerged at the end of the Civil War to become Clerk of Parliament in 1648, became assistant secretary to the Council of State in 1653, and published voluminous collections of the Acts and Ordinances of the Commonwealth and Protectorate. He would have known his fellow secretary, John Milton, well.

Rose-red Boscundle of the Trewbodys, built of red sandstone, a rare outcrop that extends on the east of the parish into St. Blazey, has been rehabilitated in our time. This manor-house stands on the eastern boundary, at the edge of the valley going up to Garker and Trethurgy[14] – all the slopes of which have been streamed for tin throughout the ages – on the other side of which stands Tregrehan, home of the Carlyons and the finest house in the neighbourhood. Though it is outside our parish, members of that family have played a frequent part in our affairs; the last of them to do so being Edmund Carlyon of Polketh, who worked manfully for the revival of the Cornish diocese and the building of the cathedral at Truro.

Half-way down the westernmost valley, between St. Austell and Pentewan, lies a very old estate with an

---

14. Garker means the garden of the caer, or round-camp; Trethurgy, the hamlet of the water-dog, i.e. otter; Tregrehan, the hamlet on the gravel.

ancient name that appears in Domesday Book, Nansladron.[15] The place was once more important, with a deer-park and was owned by the grandest of Norman families in medieval Cornwall, the Arundells. Did it pass from them to the Tremaynes of Heligan, their stewards? Both these families were Recusant Catholics in Elizabeth I's reign. The Tremaynes conformed, to become lay-rectors of St. Austell and play a part in parish affairs (though their house at Heligan lay outside), while Charles Tremayne was vicar, 1675–1696, and is buried under the altar at which he ministered. Not far from Nansladron, a little higher up the valley at Molingey – looked down upon by Mulvra, a name I love, for it means Bald Hill and that exactly describes it – was a medieval chapelry, which helped to serve the spiritual needs of the southern section of the parish. The mission-church at the end of the terrace at Pentewan may be regarded as its successor.

With Carlyons, Tremaynes, and Hawkinses, we come to families from outside the parish who have played some part within it. The most remarkable example of this is provided by a Rashleigh, Charles Rashleigh of Duporth (i.e. dark beach), who left an undying mark upon the neighbourhood – little as people realise it. He must have been an exceptional man, his story an extraordinary one. He made an improving landlord of the eighteenth century, an entrepreneur of energy and imagination, like Francis Basset, Lord de Dunstanville, Davies Gilbert and others who helped forward developments in Industrial Revolution days in Cornwall.

Charles Rashleigh was born in 1747, a younger son of the house of Menabilly, and was bred to the law. In his early forties he began to undertake the development of

15. Nansladron = the valley of the robbers, I suppose sea-robbers or pirates; Molingey = millhouse; Heligan refers to the estuary at the head of which it stands, opening out to Mevagissey.

what became – called after him – Charlestown. It had previously been known as Polmear,[16] and in 1790 had a population of only nine. But on the open downs above, on either side of the road to Porthpean, mines were being opened up, of which the dumps still remain: Polmear mine and Dally's mine. Charles Rashleigh took a hand in these and others, and built the rows of miners' cottages which became the village, called after him, Mount Charles. In 1791 he built the first pier at Charlestown, subsequently extended, while later a harbour-basin was cut out of the solid rock, and a water-course brought into it from faraway Luxulyan.[17] From that time the place became established, fishing, a shipwright's yard, rope-walk, a foundry, an hotel – the Rashleigh Arms. The open downs above and around he enclosed, formed and manured fields and farms, planted woods. At Duporth above the cove he built himself a substantial Georgian house, and shaped around it garden, park, estate. (It is all now, appropriately to the age we live in, a Butlin's camp.)

What a man Charles Rashleigh must have been, improving landlord, speculator, man of taste, an essentially creative type! What followed was long remembered in St. Austell, though forgotten today. According to Canon Hammond, he 'took into his employ a lad named Dingle, for whom he conceived a great liking and at last determined to bring him up as a gentleman. To this end he must make him a magistrate, for which the possession of a certain amount of property was then a necessary qualification.' So Rashleigh made a formal conveyance of his estate. I do not know whether the good Canon has penetrated to the heart of the matter; he confesses to having had difficulty in getting at the truth as to the transaction.

16. Polmear = big pool; Porthpean = little beach.
17. Luxulyan, pronounced Luxillion = the place of St. Sulyan.

Apparently young Dingle was persuaded by backers, enemies of Rashleigh, to claim that the conveyance was a real one, or Rashleigh may have given him to understand he would make him his heir – for his only children were daughters. The case came to law, some time towards the end of the war with Napoleon, and numbers of St. Austell people went up to give evidence. Rashleigh won his case, but it cost him his fortune; the Charlestown estate was mortgaged to his lawyers, whose representatives are now the owners. Rashleigh died some ten years later, in 1823; Dingle lived to be an old man in receipt of parish pay – and never married. Nor was Rashleigh really a marrying type: there must have been something between them. After waiting some thirty years, I have at last put the strange story into a poem – a poem giving more freedom to speculate on the inwardness of it all.[18]

The neighbouring cove of Porthpean has a charming early Victorian bow-windowed villa, with a paradise of a garden climbing up the steep hillside. The St. Austell tradition is that the founder of the Petherick family fortune, John Barratt, walked barefoot out of Cornwall to Cumberland, where he discovered the richest iron mine in the country. This is a romanticisation of the fact, which was remarkable enough. John Barratt was a Gwennap man; it was largely due to his expertise that the famous Hodbarrow mine was brought into production, and yielded some 20 million tons of the best hematite during its active life.[19] The Petherick family are the latest recruits to those families who have made a name for themselves by service to parish, county, nation.

18. The long narrative poem, based partly on documents, partly on folklore, 'Duporth', appears in my *A Life: Collected Poems*.
19. For its story, v. A. Harris, *Cumberland Iron. The Story of Hodbarrow Mine, 1855–1968*.

Such is the social lay-out of the parish. Some names that had the qualification 'gentleman' attached to them have either died out or moved elsewhere: Dadow and Rescorla for instance, Dalamine, Laa and Carne. The Dalamines were at Penrice before the Sawles moved there. The Laas (or Lees) lived at Merthen near Par, and had an exciting experience during the Civil War: Mr. Laa, a Royalist, came back to his house to find some Parliamentarian soldiery making free with his provisions, shot one of them and made good his escape, being well mounted and swimming the tidal estuary at Par. It did him no good, however; the family lost their footing.

All round one recognises the names of old St. Austell folk who farmed the land for centuries and appear constantly in the church registers: Treleaven, Trevithick, Nancollas; Trethewey, Tremayne, Vivian, Carlyon; Pascoe, Tonkin, Rosevear, Creba; Hicks, Hambly, Couch, Grose; Luke, Martin, Perry, Ede, Ivy; Hancock, Nottle, Rowe, Phillips. To them I must add my own name, for there were Rowses at Tregonissey from the time the church registers began in Elizabeth I's time. There are none there now, though they are still in the parish.

Perhaps I should qualify my contrast between Higher Quarters and the lower part of the parish with which we began. For though the china-clay villages – Carclaze, Penwithick, Stenalees, Bugle, Trethurgy, Carthew[20] – are independent-minded and self-reliant, this does not mean that the lower-lying villages – Tregonissey,[21] Mount Charles, Charlestown, Holmbush, London Apprentice, Pentewan – are less so. Perhaps they are less demonstratively, more quietly, so; still most of them

---

20. Carclaze = green caer, round-camp; Penwithick = the head of the little trees or copse; Stenalees = tin-court (where the manor court would have been held); Carthew = dark caer.

21. Tregonissey = homestead of the farm-labourer.

originated as mining villages, with the same basic spirit of independence. Hamlets mainly dependent on the squire, Charlestown, Porthpean or Trenarren, were exceptional in the scheme of the parish – and even they had their fishing and fishermen. An independent-spirited individualism is basic to the Cornish character; the study of a parish like St. Austell shows why.

Archaeology and Mining

Archaeologically the parish is no less interesting. On the top of Hensbarrow Beacon, 1007 feet, a lump on the skyline from wherever you look up, is a barrow – the burial mound of one of the early chieftains hereabouts. Hensbarrow means old barrow, going back to 1000 – 500 B.C. There would have been other prehistoric monuments in the Higher Quarters – like the longstone that still stands by the road not far from North Goonbarrow – that have now been swallowed up by the claypits. The name Goonbarrow indicates that there was another burial mound there, now vanished. For more relics we have to go to the southern half of the parish around the bay, which is richly rewarding. Even here things have been much eroded in course of time, but from what remains we can draw a picture of the life of our remote ancestors in these parts in the Bronze Age and Iron Age – say, from 1000 B.C. to A.D. 500.

Let us start at the western end. In the Pentewan valley, which has been streamed throughout the ages for tin – the detritus washed down from the rich lodes of Polgooth – Bronze Age axes and spear-heads and an Iron Age tankard have turned up. At Polruddon was a fogou, now destroyed: one of those curious, narrow underground chambers which probably served for ritual or religious purposes. Coming round the coast, on Black Head was a prehistoric cliff-fort; the defensive walls across the narrow isthmus are still there, though partly eroded, with the ditches between. It defends a protected landing beach below (like Tintagel). A little inland at Castle Gotha (meaning, old camp) above Porthpean are the remains of the circular enclosure with surrounding ditches, within which these people lived – hugger-mugger with their cattle. This site has been much ploughed in, but the southern section of the rampart remains with traces of the ditches. When excavated a furnace of Roman date was found, evidently for smelting lead-silver – Silvermine is in the cliffs below. Quite recently, and astonishingly, an Anglo-Saxon coin from the seventh century appears to have been minted at Castle Gotha. If authentic, does it throw light on the obscure historical question of continuity from Roman Britain to Anglo-Saxon England?

Along the Porthpean road, not far from the cross-roads at the by-pass, is a well preserved menhir (long-stone). Over nine feet high above ground, it bears a sinister resemblance to a human figure, particularly as observed against the setting sun. This would have been the pivot of those primitive people's religious observances – possibly human sacrifice, as at Stonehenge. The stone has attracted a certain amount of folklore. It used to be known as Tregeagle's Walking Stick – the story the usual one of the giant planting his walking stick in the ground to go after his hat that blew off. Earlier generations of Mount Charles children found something forbidding about the spot, and would never play there.

Not far away, up to 1801 when Charles Rashleigh was enclosing the waste here, was another barrow known as One Barrow, then levelled. It has been suggested that One was a corruption of wyn, or gwyn, meaning white. When opened the barrow was found to contain a kistvaen, or stone chest, containing a mass of charred human bones.

The most recent excavation brought to light a small round-camp above Trethurgy, occupied from 500 B.C. or later, into the Dark Ages (or, down here, the Age of the Saints). Evidently the precursor of the medieval hamlet, it was surrounded by an earth-bank with stone revetment; cattle in one area of the compound, huts for people in another. It was rather touching to see at the entrance the scratches in the stones by the scraping of the wooden door over the centuries. Then the village decided to move down the hill, nearer the stream that was their water supply.

One of the richest finds ever made in Cornwall was a hoard of silver treasure found at Trewhiddle[22] in 1774. It had been buried there in the reign of King Alfred of Wessex, carefully concealed in the débris of an old streamwork, at the time of the Viking attacks all round the coasts. Some churchmen had a rich amount of treasure to hide; nobody ever came back for it. It contained a silver chalice, now the oldest surviving piece of English church plate. In it was a large collection of silver coins of the Wessex kings; over a hundred of them were recovered from the finders, their dates showed that the treasure must have been buried about 875, a climax of the destructive Viking raids. One object was a knotted scourge of plaited silver wire, an apparently unique specimen. Other silver objects included rings, a pin with decorated head, a brooch and a tiny box, and mounts for drinking vessels. Some gold objects disappeared and have been lost sight of. What was left has come to rest in the British Museum.

Geologically the parish is immensely rich and diversified. Here too one notices the marked division between the granite mass of Hensbarrow and the Higher Quarters generally, and the more varied rocks of the

22. Trewhiddle: the place of the working, i.e. tin-streaming.

lower half of the parish. One might think that the social structure rose straight out of the geological formation. For geology I must rely on authority. 'This parish, important in an economical point of view on account of its mineral production, affords a vast fund of geological information. Its northern part is composed of granite; its southern part of various rocks belonging to the porphyritic group. Its granite, on the northern side, contains layers which abound in porphyritic crystals of felspar. On the western side it comprises several kinds of this rock; some characterised by the proportions of shorl that enter into their composition, and others by containing talc instead of mica, and by the felspar being prone to an extensive decay, in which state it furnishes porcelain clay, or china clay, for the potteries . . . Hornblend rocks succeed the granite, and produce a red fertile soil. These extend a little to the south of the town of St. Austell, and are followed by a blue lamellar slate in which the mines are situated. The rock is much softer, and more argillaceous than the hornblend slate, and decomposes into a light-coloured soil The matrix of its lodes abounds in chloride; it is probably a chloride schist. This formation is traversed by several beds of felspar, porphyry, and elvan courses, in the western side of the parish, which run north-east and south-west. One of these elvans, at Polruddon near Pentewan, has been extensively quarried for many centuries, and is much esteemed as a building material.' This is the famous quarry in the cliff out of which came the stone for St. Austell church, and other churches in the neighbourhood, and houses like Trenarren and Trevissick.

The parish is astonishingly rich in minerals, and in greater quantity than is usually realised: not only quantities of tin and copper, but ochre and iron, some nickel and cobalt, more uranium. From the ancient workings of Silvermine in a gully near Trenarren, we may infer that some silver was obtained, as elsewhere. To quote the geologist, J.H. Collins: 'uranium ores in considerable quantities were found many years since in the St. Austell Consols Mines', and farther west of the parish. As for iron, 'between Charlestown and Spit Point, a distance of a little over two miles, there are certainly a dozen cross-courses, nearly all of which are ferruginous in some parts at least'. One might guess that from the coloration of the cliffs all the way round from Charlestown to Crinnis – now popularised as Carlyon Bay. 'The Ruby iron lode appears to reach the coast between Appletree beach and Crinnis island; while in the killas it has yielded only a little blende and chalybite, but on entering the considerably kaolinised granite near Trethurgy it contains remarkably pure red hematite.' It was worked with some success in the Trethurgy area, at Wheal Ruby, though the quarries up there immediately under flat-topped, altar-like Carn Grey – with its superb view eastwards to Brown Willy and Rowtor, and southwards all over the bay – are a more continuing and striking feature of the landscape.

Collins concludes: 'the St. Austell mining district . . . has in the aggregate yielded ores to the value of millions, though worked only to comparatively shallow depths. The great copper mines will probably be found rich in tin if ever they are worked deeper; the great tin mines in the killas may, like the mines in the neighbourhood of Carn Brea hill, be found still richer when the lodes enter the granite.' There is no doubt about the mineral reserves still left beneath the soil – it is merely that, as things are, it is uneconomic to work them.

Such is the background; we must turn briefly to our mining history, which has been made by tin and copper.

Tin-mining developed out of age-long tin-streaming by following up the lodes into the hills. Miners could not go very far or dig very deep until the eighteenth-century

97

invention of a pumping engine to clear the works of water – apart from the difficulties of ventilation, ascent and descent by means of ladders. What hard lives our forbears of those generations lived, much harder than the open-air tin-streamers before them! Many of them died early of 'miners' complaint': various forms of phthisis and silicosis. My grandfather, whom I never knew, died at fifty from working in the bad air of Appletree mine, the workings going out under the Bay at Charlestown. All his sons were miners, several of them driven to emigrate to South Africa and America when mining here came to an end. I mention it only because it is characteristic of the lives of so many of the menfolk in those generations.

St. Austell had a smelting house as early as 1689, but that would have been for minerals chiefly obtained by the numerous stream-works. Famous Carclaze tin-mine offered an almost unique curiosity for it was a tin-mine open to the sky, worked like a quarry. All visitors were taken to see it; the popular tradition was that it went back to the Phoenicians – as indeed it might; the local people held that Solomon's temple was built of its metal. Fortunately we have an early nineteenth century print to tell us what it looked like; 'it is worked open, and the mouth of the enormous pit comprises an area of some acres. Numbers of little stamping mills work on its sides, and at the bottom is an adit to carry off the water, waste, etc. Of later years it has also been worked for china clay.' That was written in the 1870s at the time of the transition from tin to china-clay. After centuries of producing tin Carclaze became one of the best producers of china-clay. The enormous chasms in the earth, which used to be well into the downs, have now come right out to the road, several miles round.

The apogee of mining in the parish was reached in the second quarter of the nineteenth century; production had been steadily increasing in the half century before, but in the 1820s and 1830s it shot up sensationally with rich discoveries of copper. Production of tin continued to be important in the third quarter of the century, particularly with the success of Wheal Eliza. Then from the 1890s St. Austell went over wholly to china-clay.

Polgooth mine on the western skyline was the making of the town in the eighteenth century; but in the early nineteenth the mines opening up to the east of it became far more important. The case of Great Crinnis mine had an element of drama in it. In 1808 it was declared to be 'not worth a pipe of baccy'. In 1809 Joshua Rowe got together a number of associates to try once more; they soon dropped off discouraged, leaving Rowe to plough on alone. He shortly discovered a rich bunch of copper, easy to work; when the profits rolled in the former associates started a lawsuit on the claim that they had not relinquished in form. Notwithstanding the expenses of this the mine cleared £168,000 profit in less than five years. In 1817 Davies Gilbert declared that 'the most productive mine now working is the Crinnis mine . . . yielding to the proprietors more than £2000 per month'. Before it was abandoned in 1833, it had yielded profits of over half a million.

The neighbouring mines of the Charlestown area were successful in their heyday, affording employment to hundreds of miners who lived in those characteristic rows of cottages at Holmbush, Charlestown, Mount Charles, Bethel, Sandy Bottoms. Bucklers produced tin; Cuddra[23] tin with some copper; Crinnis, East Crinnis, and Pembroke chiefly copper, though Pembroke was a good tin-bearer too. There were other mines here, notably Wheal Eliza, the latest of them and a good producer, which closed down in 1892. Many of these old mine-workings are already invisible for greenery; one

23. Cuddra means the house in the wood; Crinnis, island caer (earthwork, round camp).

catches sight of the empty shells of their engine-houses among trees and flowering furze-bushes. It is rather affecting to walk down their overgrown lanes, silent now, that once hummed with activity.

These mines kept the foundries at St. Austell and Charlestown busy, the second of which continued happily in production to make its contribution in the heroic years 1940–1945. It was regularly employed in turning out equipment – vanning shovels, plates, iron kibbles – for the mines. In the 1870s the foundry built many engines and boilers both for home and abroad. The opening of Wheal Eliza in 1863 kept the foundry going through the years of general decline in mining, and the railway came to the rescue to open internal markets not hitherto accessible by sea from the little port at the foot of the hill. In the 1880s many iron railway bridges were made here, some for as far away as India. With the twentieth century lean years set in again until the mechanisation of the clay industry between the wars renewed the old foundry and kept it fully occupied. Throughout more than a century now Charlestown foundry has trained and produced many craftsmen who have gone out all over the world.

China-clay

The name of St. Austell is known all over the world for its china-clay. It is true that china-clay is produced in many parts of the world, but nowhere in such pure quality as in this home of its early development in the eighteenth century. Fortunately there seems to be no end to these deposits, now the most striking visual evidence of the extraordinary mineral wealth of Cornwall. They extend beyond the bounds of St. Austell parish into several of the neighbouring parishes, and there are outliers in other parts of Cornwall on Bodmin

Moor, and West Devon. The focus of the industry is St. Austell, the china-clay capital.

In the early eighteenth century the knowledge of how to make china-ware, hard porcelain, was brought from China to Europe. Many heads were occupied by the problem how best to make it, the optimum proportions of china-clay and china-stone, and the techniques of firing it. Among them was Cookworthy, a Quaker apothecary of Plymouth, whose frequent journeys into Cornwall gave his inquiring mind the opportunity to look out for the long-sought deposits. This was his real importance; then some twenty years after his first discovery, he began to make china at Plymouth. Local people knew of the existence of the stuff – they called it growan or killas – which often existed along with the tin in their workings. At Carclaze, for example, knowing no use for it they allowed it to run away to sea as waste. When the great potter, Josiah Wedgwood, came to Cornwall in the summer of 1775 to get a lease for a deposit for Etruria, he was told that old Mr. Carthew of St. Austell, who had used the stuff to build in a furnace, had observed that when fired it turned into porcelain. Wedgwood entered into an arrangement with the younger Carthew to lease a deposit and look after it for him.

When the proper use of china-clay came to be more widely known – its beginnings were naturally shrouded in some secrecy – the first people to dig it out were the farm-people on whose land it lay.[24] Here we find the origin of some, not all, of the St. Austell families whose names became well-known in the industry and to whom it owes practically everything: Martins, Loverings, Varcoes, Higmans, Stockers, Nichollses. Theirs were the first, and oldest clayworks extending from Carclaze in the east round the mass of Hensbarrow in a semi-

24.   I have drawn upon some of their stories freely in *Cornish Stories*.

circle, Goonbarrow, Ninestones, Gunheath, Greensplat. The clayworkers dug out the clay from small pits with the implements and simple techniques derived from tin-streaming and mining. They had it in their blood – though later on, when mining declined the miners thought it going down a step to 'go to claywork'.

For a small, growing industry that depended entirely on export, in the days before railways when bulk-transport by sea was alone practicable, St. Austell was well situated. From the clay-area it was downhill all the way to the convenient little harbours around the bay, Pentewan, Charlestown, Par. We developed our own type of china-clay wagons, a local design: I can hear the jingle of the horses, the creaking of the brakes and drags in my ears still from childhood days, as the heavy wagons went through Tregonissey on their way to the railway station. As early as 1832 there was a rail-track, for horse-drawn wagons at first, from St. Austell to Pentewan whence there was a considerable export of clay. For half-a-century Charlestown was the chief outlet, and in return imported coal and timber for the industry. Later on Par moved into first place, from 1872, with its station on the Great Western Railway line.

Later still, Fowey took first place, with its deep-water harbour for ocean-going ships, particularly after the construction of its electrically-powered jetties between the two German wars. In 1938 Fowey exported 410,000 tons of clay, Par 118,000, Charlestown 51,000. Meanwhile, in 1920 a mineral line was constructed through the Bodmin valley, which directly connected with the Great Western. Altogether the railway shifted one-tenth of the clay, mostly for inland demand; nine-tenths went by sea, some of it round the coast, most of it overseas, the biggest market being the United States.

In early days the pits were started by a group of adventurers taking small shares, just as in mining. Their resources were small – it is curious that no big capitalist saw the possibilities of the industry, no one like the Williams family in mining in West Cornwall. Returns were small and precarious, when it took a year to dig out a ship-load of clay and another year to dry it in the primitive clay-dry open to sun and wind, of which there used to be an archaic specimen by the roadside at Penwithick.[25] In 1828 Lower Ninestones was started by John Lovering and Robert Martin, in the same year Greensplat and Gunheath by Wheeler and Higman. These, like all the best pits, remained in the hands of the old clay-families of St. Austell, who knew all about clay, until the end, i.e. until the necessary amalgamation of the industry under single control in the 1930s.

The 1850s marked the first upward leap in the industry's expansion. By then there was a considerable exxport to Hamburg, still more to Antwerp – Belgium was always the best European market. With the rapidly increasing population and rising standard of living brought about by the Industrial Revolution, larger demand for pottery set in than ever before. Where the china of the eighteenth century had been a luxury for the upper classes, now its use was extended to the people. But the use of china-clay in making paper ultimately meant an immense increase in the demand. North Goonbarrow proved to possess the highest quality of bleaching clay; it was also the first pit to introduce a Cornish pumping engine, specially constructed for it at Charlestown foundry. Towards the end of the century steam-engines for pumping were introduced everywhere; in this, centrifugal pumps driven by electricity.

The 1870s saw a depression, probably set off by the Franco-German war. It came at the worst possible moment, when tin-mining was declining and an agricultural depression succeeded. This was the time when the great emigration from St. Austell began, like

25. The head of the little grove.

that of the 1840s from West Cornwall to Michigan and Wisconsin. Dr. John Rowe tells us that in the 1870s 'there were more Cornishmen working at Calumet and Hecla mines in Michigan than there were at any other copper mine in the world'. Things were not so bad in the St. Austell area, where there was china-clay to turn to. By 1874 the output was nearly 200,000 tons and that gave employment to some five thousand men in the area as a whole. In the 1880s there was a complete recovery, and by 1890 the output doubled, to some 400,000 tons.

For the next twenty years, until the outbreak of the first German war in 1914, the industry prospered. Output went up by leaps and bounds, until in 1913 production was 900,000 tons, of which some 600,000 tons were for export. I remember the little harbours crowded with shipping, as were the roads with clay-wagons and their teams. This was the good time when the leading clay-families made their money— quite a lot for small people in a small place. This was the time when their villas burgeoned on the western outskirts of the town, when they prudently – they were never spendthrift – bought their first motor-cars. (They need a John Braine to cele-brate their idiosyncracies, and amenities: he would do them justice.)

Meanwhile, the clayworkers received nothing very grand: in the Victorian age the day-labourers got 1/6d. a day, a carpenter or blacksmith 2/6d. Before 1914 my father's wage was 18s. a week. As against this, the work was healthy, hours were not long, eight hours a day, and many clayworkers had a second string to their bow, a small holding, a part-time job, a small shop. Moreover, they were individualists, self-reliant, used to looking out for themselves. So there was very little trade-unionism in the area. Radical impulses were directed to left-wing Liberalism – so long as St. Austell gave its name to a constituency it returned a Liberal; Lloyd George was its hero, not Karl Marx – of whom indeed it had never heard. For the rest, these impulses went skyward in the chapels.

So that when the one big strike in the history of the industry broke out at the end of July 1913, it came spontaneously and independently of the General Workers' Union, which had only a small membership. And its leadership came from the more radical Nonconformist chapels, its real leader one of their popular ministers. By mid-August most of the pits were idle, and nearly 5,000 men were out. They had not the resources to stand the struggle, though they held out stubbornly for nearly three months. Medland Stocker, head of the West of England Company and the biggest-minded man in the industry, accepted the men's demand for a small increase of pay; and though they were defeated at the time, this later became accepted throughout the industry. The defeat of the strike led to a considerable increase in union membership. There was never any ill feeling, let alone class-hostility, between the workers and the owners and 'captains' of the works: they were all still too close together socially and culturally for that; they came from the same people, they attended the same chapels, they shared the same tastes – football and brass-bands. Were they not all Liberals?

The war of 1914–18 ended the old world in the clay-trade, as in so much else. In 1919 the production of clay was about half what it had been before the war, the export less than half. Export markets had been lost, the pre-war organisation damaged and contacts broken; other countries had been given the opportunity to develop their own resources. The St. Austell industry fell on hard times and was ill-equipped to meet it; it had grown up in an era of individualism; the many and diverse concerns found it impossible to co-operate even to meet common dangers, or in constructive steps to achieve a common marketing scheme. There was also a fundamental division of interests between the producers of high-grade clay and those of low-grade, and this held up effective amalgamation all through the 1920s.

In the nineteenth century the industry owed everything to the individual capacity and nose-for-clay of the 'captains' – each pit had its captain, and a characteristic body of men they were, regarded with proper respect. Labour was cheap, cheaper than any mechanisation, until the depression of the 1920s. All these factors worked to decrease the number of men needed, so that another wave of emigration was a feature of that post-war period.

It was not until the world economic crisis of 1931 that a complete reorganisation was forced upon the industry. Only the strongest of the diverse units, the old producers of the best clay, could hold out in the blizzard. Smaller, and more uneconomic, concerns had to confess themselves defeated. This produced the circumstances, and the atmosphere, in which a complete reconstruction could be carried through. We cannot trace the steps in detail – that more properly belongs to a history of the trade. But it was a St. Austell man who gave true leadership at that time, brought a constructive mind to bear on those difficulties, and ultimately led the industry to the right solution. This was Medland Stocker, one of the small ring of families who had been in clay all their days. Head of the West of England Clay Company, he piloted the attempts to control production and prices by agreement, and formed the co-operative associations to this end in the 1920s. These were steps in the right direction, though the problems of the industry could be grappled and resolved only by a policy of amalgamation and centralised control. In this he was the pioneer, and set the first model with English China Clays. The world crisis hastened the pace and enforced the right policy. In 1932, at the nadir of the depression, a combine of leading firms followed, E.C.L.P. (English China Clays,

Lovering and Pochin) which thus achieved control of three-quarters of the industry.

Within his own firm Medland Stocker developed and gave his name to Stockalite. A truly creative man – if we were a more literary, or at least a more literate, people he too would have his name in the *Dictionary of National Biography*. What he accomplished was something of importance to the nation. It was his discerning eye that selected the man who came to succeed him as leader of the unified industry, and it was by something of historical propriety that he should come from the Potteries, from the country of the Wedgwoods, Sir John Keay. With him in control, by 1939 some 90% of the industry was unified and under central direction, in time to stand the strains imposed upon it by a second world-war and to plan its rehabilitation and part in world-trade with the peace. Nor has it failed to take a bigger and more generous share in the life of the community of which it is the mainspring and undoubted focus, successor to so many little concerns and small enterprises, the work of unnumbered individuals of the parish who have now vanished into the limbo of time.

Though the industry has been going for two hundred years it is only recently that it has had its history written.[26] One reason why that was so is because of the secretiveness that has prevailed from the beginning. Cookworthy got a monopoly at first, or else it is possible that potteries might have developed in Cornwall – but the tinners as well as the potters were opposed. Josiah Wedgwood, richest capitalist of his day, made his own arrangements for supplies and eventually broke the monopoly. But the local people from very early got control of production, not the principal landowners, of whom there were over fifty – from Lord Falmouth, the

26.   R.M. Barton: *A History of the Cornish China-Clay Industry*.

Pitts and Fortescues downwards – but St. Austell tradesmen, grocers, saddlers, drapers, even one doctor. It was from these that the 'china-clay families' came, many of whom I have known about from my childhood – to whom the industry owed its development, quietly, unobtrusively, stealthily.

As the *Mining Journal* observed a century ago: 'St. Austell will tell its own tale, to see new mansions that have been lately built by persons who only a few years since were standing behind the counter or working at their trades and are now independent gentlemen.' But St. Austell did *not* tell any tales; the china-clay families were shrewd and secretive; they kept to themselves, married among themselves and did not move far out of the district. The original secrecy of the Chinese seems to have descended to them. Just as their forbears were said 'to knaw tin', so they had a nose for china-clay, knew the different qualities of clays and of china-stone, the proper proportions of rain-water to spring-water to obtain the best results; they made improvements in the drying of the clays, the kilns, the design of the settling pools, the mica launders to run the stuff, methods of extraction. But they were not letting on; with Cornish secretiveness they kept their know-how to themselves. The description of the other end of the industry, as early as 1799, applies also to the producers: 'the chosen knot of china folks, whose interest is to make china ware and opake information.'

In 1807 there were seven clayworks active, each with its necessary china-stone quarry, in the original St. Stephens area. (The Post Office has imposed its foolish form 'St. Stephen' on people, and on the author of the book, but there is no reason why Cornish folk should put up with it). By 1850 there were 100 small pits, but half the industry was in the hands of half-a-dozen individuals, who made no noise. *The Mining Journal* observed, 'It has been done so quietly, with so little demonstration, with no speculative risk, that I wonder that it can have been going on under one's own eyes. When will capitalists open their eyes and invest in Cornish clay and stone?'

The answer is that they never did, effectively, until our own time, when large-scale English capital bought the Cornish out. In 1850 fortunes were being lost in the decline of the dominant Cornish copper-mines; the tin-mines were always speculative, and declined decisively from the 1870s. By the mid-nineteenth century china-clay employed some 7,000 men, women and children. The miners thrown out of work thought it inferior to 'go to clay'; for the most part they preferred to emigrate to go on mining all over the world, taking their skills with them.

In the St. Austell area there was an intimate transition from tin to clay. The famous open tin-mine, Carclaze, also produced clay: in 1866 it raised 5,000 tons of clay 'entirely out of the profits made on tin' – a good proposition for the Lovering family who owned it. Some of the steam pumping engines thrown out of work by the closing down of tin-mines were installed in the clay works; a few of the old foundries, like Charlestown, were taken over by them. The period 1850–1900 was one of slow and steady technical improvements, all on a small scale: the deepening of pits, a first experiment at night-washing by electric light (St. Austell was the first town in the county to use electric light for domestic purposes), the piping of liquid clay to the clay-dries increasingly located by railway sidings or harbours. Gradually there was formed a network of railways around that central *massif* that dominates the landscape behind St. Austell.

Relations between the producers and the landlords throughout the period were friendly and co-operative. The land-owners were understanding and ready to make concessions when necessary. This was just as well, for –

with over fifty leading owners of mineral rights in a small area – it formed a 'tessellated pavement' of much complexity. Gradually these rights were bought out and consolidated – until only Lord Falmouth stands outside today, with one of the best pits, Goonvean.[27] But in the clay industry there never was an instance like the notorious case when Dolcoath mine – most famous of Cornish mines – was swiped £25,000 for a renewal of lease by the Bassets of Tehidy. This created lasting resentment in the Camborne area.

It is impossible to recover now anything beyond the outlines of those silent burrowing personalities, whose names have come down to us, though we never knew precisely for what – anyway, they were not particulary literate. William Pease was – he kept an invaluable Diary; but then, a man full of ideas before his time, he was not a Cornishman. The two John Loverings, Senior and Junior, must have been men of mark; old Rebecca Martin a strong personality in her own right. In the 1930s the old family concern of the Loverings sold out for something like half-a-million pounds – no one knew the precise figure. There is nothing at St. Austell to show for it or them.

The ultimate shape the industry would take was portended by the incursion of an 'up-countryman', the Midlands chemist and industrialist, H.D. Pochin. He developed ways of using china-clay in the manufacture of paper, as well as in chemical and pharmaceutical products. This was the ways things would go: china-clay today is used in a wide range of those products, besides other domestic uses, textiles, plastics, paints, linoleum, not to mention cosmetics; the original use, to make china-ware, must now be a tiny proportion of the whole. From 1879 Pochin began acquiring his own clay-works for his rapidly expanding needs. The Aberconways

27. Goonvean means the little down.

inherited his family interests; the first Lord Aberconway headed the great combine on its formation.

Today accountancy rules; the day of the local men who 'do knaw clay' – Elias Martyn and John Martin, John Lovering I and John Lovering II, the Stockers and Parkyns, the Higmans, and Nichollses, and old Dr. Stephens as we saw him in top hat driving round in his carriage and pair – is over. So, I suppose, will the industry be one day. As Mrs. Barton says: 'Like Cornwall's other two great extractive industries, tin and copper, that of china-clay also will pass entirely into history, the quays of its ports deserted, the "great, white road" weed-grown and silent, and the wide uplands of Hensbarrow again a desolate land where "scarcely a goat can live in the winter".' That time is not yet, and so, even the enterprise of many generations will long be recorded in a miniature landscape of sharp, green hills and countless lakes, turquoise and white cliffed, the burrows and pits of time past.

Place, Fowey, and the Treffrys

The fascinating and historic town of Fowey is entirely dominated by the no less historic and fascinating mansion of Place, to a degree rarely paralleled. And few there are who have penetrated within those bulwarks, to look down on the rooftops, narrow opes and quays below, the estuary opening out to the Channel. The name Place refers to the monastic barton of the priory of Tywardreath, which owned the manor – as Elizabethan Place as Padstow belonged to Bodmin priory, and Place at St. Anthony-in-Roseland to the monastic cell there. The name Treffry means the homestead on the hill, and is pronounced, as usual with Cornish names, with the accent on the second syllable – though in New England, where there are rather more of the name, they pronounce it in the English manner, wrongly, with the accent on the first. We should say Tre-ffrý.

The name comes from a small farm just outside the park at Lanhydrock near Bodmin, where now is a pretty slate-hung Queen Anne farmhouse. The family was indigenous there, until they married Elizabeth Boniface, heiress of Place, when they moved thither. There is an old tradition in the family that one of them was a standard-bearer for the Black Prince at Crécy – likely enough, and this has been commemorated in the name de Cressy with them.

However, they do not emerge into the daylight of history until the 15th century, really with this Elizabeth. The Middle Ages saw constant raiding to and fro across the Channel, in which the 'Fowey Gallants' gave as good as they got. On one such raid, in 1457 – Henry VI's troubled time – the French raided the town one night and attacked Place. In the absence of her husband, Thomas Treffry, his wife repelled the assailants with boiling lead over the bulwarks. I often think of it as I walk under their shadow jutting out over the cliff path.

Their son married a co-heiress of the Michelstows, that piratical family which lived up the creek from which they got their name and which we today pronounce Mixtow. In the church at Fowey are three pretty nameless brasses, of two men and one lady in 15th century dress, inscriptions ignorantly destroyed. But the useful Cavalier Captain Symonds, who employed his spare time noting antiquities, tells us that they were of Thomas I and Thomas II and their wives. Let us hope that the sole remaining lady is the brave Elizabeth who repelled the French raiders: she had a double motive for doing so since Place was her inheritance; and there she was given a statue later in commemoration.

The sons of Thomas Treffry II were three brothers, John, Thomas and William. Like their neighbours across the river, the Trevelyans of St. Veep, and indeed the bulk of the West Country gentry, they were loyal to the Lancastrian royal house, and broke out into open opposition to Richard III's usurpation. They made a premature rising against him in 1483, after which John Treffry took refuge with Henry Tudor in Brittany – to return with him to Milford Haven where he was knighted on their happy landing.

Thus the apogee of the Treffrys was the early Tudor period, particularly that spanned by the three brothers. Close in the confidence of Henry VII – as far as anyone ever was – were Sir Robert Willoughby de Broke, Receiver of the Duchy of Cornwall, whom we see on his fine alabaster tomb (disgracefully manhandled) in Callington church, and Sir Richard Edgcumbe of lovely Cotehele beside the Tamar, perfectly preserved to us and cared for by the National Trust. When Sir Richard sailed in 1488 to receive the submission of Yorkist Ireland (anything to be out of step!), he voyaged in a Fowey vessel, accompanied by Sir John Treffry in another. A year later he went with Edgcumbe on his last mission with several Fowey ships of war, to Brittany where Sir Richard died, and is buried in the church at Morlaix ('Mords-les!' Bite them, was the town's motto).

Sir John Treffry died in 1500, his will revealing the full panoply of medieval faith in the generation before the Dissolution of the monasteries and its end. To the priory of Tywardreath – of which not a stone remains, except the gravestone of the last prior – he left a gown and two vestments of blue velvet, two silver cruets and other items, in return for prayers for his soul daily and yearly as for the Cardinham founders. 'And I will that there shall be an honest priest singing within the church of St. Barry [Fimbarrus of Cork] in Our Lady chapel by the space of three years next after my decease, to pray for my soul and all the souls that I am bound to pray for, having for his wages for three years – £15'. A quarter-share in the vessel *Mary Hardford* was to go to brother Thomas, and a quarter-share in the *George* to nephew, John Trevanion. To brother William his best basin and ewer of silver, his best dozen of silver spoons, three silver candlesticks, and a ring of gold with a sapphire. Sir John had been several times sheriff of Cornwall. He had an only daughter, but the heir to his property was his next brother Thomas.

The youngest brother William also received marked reward for the family's loyalty; a few months after Bosworth Field he was given grants for life of the offices which made his fortune: Surveyor of Customs for the port of London, Constable of the Coignage of Tin for Devon and Cornwall, Keeper of the Duchy gaol at Lostwithiel (which he would have performed by deputy, receiving the fees), and most important, Gentleman

Usher of the Chamber, which meant intimate attendance upon the King. His will, of 1504, shows him to have become a rich man, and it is the most revealing early Tudor will that I know.

Evidently the Treffry chapel at the end of the south aisle was not yet built, for 'as soon as the ambulatory is made' he wished for a tomb to be made with three images of himself, his wife and brother, 'like unto a tomb which lieth on Mr Browne in the Crutched Friars of London with the Pity of St. Gregory', with similar scriptures and apparel.[1] To Lord Willoughby de Broke he left a large board-cloth of damask, and a tapestry portraying the childhood of Our Lady, which is in 'a chest with sheets in my great chamber in my house in London.' To Sir John Arundell of Lanherne, another large piece of diapered damask; another piece along with plate to remain in the Grocery at London to be kept for nephew Thomas Treffry. He was also to have 'my best basin and my best ewer of silver, two pots of silver parcel gilt, three candlesticks of silver parcel gilt with their prickets for wax and their sockets for tallow; also my smooth standing cup clean gilt with a cover, also my best praunge [pot] for green ginger, also a Spanish dish of silver all gilt on the inside; also a white layer pounced [punched] of silver, also a dozen spoons of the Apostles [today worth a fortune in themselves], their names written on the back side with enamel, and one spoon of Our Lord which make thirteen.' All this to rest in the Grocery until his nephew reached twenty-one.

Lord Broke and Sir John Arundell were to receive a hundred shillings as overseers, but the executors to be William Holybrand 'my fellow', Robert Rydon, and nephew Trevanion: these were to have his best, second and third gowns. We must remember how valuable, and durable, clothes were then. Holybrand and Rydon to

1. This church stood nearby at the corner of Hart Street.

have coverlets of silk verdure; nephew Henry Treffry 'half-a-dozen Paris bottles parcel gilt with their covers and the half-months of the year contained within the same, also my worse basin and mine ewer of silver parcel gilt' – to remain in the Grocery until he was twenty-one. Nephew William, his godson, was to have a great silver standing cup, and twelve Apostle spoons, also another praunge for green ginger – likewise to be kept until twenty-one.

Sister Genet Trevanion was to have 'a great plain Paris bowl' with a silver cover; brother Thomas' wife a little cup, silver cover with little low foot, to be kept in the family as an heirloom: all the rest of the plate in the Grocery similarly. John Trevanion: a small flat silver cup, half-a-dozen small silver spoons, 'a goblet with a cover with enamel of violets, with other broken silver which is in a standard of iron in my Counter at London.'

'Master Holybrand, I took out of the King's money £10 and a noble [6s 8d], which I pray you take out of my fee-reward gathering money for the cloths and boat-hire money. For I have taken no money of the said parcels of all this year past.' To his maid Margaret £20 more at her marriage, and Alice 20 nobles for her good service. A sum of £200 was to be completed by selling over forty bales of wool or 'with my fees and rewards of the Custom House'. In his coffer were two chains of fine ducat gold, 'with other old Henry nobles, crusados [Portuguese coins] and ducats, and two sovereigns', making up some £200. Also there, two collars of gold, one with eighteen pearls and five rubies, the other with black enamel.

A very large piece of purple velvet was to make an altar frontal for his London parish church, St. Olave, Hart Street, and another above; the rest for a cope and vestment for the Crutched Friars 'if it will stretch thereto – they to have me in their prayers'. The above collars and chains were to provide £20 for the church of St. Barry in Fowey, and to buy land sufficient for a priest to sing perpetually there for the souls of father, mother, brother Sir John, 'my wife, father-in-law and me'. He repeats his request for the tomb to be made of Purbeck marble.

Smaller sums of £10 and less were to be distributed among the poor of Fowey, among his tenants and the poor at Trenwith, St. Veep, Treffry, Lanhydrock, Tywardreath, St. Pinnock and Lansallos. The vicar (of Fowey) to have his best horse, the next with 40 shillings to Thomas Clark, 'my servant, beside his wages and his winter clothing'; his horsekeeper John Penhale, his third horse, 40 shillings, his quarter's wages and winter clothing; Thomas Hackthorp similarly, without horse; Thomas, 'of my kitchen at home at London his winter gown and four nobles'.

The sale of jewels and goods was in order that 'my building at Fowey may go forth according as it is begun and my nephew John Trevanion can show you the plans thereof.' The goods in his house at Fowey to go to his younger brother and his children. For Mrs Holybrand a flower with a pointed diamond, three rubies and three pearls – such as we see in the Holbeinesque portraits a little later; for Lady Arundell a pawnce [? girdle] with diamonds and a great pearl hanging under. For Lord Broke 'an ouch [brooch] for his pleasure – a hart enamelled wrapped in a towel, wherein is couched a fair diamond, a ruby, and a pearl.' For Mrs Rydon a ruby in a white flower, three pearls hanging under. Sister Genet Trevanion – a pomander [perfume-ball] of gold 'which is in my standard within my Counter, as I understand'; sister-in-law Genet 'a little ouch of gold, with an amethyst, a sapphire, and a pearl'.

Sister Trevanion – 'a girdle best harness with gold, with a bonnet of black velvet; nephew, her son, 'to help him to his marriage a bonnet of velvet with the best frontlet of gold with the next girdle of gold'; William Trevanion's wife the third similarly. Brother Thomas'

117

wife ditto, 'if there be any more left, as I am sure they be'.

Henry Pester to have the house he dwells in, in debate between him and Treffry – Pester to pay 'my brother after his conscience'. His chantry priest at Berkeley to choose a gelding and a gown furred with black budge [lambskin]; £3 to pray for him, also several pieces of linen. Brother Thomas – a gown lined with sarsenet, another of damask, and 'my best doublet of tawny satin'. 'My fellow, Hugh Denis' – evidently in the King's service – 'a piece of crimson chamlet [silk and wool] to have me in his memory.' Mr Shirley, Clerk of the Kitchen, a good piece of chamlet or else a gobbet of fine linen.

'Also I will that Mr Weston of the King's Chamber have another piece of fine black chamlet. Mr Hugh Denis and Mr Weston, I beseech you commend me unto my sovereign lord the King, he to be good and gracious lord unto my nephews; and show his Grace that I never had none of his money untruly in all my life.' This has the ring of truth about it – in those last years of Henry VII when he was scrutinising more closely than ever the revenues of the Crown, for his son to spend. Mr Weston here was the father of Sir Richard, who built splendid Sutton Place in Surrey; grandfather of young Sir Francis, whom Henry VIII executed, wantonly and falsely, along with his Queen, Anne Boleyn.

All movable goods at his house in London and in the King's place at Wanstead were to go to garnish his house at Fowey. Nephew Trevanion to have a silver salt 'which goeth about in the house'; nephew Thomas Treffry the best salt, his brother Henry the next, brother William the third. Thomas also to have 'my bottle chain with a device enamelled which I wear daily'. All his lands and tenements in Cornwall, Coventry and Berkeley were to come to brother Thomas and his heirs.

What a will this is! I have given it at length for it is all that we know of him, as also for its rarity and intrinsic interest. He was evidently a busy man with his offices in the port of London and at Court, his houses in St. Olave's, Hart Street and at Fowey. In 1500, four years before his death, he was sheriff of Cornwall. We learn his close friends in the service of Henry VII, whom he would have known well. We see from his will the luxury of his possessions – plate and jewels were also a form of investment in the absence of banks. Overriding is his family feeling; having no children of his own, he makes generous disposition among all his kin, remembering everybody. Having accumulated so much, it is remarkable what he remembers in detail, though occasionally he is not sure where an item is laid up. Above all, he repeats the provision for prayers for his memory.

The tomb which he was so anxious should look like that of Mr Browne in the Crutched Friars that he repeated the request, was not made according to it; it was not made of Purbeck marble, it did not carry the Pity of St. Gregory, nor did it include his wife. When made, altogether less expensively of local stone, it had incised upon it, in curious rustic outline, the three brothers, Sir John, Thomas and William.

Thomas died in 1509; his son Thomas Treffry V continued the family, marrying Elizabeth, daughter of John Killigrew, of another sea-port family, of Arwennack on the harbour at Falmouth, Captain of Pendennis Castle. Thomas became Captain of St. Mawes Castle, on the opposite side of the harbour: the beautiful trilobe fort designed by German engineers, still in perfect shape, the building of which he supervised – part of Henry VIII's fortification of the Channel coast provided for by the Dissolution of the monasteries. Treffrys and Killigrews threw in their lot with the Reformation and became Protestants. Perhaps this also partly accounts for the reduced form of the family tomb.

We find Thomas Treffry in the personal confidence of Thomas Cromwell, wholly in favour of the new deal and ready to bully the monks of Tywardreath, under their drunken old prior (the last), out of their ancient hold upon the town of Fowey. Cromwell wrote by Treffry. 'I require you to agree with the inhabitants . . . that their liberties may be extended amongst them. For his Highness thinketh that the said port ought to be his, so that his Grace intendeth from henceforth to have it well provided for defence against the enemies of the realm. Wherefore his Highness thinketh that ye be very unworthy to have rule of any town that cannot well rule yourself.' This was true enough. The days of monasticism were over: henceforth secularism was to prevail.

In the Reformation Parliament which confirmed and forwarded the new deal Treffry served, through all its six years, as Member for Bodmin. For Queen Mary's third Parliament we find Treffry elevated to be knight of the shire – so he had the confidence of the county, though not in sympathy with her proceedings. From 1540, in connexion with the fortification of the south coast, we have a remarkable illustrated map of the whole of it, in which Place appears beetling above the town of Fowey: a plain façade recognisable still except for the Regency bays, with the tower beside which had to be rebuilt later.

John Leland, the King's antiquary, travelling about the country in those years recording what he saw, was entertained by Treffry, from whom he got information. After the French assault in 1457 Thomas Treffry II 'builded a right fair and strong embattled tower in his house; and embattling all the walls of the house in a manner made it a castle. And unto this day it is the glory of the town building in Fowey.' It still is, further glorified in the Regency period. Leland gives us a brief account of Fowey's history, which he learned from his host, who had 'devised a block-house on the western entrance to the harbour, made partly by his cost and partly by the town.' At St. Mawes Leland made for Treffry the Latin inscriptions we still see carved round the walls, to the honour and glory of Henry VIII, to the terror of his enemies, and the fame of his son Edward now Duke of Cornwall, etc.

In 1545 Lord Russell, as President of the West, found great lack of powder at St. Mawes and Pendennis, while 'Treffry's house has great miss of the ordnance which was taken away' – evidently for Henry VIII's expensive third French war. War always increased privateering and piracy in the Channel – sometimes difficult to distinguish. Treffry lent money to rig out a ship for the Lord Admiral, but had trouble in getting his money back, while a son of his was taken prisoner. Thus he was given a license to bring in French wares to raise enough money to ransom his son, rated at sixty Frenchmen!

In Edward VI's reign Treffry was involved, with other prominent new-dealers, in rounding up the medieval church plate of the county, to replenish the virtually bankrupt national exchequer. Over 6000 ounces of silver and silver gilt were collected from Cornwall, under this deplorable act of nationalisation, and lodged in St. Mawes under Treffry's care. On Queen Mary's accession he was sent up to the Jewel House with some 300 ounces, already defaced. In the upshot little was left to the churches, and some of it stuck to people's fingers. Mary, for all her Spanish fanaticism – a female Canute – could not hold up the tide. We learn that Treffry had been present with the leading gentlemen of the county at the proclamation of Queen Jane, but was able to excuse himself. He died in 1563, his large stone slab relegated unrecognisably from the family chapel to the exterior porch.

Little is to be said of the Elizabethan Treffrys: John, who succeeded his father in 1563 and had a longish reign to 1590, and William who, born in the first year of the

Queen's reign, died a month before her in February 1603. One exciting event lights up the scene at Place. John Hawkins' third Voyage to the Caribbean, in 1567-8, had been treacherously overthrown at Vera Cruz with great loss of life, ships and goods. A fine opportunity for recoupment occurred in 1569 when Spanish ships carrying treasure for the troops in the Netherlands were driven by storm to take refuge in harbour at Plymouth and Fowey. The bullion had been borrowed by Philip II from banks at Genoa: Queen Elizabeth felt the need to borrow it herself. At Fowey the two pinnaces carried thirty-two cases, each containing 20,000 reals. These the Spaniards lugged up to Place, where they were locked and sealed, and a guard placed over them until the government's orders came down. (Meanwhile, the Spanish army in the Netherlands mutinied, and Spain could never regain control. The Queen repaid her borrowing in her own good time.)

The conflict with Spain was getting more acute, and with it the government's struggle with the Catholic opposition, infiltrating priests and seminarists into the country contrary to the laws. The fire-eating Richard Grenville drove forward a campaign against the Cornish Catholics, as sheriff 1576-7. The first of the seminary priests was caught, and hanged at Launceston. While he was addressing the crowd, John Treffry as J.P. cut him short by commanding the hangman to put the rope about his neck, and 'let him preach afterward'. The priest's skull is preserved, and venerated, at the old Arundell home, the Carmelite convent at Lanherne. For his service to religion and country Grenville was knighted. Such are humans.

John Treffry had some seventeen children – this must have been a strain on his resources providing for them all, or most of them. The eldest son William married Ursula Tremayne of the Protestant Devon line (the Cornish remained Catholic). While the newcomers to the town, the Rashleighs, pushed forward in trade and shipping, buying up houses within and lands without, William Treffry concerned himself more with county affairs, reporting constantly to Sir Robert Cecil on activities of the enemy. In 1595 a force of galleys from Spanish-occupied Blavet in Brittany raided Penzance, burning Mousehole and Paul. Cecil himself recommended Treffry for the Commission of the Peace, for his vigilance at the invasion.

In 1599 he is reporting a concentration of ships and galleys at the Groyne, i.e. Corunna – were they for Ireland, aflame with O'Neill's rebellion? Examining a suspicious ship in harbour, he encountered an obstinate Catholic, who refused to take the oath of Supremacy; and in a hogshead of salt was concealed a barrel of Papist books and propaganda to serve the faithful and trouble the régime. Next year he is reporting shipping movements for the Lord Admiral and the activities of a Dunkirk privateer, which has captured a Fowey bark and three other West Country vessels. Meanwhile, brother Thomas the lawyer, advises Cecil as to the sale of the Cornish manors he had bought, and in return receives a profitable wardship. Then, in 1603, William died aged forty-two, leaving John, his son and heir, only eight years old: Hannibal Vyvyan of Trelowarren puts in for his wardship.

William's brother Abel remained at Oxford to be provided for, a scholar at St. Alban Hall, for in 1599 the Queen recommended him for a Fellowship at All Souls, another small *douceur* for family services. The College replied that it had no vacancy; and next year, when Cecil renewed pressure, the Warden and Fellows returned that they had not found Abel altogether answerable to that which had been delivered Cecil in his behalf, so that they were not able to satisfy his request. However, he got a Fellowship in 1602, and we find him contributing Latin verses, from All Souls in 1603, to the volumes from the university commemorating the Queen and welcoming James I. By 1610 the young Fellow was dead.

Cornwall was in the front-line of the war, brought home to the coast by the armadas of 1588, 1596 and 1597. Treffry was kept busy as Master of the county ordnance, with four troops of a hundred each under his command. He served only once in Parliament, that of 1584 which, on the threshold of open war, severely increased the penalties for recusancy, refusing to attend church, and undermining the régime by bringing in Jesuits and seminary priests. In the Parliament of 1597 his brother Thomas, counsellor at law and mayor of Lostwithiel, represented Fowey, sharing it with John Rashleigh, who had already served in 1588 – William evidently was too busy.

In the year before he died he had received a generous tribute in Richard Carew's *Survey of Cornwall*, mainly for his work for defence of the county and Fowey harbour in particular: 'a gentleman that hath vowed his rare gifts of learning, wisdom and courage to the good of his country, and made proof thereof in many occurrents, and to whose judicious corrections these my notes have been not a little beholden. His fair and ancient house, castle-wise builded and sufficiently flanked, overlooketh the town and haven with a pleasant prospect, and yet is not excluded from the healthful air and use of the country. Which occasioned his ancestors – though endowed elsewhere with large revenues of their own and wives' inheritance – for many descents to make here their ordinary residence, as is witnessed by their tombstones which I have seen in the church.'

Elizabeth I's reign is marked by the establishment in Fowey of the Rashleighs from North Devon. From their house below Place – now the Ship Inn, with their great chamber upstairs, Elizabethan panelling still *in situ* – they came to take an active part in the town's affairs and to buy up many properties commanding votes for Parliament, under the borough's scot-and-lot franchise, and controlling the corporation. Treffry and Rashleigh co-operated well enough during the long war with Spain, later to develop some rivalry, and later still a contest for political ascendancy. This is not the place to tell the story of the Rashleighs, merely to note that their monuments crowd the north aisle of Fowey church to counterpoise the Treffrys on the south.

Two of William's sisters acquired fame through their progeny. Anne married Edward Herle of Prideaux on the edge of the lovely Luxulyan valley. Their son Charles Herle became a leading Puritan of a moderate persuasion, a favourite preacher before Parliament, a decisive figure in the Westminster Assembly of divines, eventually becoming its Prolocutor. Both a learned man and a reliable committee man, he had a large hand in drawing up the Presbyterian confession of faith. Though he detained the Assembly some three weeks over the manner of receiving communion – knees or no knees – he was trusted with the arduous business of composing their wrangles over doctrinal nonsense. Himself contributed largely to it in numerous indigestible publications, today unreadable.

He had been educated at Exeter College, Oxford, with its West Country affiliations; then becoming tutor to a future Earl of Derby, he was elevated to their fat rectory of Winwick in Lancashire. Like other respectable Presbyterians he was shocked by the killing of the King and withdrew into retirement at Winwick, where he had leisure to reflect on the consequences of his earlier enthusiasm for Parliament. He is an important enough figure historically to deserve a biography.

Another sister, Martha, married Thomas Dyckwood, alias Peters, and in the same year that the respectable Herle was born gave birth to the very unrespectable

Hugh Peters. Peters was not as bad as he has been made out to be: true, he was an immoderate Puritan, and that was bad enough. Chaplain-general in Oliver Cromwell's army, he preached up the war and the execution of the King; but he was not a regicide, though at the Restoration he was executed unjustly for one, when John Milton, who was the principal defender of the King's execution, went scot free. Hugh Peters had no one to defend him, and everyone against him; his enthusiastic temperament betrayed him – he had been all too effective as Army chaplain, preaching to the soldiery. Actually, for a Puritan, he had done quite a lot of good works.

A Cambridge man, of Trinity College, he consorted with Puritans there and absorbed their fantasies; a *mauvais coucheur* like all of them, he left the country for Holland, and then for Massachusetts, where they were 'set, as it were, upon an hill', as an example to lesser mortals. There he had a farm called Foy at Marblehead, which might well have settled for the name. Peters took a leading part in the affairs of the colony, and in the establishing of Harvard. He was a chief persecutor of the insufferable Mrs Hutchinson, and excommunicated the free-wheeling Roger Williams for his heterodoxy. Sent back to England as agent for the colony, he was in a position to make hay while the sun shone for the Puritan cause, both as popular preacher and war-correspondent propagating the news. Settling into Whitehall under Cromwell, he was his principal adviser in Church matters, something like a Cromwellian archbishop.

His biography has been written at some length;[2] we must confine ourselves to the family. The Dyckwoods were Protestant refugees from the Low Countries, with which Fowey, and the Treffrys, had shipping connexions. Settling in Fowey the Dyckwoods became

2. R.P. Stearns, *The Strenuous Puritan*.

allied with the Peters family, of which Robert, several times member of Parliament in Elizabeth's reign, had served in the Netherlands. Evidently Hugh Peters, who was born at Hill-hay, now a Treffry farm a mile or so up river, inherited a curious, marked temperament from his mixed ancestry, with a vein of comic play-acting in his preaching. His end was not at all comic. Place has a rather unfeeling portrait of him, bold and rustic-looking, big nose, large eyes, heavy brows – sad in expression, as clowns are apt to be: not a Cornish face.

The Civil War was a devastating experience for Cornwall – three armies marching down and up, its own manpower drained in fighting up through the West Country. In 1644 a Parliamentarian army under Essex invaded, hotly pursued by the King. Essex' army was cooped up on the western side of the Fowey peninsula, which it ate up before its surrender, denuding the Rashleighs' estate and farms at Menabilly and Combe of cattle, sheep, everything – their losses were never recouped.

John Treffry, who had succeeded so young, was head of the family through all this disturbed time, while his cousins were so deplorably active, making history. Like Charles Herle, he had been at Exeter College, to which in 1611 he presented a silver tankard of 27 ounces. Back at Place, he narrowly escaped involving himself in the King's misfortunes, for at the beginning of the Civil War he took a hand and rounded up the town's ordnance on his behalf. This was brought up against him by the victorious Parliament later. Meanwhile, in 1644, Fowey was the scene of exciting events, when Essex led his army into Cornwall, hotly pursued by the King. The Parliamentarian army was shut in in the narrow peninsula west of the river, eating up the land. Essex and Lord Robartes scuttled away in a fishing boat to Plymouth before the surrender.

At the end of the war the Rump Parliament scrutinised everybody's record who had been against them, inflicting heavy fines to raise money for their purposes, confiscating all Crown and Church property. It amounted to half a revolution, and many families were squeezed down or out. John Treffry's case came up several times before the County Committee. We need not go into the details, but in 1653 the votes were equal on whether he was to be discharged, and next year his case came under the Act of Pardon. He was lucky to have friends on the other side and to get off scot-free. Four years later he was dead. He had married Bridget, daughter of Sir Arthur Champernowne of lovely Dartington. The marriage took place at St. Kew, where the family owned the farm of Rooke – one sees the gravestones of Treffrys in church and churchyard there. No children of the marriage, the succession came to Thomas Treffry of Rooke.

His son John, born in 1650 during the upheaval of war and Puritan Revolution, lived long into the quietude of the Hanoverian succession, not dying until George II's reign, in 1731. Educated as usual at Exeter College, Oxford, he served twice as Member of Parliament for Fowey. In 1679 he shared the representation with Jonathan Rashleigh, in 1685 with Bevil Granville. The year 1700 saw something new in the family record – a literary event, if a modest one: John published *Poems on several occasions*, 'being the result of idle hours, to please the desire of some friends'. Most of his hours seem to have been idle: he did not exert himself in any other way. In 1711 he sold off Rooke to Edward Treffry of Mevagissey. He made an unambitious marriage to the daughter of a Fowey townsman: again no children. We find the males of the main line at Place petering out, the succession passing through females in several generations. However, with such an old stock, Treffrys in the male line are still about in Cornwall as in the United States.

Sister Jane married another Fowey townsman, John Toller, Collector of Customs, mayor in 1716. On

succeeding his uncle, William Toller assumed the name
of Treffry by Act of Parliament. He lived only four years
to enjoy it, but put up a memorial in the church asserting
his descent. 'Here lieth the body of John Treffry,
Esquire, who married the daughter of Philip
Champernowne of Modbury, by whom having no issue
gave his estate to Thomas Treffry of Rooke from his own
sisters, for the support of his own name and family. Who
left it to John Treffry, Esquire, his eldest son, who
having no issue has settled it on William Toller, his
sister's son, and the heirs male of him the said William
Toller for the same intent and purpose, and inserted it
here to prevent all future disputes and cavils, and that
mine ancestors' and my intent may always be fulfilled.'

All his children died in infancy, except a fourth son,
Thomas, who married the daughter of a Fowey
merchant. This was becoming a habit, in the decline of
the family, and of Fowey, in the 18th century. Thomas
served as sheriff in 1766, dying ten years later, leaving an
only son William Esco Treffry, who survived his father
only three years. Once more the male line failed: the
females of the stock showed much greater vitality and
staying power.

This was evident in his sister Susanna, on whom
William Esco settled the estate. She had married a
Joseph Austen of a Cornish family at Plymouth, and was
early widowed, with one son and a daughter. She took
up residence at Place, the estate run down, the mansion
in disrepair, the medieval tower in ruin, the family
impoverished – only a few farms left, which she
proceeded to manage herself. Born in 1748 she held the
fort there into the full flight of the Victorian age, dying
in her nineties in 1842.

Hers was a remarkable achievement, but not the least
was her son, Joseph Thomas Austen, who ultimately
acquired the name of Treffry, and proved himself the
most remarkable of them all. Last of the great leaders of

the Industrial Revolution in Cornwall, he rehabilitated the family fortunes and Place. He kept the historic house intact, medieval and Tudor, adding as much again in Regency Gothic, outside and inside; above all he rebuilt the crenellated tower once more to dominate the town. The splendid house – once more 'the glory of the town building in Fowey', as Leland had called it – remains a monument to him, but not the only one.

Joseph Thomas Treffry:
Industrial Leader

Joseph Austen, 1782–1850, who took his mother's name of Treffry, was the last of the leaders of the Industrial Revolution in Cornwall, and the least known. At last a biography of him has appeared, full of meticulous detail, by one who has devoted a lifetime of research to Fowey.[1] Now we have the opportunity of estimating Joseph Austen at his true worth and appreciating what he did with his dedicated life, with its singleness of purpose. He was not an easy man to know.

William Esco Treffry who died in 1779 left two sisters. Jane, the elder, by a second marriage left progeny which ultimately succeeded to Place to constitute the present line there. Curiously enough, the younger, Susanna, came in for Place – it would seem by her brother's will; certainly she had the will-power to make a go of it. This led to some family ill-feeling, until Susanna's son many years later decided to make Jane's grandson, his heir. Susanna married at Fowey in 1780 Joseph Austen, a Plymouth Cornishman, who shortly died, leaving her with a son, born in 1782 and two small daughters.

Joseph Thomas Austen proved a very remarkable man. The early Industrial Revolution leaders belonged to the mining area of West Cornwall, particularly the three, if not four, generations of the very able Williams family. They made an immense fortune, married into the

1. John Keast, *The King of Mid-Cornwall*, 1982.

131

old county gentry, bought up estates all over Cornwall, and proceeded to make a second fame as gardeners of genius. Joseph Austen was exceptional in that, a scion of an historic family of gentry, he turned himself into a mining and industrial pioneer, in Mid-Cornwall something new. True, the opportunity was there at the end of the Industrial Revolution: he made the most of it.

Susanna sent him, as usual with the family, to Exeter College, Oxford, where he interested himself in mathematics and history, and he was always good at drawing and surveying. These studies stood him in good stead. At home his mother busied herself building up a dairy-herd, selling butter in the market in the arcade under the old 'King of Prussia' inn (Frederick the Great, of the Seven Years' War), which appears in Q's stories of Troy Town (Fowey). When Joseph was old enough to join her, he set to to repair the depleted inheritance, so long neglected; for years there was a remarkable partnership between mother and son – and the son never married, thus ensuring singleness of aim as of life.

He began in a small way, building little ships on the slips up-river, installing lime-kilns, bringing in limestone, culm, coal; tree-planting up the valley by Penventinue (pronounced Pennytinny, it means the head of the springs). He started as an improving agriculturalist, pulling the estate into order, giving employment.

As a young man he was deflected into politics and wasted valuable time on it, as young men will. He was a radical Reformer, and there was plenty to reform in the corrupt old borough of Fowey, largely in the hands of the Rashleighs, who occupied one of its two seats in Parliament for nearly a century, 1727 to 1802. It was perhaps surprising that the young squire in the decayed mansion up above should have been the leader for reform, and this won him much unpopularity in the town below. I suspect that this was the usual middle-class jealousy of the gentry, which has won out in our time, with its deplorable consequences for the country houses, which were the glory of England, and their way of life, which set the best model of living the world has seen (copied by the Byrds, Washingtons, Jeffersons, Adamses, Wadsworths and so many others all over the old Colonies which created the United States).

It is interesting that in all that period there was never a Treffry mayor of the town, until this century, with a new dispensation and a new borough charter, when a squire condescended to step down from his bulwarks into the mêlée of civic affairs – as also did my friend Q. In those early days leading up to the Reform Bill of 1832 Joseph Austen attacked the crusted Corporation at its most vulnerable point, its mismanagement of the Town Lands. We must remember that scot-and-lot voters, i.e. holders of small tenements which qualified them to vote, were up for sale, expecting not only cash, but jobs from government, in the Navy or Customs, tide-waiters, what not. Reform was naturally not popular with them, nor was the aggressive young squire, filled with energy, zeal and himself. Everybody remarked on his egoism; but all remarkable men have something to be egoistic about, their egos a great deal more interesting than the non-egos of the feeble and uninteresting.

George Lucy of Charlecote near Stratford, with its Shakespearean associations, took an expensive hand in Fowey politics and elections to Parliament. At first on opposing sides, the Blues against the Greys, with their respective inns as headquarters, eventually Austen and Lucy came to a private accord – to the chagrin of partisans out for fun and flinging mud, the small change of local politics. This earned a further measure of unpopularity, when young men, with the discretion of maturer years, move to the right. Later, we find Austen and his mother spending Christmas at historic Charlecote, where Lucy was making extensive – and expensive – additions and 'improvements' to the Elizabethan house Shakespeare knew.

These may well have played a part in suggesting Austen's restoration and additions to Place. The Regency period was a great time for improving architecture – his now remote kinsman Trevanion, Byron's cousin, was engaged in making a romantic Nash castle of Caerhays further down the coast.[2] Austen had first the ruins of the medieval tower to clear away: he used them to fill in ground and make a carriage drive sweeping round to the front of the house, and then characteristically proceeded to extend his grounds. In the course of it he brought up a prehistoric urn from the site, about which he wrote a paper. Over years he engaged in a correspondence about such things with the historical topographer, Lysons, which has silted up in the British Library and would repay investigation.

With the end of the long-drawn war with Revolutionary and Napoleonic France began the major interest of Austen's life, his mining ventures. And a good thing too for Cornwall, for peace brought agricultural depression, men out of work on poor relief, poverty and want, in the industrial district of Lancashire riots: after Waterloo – Peterloo. Austen's development of the mines in Mid-Cornwall gave work to hundreds of families (who thereupon began to breed automatically). In the end it was calculated that the mines with which he was connected gave work to some 3,000 people, men, women and children.

The egoistic squire proved a more humane man than the faceless men. Later on, the 1840s saw another period of depression, and consequent food-riots. My own ancient grandmother remembered the tradition of the 'Hungry Forties'. Dr John Rowe, in his admirable book,

2. v. my *The Byrons and Trevanions*.

Joseph Thomas Treffry: Industrial Leader

The Industrial Revolution in Cornwall, tells us that Treffry – he had by then taken back his mother's old name – 'induced his fellow mine adventurers to subsidise the sale of flour and grain to their employees, besides advancing loans to the more needy, unfortunate and distressed tributers', i.e. independent miners working on their own. That was to be in the future.

Meanwhile, the 1820s and 1830s proved a prosperous time for mining in Cornwall, when the little land produced the greater part of the world's copper. Hitherto production was concentrated in West Cornwall of the Bassets, Williamses, and Bolithos. Austen was fortunate in that Mid-Cornwall lay open to his energy and vision. On horseback he rode all over this countryside, keeping his eye open for potentialities and 'capabilities', in Capability Brown's phrase, everywhere and of every kind, not only mining.

On the great shoulder of hill between Fowey and the Luxulyan Valley there was a small mine, Wheal Treasure, yielding not much treasure, actually in default. Austen took it in hand, raising capital from the North Cornwall Bank, with which he was already connected and to which he was heavily indebted. People regarded him as a daring speculator: they did not see the hard-headed calculator, good at planning, surveying, statistics, beneath the outer man, all enthusiasm and energy.

He was also a first-class judge of men, well served by the fellows he chose as managers and for his business office, as well as his engineers, who worked for him all their lives. That speaks for itself. For mine-captain he chose Thomas Petherick, of that experienced mining family. Together they made a great success of Wheal Treasure, justifying its name, and then extended operations to the group of mines up on those moors.

Brought together in one concern, Fowey Consols, they made mining history, rivalling the Western area.

As the lodes deepened so the necessity of greater power grew: in the first place the complicated business of making water power available, bringing streams across the land of other landowners; secondly, the installation of steam-engines to pump the deeper levels out. The development of the famous Cornish pumping engine kept pace with the need:[3] eventually Austen installed one of the finest, under the aegis of his chief engineer, William West, which became known as 'Austen's engine'. This so much impressed the visiting King of Holland that he ordered from its makers, Harveys of Hayle, the biggest of its kind to pump out the Haarlem Meer: now laid up as a national monument in Holland.[4]

The results were prodigious: the mines proved rich – right up to the later 1840s – and Fowey Consols came second only to the most famous of all Cornish mines, Dolcoath at Camborne. Today all silent and deserted: there on the skyline is the great gaunt ruined engine-house of Fowey Consols, another monument to the energy and vision of the man who brought it into being – the whole hillside alive with men, like ants, in his day. Motoring up steep Penpillick[5] Hill, his works above and below, I often think of him.

With production from his mines increasing, the urgent problem became that of transportation to a port on the coast. Naturally he first thought of Fowey and his own quays already in work and building small barks up-river. The land it would be necessary to cross belonged to the Rashleighs and, though their tenants were willing, the fellow squire at Menabilly was not. Austen tried again and again, but in vain.

At last, surveying St. Austell Bay from the heights, he saw that the answer lay below him in the little porth at

---

3.   cf. D.B. Barton, *The Cornish Beam Engine*.
4.   cf. E. Vale, *The Harveys of Hayle*.
5.   i.e. the head of the little creek, which once ran up to St. Blazey.

Par, where small vessels unloaded on the beach. If only he could make a harbour there, and connect up with the mines on the hills above! – it was considerably nearer than Fowey. The precipitous hill down which the ores would be carried offered no problem. The roads were already being worn out by hundreds of waggons, horses, and mules, and he was the recipient of protests from those trying to keep them in repair.

His reply was waggons on rails on the inclined plane downhill, the filled ones as they went down drawing the empties up. The course of the stream running down Luxulyan Valley he straightened and canalised to its mouth at the porth – one glimpses it today as one goes over the level-crossing. Barges would take the ores to harbour. The great feat was the creation of the harbour at Par. The approach was difficult, and even dangerous, from a reef running out from the west, giving the name Spit to the beach there. This he built up into a breakwater with thousands of tons from the cliff quarry at Polruddon, between the Black Head at Trenarren and Pentewan at the western end of St. Austell Bay. Quays were built, the approach deepened; the harbour not only accommodated numbers of small ships but became a hive of industry.

In time there grew up the export of ores, and also that of granite from the quarries in the Valley, china-clay and china-stone from the moors inland, with corresponding imports of coal, timber, grain and flour. Behind the quays granite-polishing of the finest quality was established. Once there came from the Valley a rare specimen of granite of a crimson tinge, which under the name of 'Luxulyanite' was sent up to St. Paul's for the Wellington monument in the cathedral. Ordinary white granite, but of the best quality, went into the making of the great Plymouth Breakwater, the Bute Docks at Cardiff, market-houses and public buildings at Exeter and in London; and some of it went up for the Prince Consort's own favourite Osborne House in the Isle of Wight. The little ships went loaded from the Master's creation at Par.

Somewhat later when lead-silver and iron mines were developed inland and across the county to Newquay – again by his inspiration, and connected up by his rail-tracks – a smelter was installed at Par. In our time the harbour and its works have been taken over and further developed by the big combine, English China Clays; even so there long remained by the road-side as one passed the original office with its signboard, 'Smith and Treffry'. And opposite – as I never forget – the vacant space of the house, upon which fell one of the German bombs aimed at the harbour in the dark days of our Forties, killing all the soldiers within: a characteristic memento of our time.

William Pease was the good fellow who devotedly ran the harbour's office all through Austen's time, one more example of his unerring judgment in men. Pease left a Diary, tribute to the good teamwork those men did together. Typical of Austen's spirit, in confronting risks to one of his ships, is his express wish: 'I hope the men who work the *Hydra* will never let an opportunity slip of getting a cargo of stone, whether by day or night.'[6]

Austen was never a man to let an opportunity slip; but his imagination conceived one great project which was never fulfilled. In those days hilly Cornwall was behindhand so far as roads were concerned, and before Macadam were very unsatisfactory; the main artery was the ancient ridgeway down the central spine, crossing mostly empty moorland, the present A30. Austen planned a coastal road to connect up the towns, chiefly on the south coast, to link with Falmouth and its (then) Packet Service overseas. Austen constructed a few stretches of it, one approaching St. Austell from the

6. q. Keast, 139.

east, through the mines by Boscundle and Cuddra; most impressive is the main road into Fowey from the west, which he cut through the living rock. Again one thinks of him as one goes down that declivity, his granite tower at Place rising into view.

He planned what would have been another monument: there exists a depiction of his projected suspension bridge across the river Fowey, a beautiful object like the Clifton suspension bridge, with its early Victorian Gothic towers. Neither this nor the coastal road came into being, to the town's loss: Fowey was left high, if hardly dry.

A no less splendid monument did come into existence to delight the eye and ornament the scene, though no longer serving its original purpose: this is his combined viaduct and aqueduct spanning the Luxulyan Valley and built of its magnificent granite. Everyone who knows the scene will appreciate the splendour of its design: our Pont-du-Gard, no less Roman in grandeur and appearance.

This came into his mind with the extension of his interests into the china-clay *massif* in the hinterland of St. Austell, and beyond to the mines near Newquay. In 1836 he purchased the manorial rights and harbour of Newquay, then a tiny fishing village with a few cottages and an inadequate pier, which he at once repaired and strengthened. On the way thither he had an iron mine at Withiel – where there was also porphyry: one sees the disused stack as one follows the sequestered road that coasts Bryn (birthplace of the famous Sir Bevil Grenville of the Civil War).

Then he planned a rail-link to connect Newquay with the south coast, with out-liers to the china-clay area around St. Stephens, on the western side of the *massif*, though these did not come into existence – he always had to face a good deal of opposition from the unimaginative who could not see the potential he saw. The railway to Newquay, however, was built, crossing the approach over Trenance Valley by another viaduct, with timber arches – over the use of which he was in agreement with the brilliant Brunel. Once more he recognised the quality of an equal, and henceforward cooperated with Brunel, whom the conventional military man, Lord Vivian, could not abide. At one point, angered by ordinary folks' delays and obstruction, he breaks out: 'You have no idea how much my motives have been misconstrued by people viewing all that I do with a jealous feeling.' Well, of course, he was a man in a hurry, who did not amble at the pace of ordinary humans.

Following in the footsteps of Trevithick he had always seen the crucial importance of railways for his mines – he calculated that the linkage of Fowey Consols to Par saved the Company £3000 a year in transport, as well as the wear and tear on the roads. (The Luxulyan viaduct, with granite on the spot, cost him only £3000.) He realised that knitting Cornwall together by railways was the clue to its future, but the job was a long and a hard one, costly on account of the hills to be tunnelled and the valleys to be bridged. However, he was not the one to lose heart, though he did not live to see the plan fulfilled or what it did to save Cornwall in the next half-century, with the mines closing down and scores of thousands of families having to emigrate – and help to build up the United States, and Canada, Australia, New Zealand and South Africa.[7]

In the 1840s, along with the depression in agriculture, Peel's reduction in import duties on foreign copper and tin, threatened the Cornish mines already on the way

7. cf. my *The Cornish in America*, with which I have given a lead. Why has it not been followed up by similar books on the Cornish in Australia, etc? No imagination or energy? – when academics waste their time on less interesting and rewarding subjects.

downward. Treffry led a delegation to the government to protest, but got little satisfaction – Peel was on the way to Free Trade. In Cornwall Treffry took the lead: we see him in action through the eyes of a bright young Quaker, Barclay Fox of Falmouth. At a county meeting 'Treffry held forth with great enthusiasm on the national and provincial importance of the mines, and the vast evils to be apprehended from their stoppage'. Then the inevitable, supercilious comment: 'What a sincere advocate a man becomes when his interest is touched'.[8] In the event, after Treffry's death, the decline of mining was an appalling disaster for Cornwall: what was wonderful was the way the poor little land surmounted it, though with the loss of a quarter of its population abroad.

It was the completion of the railway system that contributed largely to eventual recovery. Here Treffry, with his ardent spirit and singleness of purpose, was again the leader. For some years he was a director of the local Cornwall Railway; when he became Chairman he was no longer content for it to be confined within its boundaries. Barclay Fox responds more favourably to the man's spirit, when he heard him speak at a great county meeting at Truro in January 1844. 'Treffry made a capital, practical, statistical speech, showing from his own experience how cheaply a railway may be constructed in Cornwall. His did not cost £3000 per mile.' This was optimistic; still, 'pour agir il faut espérer'. This time he carried the meeting with him with immense applause; some £70,000 was raised at it, and he was named to lead a deputation to London to clinch the matter with the Great Western directors.

In a brilliant essay on 'The Railway in Cornwall, 1835–1914', Professor Jack Simmons sums up what Treffry did by his leadership: 'it was one of the railway's

8. *Barclay Fox's Journal.* ed. R.L. Brett, 264, 367.

misfortunes that he died early in 1850'.[9]

We cannot sum up here all that flowed from his imaginative enterprise, after his death: the development of Newquay as a summer resort, of Fowey as a winter resort. The Great Western opened up the Cornish Riviera; and, in place of copper and tin, the railway carried up-country milk, fish, early vegetables and flowers; and the ever-expanding tourist traffic westward. While Treffry's Fowey and Par, under the aegis of the giant E.C.C., became the principal ports for the export of china-clay, and that the leading export of raw material, in the decline of coal, for the whole country.

In the 1840s Treffry at last brought his work on Place to completion, inside and out. At various periods works of repair and restoration had been going on – at last he was in a position to rebuild the tower, or, rather, build it anew in his own white granite according to a Regency Gothick design. The ground floor was occupied by his grand hall of polished porphyry. Within the old part of the house much renewal had had to be done at intervals. At one point he bought fine oak timbers from the *Bellerophon*, which thousands of West Country folk had swarmed around in Plymouth harbour, to see Bonaparte on board. Hence amid the admirable Regency carving around the dining room one sees Wellington and Napleon carved on the grand side-board. He gave his patronage too to the young Cornish sculptor, Burnard, to execute carving, sculpt a memorial tablet in the church, and make the pedestal for a bust of the child Prince of Wales.

The crown of his efforts came in 1846 with a visit from the young Queen Victoria and the Prince Consort. Some 5000 people crowded into the little town; Queen and Prince landed at the Town Quay, where, as a boy, I

9. *Journal of the Royal Institution of Cornwall*, 1982.

used to be impressed by the tiny feminine footprint preserved to register the event. The royal entourage processed through the principal rooms of Place, finished at last, admiring everything, especially the Porphyry Hall, so expressive of the man who created it – he was himself a piece of granite, if unpolished.

He was already ill, not old – in his early sixties, but worn down by his life of hard labour and exertion, the enthusiasm he had put into his life. His mother, Susanna, had accompanied him most of the way, dying only eight years before he did. She was so old that it was said she had known an ancient servant, who had known someone who saw Essex's troops in Fowey in the Civil War – but perhaps that was tradition. Now, ill and failing, he was left alone: there had never been any other woman in his life – one reason why he had accomplished so much. No distractions, he had lived a plain-living, rather Spartan life, no Regency extravagances like the Byrons and Trevanions, and none of their *égarements* either. He got up at five every morning, making his appointments to conduct business from 6 a.m. onwards; while a peasant would scarcely envy his plain and abstemious fare. No riotous Regency living with him!

It was a time for reconciliation; even the town seems to have come round to him from the time of the royal visit, when Place opened the great gate he had built to the townspeople. He had already decided to make Aunt Jane's grandson his heir. This was Edward John Wilcocks, educated traditionally at Exeter College, a cleric and Headmaster of Berkhamsted School; however, he was a distinguished young man in his own right, and had the saving grace of being nautical. (When he came to die his demise took place on board his yacht off Fowey.) On his succession in 1850, he also was to take on the old name, and, with nine sons and two daughters, the continuance of the family was well provided for.

What the Reverend Doctor could not continue was his precursor's leadership in Cornish industry. But the great days of that, in which Treffry had played so creative a part, were passing, and the decline of mining would have grieved him. Already in the forties he had lost £10,000 on Par Consols, which had hitherto done well. It was partly owing to declining health that his projects for Newquay and linking up with the china-clay district were not pushed through. But if he had only lived into his seventies he would have seen the completion of his protégé Brunel's Saltash Bridge and would have presided over the through line into Cornwall opened in 1859, delayed by some years for want of his push.

He died at Place on 29 January 1850. His portrait there does not give much away, hardly anything of the inner man. Perhaps there was not much of an inner life, it all went into his outer projects; still, those were the extrapolations of his inner spirit. He was recognised to be a kindly, hospitable man, and a devoted son; but, a remarkable man, he was constantly subjected to criticism by the unremarkable. This, with his impelling energy and singleness of purpose from which he refused to be deflected by anything or anybody, they called egoism. Of course. There he stands, ships in the background under a stormy sky, one hand on table with open ledger and roll of map, the other unrolling map or survey for some characteristic project. The face is not after all hard to read: stance erect, unbending; a rather ascetic look, thin lips, a straight, uncompromising stare; the expression not without a certain grave nobility.

Nicholas Roscarrock and his Lives of the Saints

Nicholas Roscarrock's Lives of the Saints,[1] though known to hagiographers, have never been studied or received much comment. My interest in the manuscript is not hagiographical but historical: in the personality of Roscarrock, in the light he throws upon the observances of saints' days and the survival of medieval customs in the Cornwall of his youth, in the mind and attitude of a Catholic antiquary, who had suffered for his faith, caught in the conflict of Counter-Reformation with Protestantism, in the critical blast of scoffing Protestants at his beloved subject. He had an uncomfortable time of it, though he came into haven at last; he was in an awkward situation: it makes him interesting.

Roscarrock was a Domesday manor, the chief holding in the parish of St. Endellion. It is situated on the north coast of Cornwall near Port Isaac, on the east side of the Camel estuary, which can be seen from the old mullioned windows at the back of the house, the pleasant Georgian front looking south over the gull-speckled fields. The family had been there since at least the end of the twelfth century: one of those families of small gentry of Cornish stock going back a long way – not grand like Norman Arundells or Grenvilles, but with their own pride and coat of arms. Roscarrock's father, Richard, married Isabella Trevennor, heiress of a similar

1. Cambridge University Library, Add. MS 3041.

family and had a large number of children, of whom Nicholas and Trevennor were the youngest sons. The father provided for them during his life-time, settling Penhale, Carbura and Newton in St. Cleer and St. Germans on Nicholas, and Trentinny near St. Endellion on Trevennor. Richard died in 1575, leaving his eldest son Thomas to succeed him: he had been sheriff in 1550 and in 1562, so that under both Edward VI and Elizabeth he had had no difficulties of conscience. The family, closely related to the aggressive Protestant Grenvilles, conformed. The eldest son followed in his father's steps and became sheriff in 1586, when his brother Nicholas was in the Tower.

What accounts for the passionate, undeviating Catholicism of the two youngest sons, Nicholas and Trevennor?

It would seem that the atmosphere of Exeter College, from which Nicholas supplicated for his B.A. at Oxford in 1568, is the answer. Exeter was, along with St. John's, the most strongly Catholic in its sympathies of all Oxford colleges at this time. Its Rector, John Neale, was deprived by Elizabeth's Visitors in 1570 and went to Douai. His successor, Robert Newton, resigned in 1578 to be received as a Catholic. A list of the members of the College in 1572 brings home the situation.[2] Of the Fellows, Richard Bristowe – who, like Campion, had shone at Elizabeth's visit in 1566 – went into exile in 1570, became President of Douai College and one of the translators of the Bible. Ralph Sherwin was martyred with Campion in 1581. Edmund Lewkenor resigned in 1577 and went to Douai; John Curry became a priest and was for some time chaplain to the Arundells with John Cornelius, a student a little later, who was martyred in 1594. Among the students we find, along with the two Roscarrocks, members of known Catholic families, Fitz-

2. C.W. Boase, *Registrum Collegii Exon.*, 68.

herberts, Habingtons, Coningsbys, a Throckmorton, a
Fulford, a Bawden.

We shall come across one or other of these in
association with the Roscarrocks. They formed a
conscious group, devout and loyal to each other: tribute
to the strength of the early influences they received in
that atmosphere at Oxford.

In November 1572 we find Nicholas Roscarrock
admitted as a student to the Inner Temple, at the same
time as Tichborne, of that ardent Catholic family, and
Edward Coke who was no less ardently the other way.[3]
The year before, William Camden and Giles Risdon were
admitted: whose antiquarian interests Roscarrock shared
to the full. Camden and he remained always friends.
There is no indication that Roscarrock intended to follow
the law; indeed one of the two dominant interests of his
mind, antiquities and heraldry, is revealed at this time in
the long verses he wrote – pedestrian enough, but no
worse than many such Elizabethan exercises – to preface
to John Bossewell's *The Workes of Armorie*. These verses
are entitled 'Cyllenius censure of the Author in his high
Court of Herhaultrie', and are a long and tedious conceit
about the court resplendent which no man may enter
unless he has the herald's art:

Within these sundry rooms, through walls ybuilt of
crystal clear
Each thing that longs to herald's art doth perfectly
appear.

And so on, with a reference to Pegasus, the patron of the
young men of the Temple, to cite the names of these
friends-in-heraldry – Gerard Leigh, Alan Sutton and
Upton – and to a final complimentary flourish in honour
of Bossewell.

3.   W.H. Cooke, *Students Admitted to Inner Temple*, 71.

Four years later, we find a better set of verses prefaced to a better-known book, George Gascoigne's *The Steele Glas*, by N.R.: these initials have always been taken for Roscarrock's, and his verses stand next to those of a very different spirit indeed, though a fellow West Countryman – 'Walter Raweley of the Middle Temple, in commendation of *The Steele Glasse'*.

Meanwhile, at home at Roscarrock the kindly, hospitable life continued, with friends and relations always in and out of the house, dining together, playing at bowls or at cards, business of the county or the family. It is lucky that the Diary of William Carnsew, their neighbour of the next parish, St. Kew, should cover just this year: it provides some helpful touches where so much is dark and there are so few facts to go upon.[4] On 2 February 1576, Carnsew rode over to Roscarrock and lay there that night, for there was a great storm: 'won at play, lost health'. Early next month, he sent for the Roscarrocks to dine with him: Thomas came over to dinner, and John at night; they stayed and played at saint, at which Carnsew won. Ten days later he went over to his friends and there met Richard Grenville and Mr. Arundell of Trerice – of the Protestant and seagoing branch of the Arundells: 'lay there at Roscarrock all day playing and trifling the time away'. And so on throughout the year these agreeable visits continued, just as Carew charmingly describes them; Carnsew meets Grenville once again with the Roscarrocks.

But at the end of March, a more urgent note in relation to Nicholas Roscarrock, who does not otherwise appear in the laconic Diary, slips in. 'March 24: Sent letters to N. Rosca: and received answer. 25: Wrote to him again. 26: Wrote to Nicholas Roscarrock, but he was gone before my letters came to him. 27: W. Penkivell rode into Devonshire. Sent my letters to N.R.

4. SP 46/16. PRO.

to be carried to him by young Nance to Oxford.' In September Thomas Roscarrock was with Carnsew at Bokelly on his way home from assizes at Launceston. Could they have known that in time for next year's assizes, their friend Grenville would have struck with all his vigour and harshness at the important circle of Cornish Catholics, bringing the first of the seminary priests, Cuthbert Mayne, to execution, involving the life-long imprisonment of his patron, Francis Tregian, exposing the young Roscarrocks as recusants, condemning them to an unending opposition to the whole course of the nation, uprooting them for ever from their home?

For that was what was involved by Grenville's campaign. No need to go into here, still less to defend it.[5] At a time of increasing danger, with the declared policy of the Papacy to absolve the Queen's subjects from their allegiance and drive her from her throne, with Allen's first seminary priests arriving in the country – and Mayne had the full Counter-Reformation position, the duty to support an invader and the rest of it – here was a fifth column. The government was being openly defied by an important group: what exacerbated feeling was that they were a section of the governing class. Grenville was determined to bring this more or less open defiance of the law to an end in his sheriffwick; he was encouraged and supported by the Privy Council in order to round up the group. Among the haul of prisoners at assizes at Launceston in September 1577, Nicholas Roscarrock was indicted for recusancy, his estate rated at £20 p.a. in lands, his goods and chattels at £40, for the payment of Recusancy fines. For the young Roscarrocks it was the end of the old pleasant life: henceforth it was opposition, defiance, danger, imprisonment, torture, expropriation – and what consolations the inner life of devotion, the

5. Cf my *Sir Richard Grenville of the 'Revenge'*, c. vii.

outer interests in antiquities and scholarship, could give them.

With the 1580s the crisis heightened, the danger of invasion grew near; the infiltration of the Jesuits and the considerable success of Campion and Parsons' mission in 1580 gave alarm to the government. In London an association of young Catholic gentlemen was formed to aid and conduct the incoming seminary priests, to provide them with money and supplies; they took an oath to restrict themselves to bare necessities and bestow all they had on the Catholic cause. They were fanatics and they were dangerous. Their association was blessed by the Pope in April 1580. Among their members we find the names of Babington and Gunpowder Plot conspirators, some later exiles, others from the old circle of students at Exeter in Oxford days: Anthony Babington, Chideock Tichborne, William Tresham, Edward and Francis Throckmorton, Charles Arundel, Charles Basset, Edward Habington, Thomas Fitzherbert, George Gilbert. Nicholas Roscarrock was one of them. In September we find him journeying to Rome in the company of Cresswell, who became a Jesuit there and succeeded Parsons as Rector of the English College: the two of them spent twelve days at Douai on the way.[6]

These activities did not escape the attention of the authorities. Shortly after Roscarrock's return to England, Ralph Sherwin – who had been at Exeter with him and was now a seminary priest – was taken in the act of preaching after mass in Roscarrock's chamber. They were apprehended by Hunsdon, the Lord Chamberlain; and the Privy Council ordered their examination, 'forasmuch as the said Roscarrock, by certain examinations heretofore taken of certain persons as evil-affected towards her Majesty and the present state, hath been detected to have been a practiser with foreign states and

6. T.F. Knox ed., *First and Second Douai Diaries*, 169.

a conveyor of letters both abroad and into this realm'.[7]
This was a dangerous charge, and upon the result of their
examination they were both consigned to the Tower.
On 15 and 16 December Sherwin was racked – it is said,
in a cell near Roscarrock, *pour encourager l'autre*, no
doubt. On 14 January Roscarrock was put to the rack. In
December Sherwin, Campion and Bryant were hanged,
drawn and quartered at Tyburn. Roscarrock remained in
the Tower, unyielding, obdurate. In April 1581 we find
his servant Greene passing through Douai, evidently on
some mission. A priest, writing to Dr Allen in
November 1582, says that 'Pound, Brinkley and
Roscarrock, laymen, have – I am ashamed to say –
shown themselves braver than many priests'.[8]

Roscarrock did not desist from his activities, or from
taking risks. In 1584 the Scottish Jesuit, Crichton,
captured at sea, was imprisoned in the Tower; he was a
political, who had been a chief agent in the schemes for
capturing the young James VI for Catholicism and was
now engaged in furthering plans for Mary Stuart's
liberation and the invasion of England. (Because
Crichton had declared to a Catholic conspirator that it
was unlawful to kill the Queen, the government handsomely released him.) While in the Tower Crichton was
lodged over Roscarrock, who contrived to open two
doors between them and to converse with Crichton at
leisure; and then to smuggle his letters out of the Tower
for him, through his own window near the ground, by
the hand of a girl who took them to one of the Catholic
companionship in the city.[9] A government note of
prisoners in the Tower, 27 May 1585, states: 'Thomas
Pound, Nicholas Roscarrock: for religion only
committed and for intelligence with Jesuits and priests,

7. *A.P.C.*, *1580–1*, 264–5.
8. Catholic Record Soc., *Miscellanea* iv. 74–5.
9. SP12/178, 11, 74.

two dangerous men and apt for any practice; fit they should be banished'. Roscarrock, as a gentleman of means, was in the Tower at his own charges; and on 6 March 1586, the Lieutenant of the Tower, Sir Owen Hopton, renewed his old suit that Roscarrock might be released upon bond, upon condition he were forthcoming at all times when called for; since he had been a prisoner for over five years and was now £140 in debt to the Lieutenant for his diet and charges. Roscarrock had taken part in no political conspiracy, and about this time he seems to have been released as well as Crichton.

Meanwhile, his brother Trevennor was in Newgate prison in 1583 and 1584 for hearing mass and refusing to come to church. Both brothers remained obstinate recusants. Nicholas was in trouble again in the 1590s, when we find him in the Fleet with Francis Tregian – their movements spied on and reported to the government by a Catholic spy, Benjamin Tichborne alias Beard, whom they entertained, perhaps not wholly unawares, as a host its parasite. In December 1593 Beard was writing to Sir Robert Cecil, 'I was with Roscarrock continually private in his study, and might have effected something ere this'.[10] Roscarrock was now living in conditions of some comfort. It was a cultivated Catholic circle that lived together in the Fleet in those years, with plenty of opportunity for entertaining friends, and much coming and going; music, antiquities, versifying, conversation. Nor were they deprived of the consolations of religion: plenty of opportunity for secret masses in the Fleet, and there were always priests in and out. But the spy complains that Tregian and Roscarrock do not wholly confide in him. In May 1594, a man known as the Green Man was taken, who had lately been sent over from abroad; Mrs Tregian let out to Beard

10. H.M.C., *Salisbury Mss.*, iv. 432.

that he was a seminary priest. The spy reports to the government that 'there is one now in the Fleet who is greatly suspected about his taking [he means himself], but not one word is spoken of him by Tregian or Roscarrock', which makes Beard think the man the more dangerous.[11] Later on, in 1599 a Middlesex jury found a true bill against Roscarrock for not coming to church. Neither of the brothers ever did attend church – and they paid for it with their inheritance.

From the 1590s we can watch the process in the Recusants' Rolls. Two-thirds of a recusant's lands were taken over by the Crown and leased out to pay the Recusancy fines. Year after year in the Recusants' Roll for Cornwall we find two-thirds of Trevennor Roscarrock's remaining possessions returning their small sum: 31s. p.a. for the farm of half of four messuages in Tregonan, two messuages in Tregarrick and four messuages in Gear, parcel of the manor of Lamoran. In Devon we find a still smaller return (10s. 8d. p.a.) for the farm of two parts of the half of two messuages in Smith's hill and Ashwater, in the hands of the Queen by Nicholas Roscarrock's recusancy. But what had happened to his property in Cornwall? It was evidently no longer in his hands; most probably he had had to sell it in order to exist. He may have turned it into cash, or into an annuity, as a precautionary measure. Recusants were driven to all sorts of expedients – as with penal taxation today – in order to protect themselves from the full harshness of the law.

With the accession of James and the end of the war with Spain, there was – in spite of the idiocy of Gunpowder Plot – *a détente*, a relaxation of the severity for Catholics. Nicholas Roscarrock came into port at last, and a very pleasant port it was.

11. *C.S.P. Dom.*, *1591–4*, 499.

In his last year in the Tower two important Catholic persons came to join the select company there: two of the dead Norfolk's sons, Philip, Earl of Arundel who had designed to leave the country – to lend himself to what dangerous purposes his godfather, Philip II, intended – and his brother, Lord William Howard. It must have been then that Roscarrock became friendly with the Howard brothers; Lord William was released about the same time as Roscarrock, Arundel remained there till he died in 1595.

Now, with James's move south, Lord William was free to move north and consolidate his – or rather, his wife's – splendid inheritance on the Border. She was one of the Dacre coheiresses whom the Duke had providently marrried to these two of his sons. From about 1604 Lord William was engaged in making Naworth, the chief Dacre castle in Cumberland, ready to live there: rebuilding and repairing, for it was in a state of complete disrepair, planting, making orchards and gardens round about, bringing stained glass for the windows, timbers and carved roofs for the rooms, restoring the chapel. For he, too, was a Catholic: brought up by Gregory Martin, another of the Oxford men of the 1570s who had gone to Douai. And when Lord William settled at Naworth, he brought Roscarrock to live there as his companion. Here, on the Scottish Border, within those rose and grey walls looking up to the high fells, the Waste of Bewcastle, the pleasant pastures of the Irthing beneath the walls, the sound of the river mounting up to the windows – so different a scene from his native Cornwall – Roscarrock passed the rest of his life.

He and Lord William had the two chief interests of their lives in common: religion and a love of antiquities, books, scholarship. These two archaeologising buddies – freed from their worries and from persecution in middle age – set to work to form a collection of Roman antiquities from the Wall near by. They had a wonderful opportunity and they made the most of it: the sheltered garden was full of Roman altars and gravestones and inscribed slabs. When Stukeley visited it in the eighteenth century, he found it in a state of great neglect, the stones being cut up for gate-posts; later, it was completely dispersed.[12] Lord William also gathered a fine collection of manuscripts; here too with the cartularies of Northern monasteries, he had a grand opportunity. They have all been dispersed, mostly disappeared. In this field Roscarrock would be specially helpful: he was a collector himself. We know from his Lives of the Saints that he possessed a few manuscript *Vitae* of Cornish saints. But only two of his manuscripts have been identified. The Bodleian possesses a fifteenth-century illuminated MS., John Dade's *De Arte Heraldica*; this seems to have belonged first to George, Lord Bergavenny, and then to Henry Ferrers, one of the group of Catholic antiquaries, like Erdeswicke and Habington: Ferrers intended to write a Perambulation of Warwickshire, which Dugdale later accomplished: he was a friend of Roscarrock's and may have given him the MS. Later, it came into the possession of Sir William Waad, Lieutenant of the Tower, by the good offices of King James: 'Wy. Waad lieutenant of the Tower to our Sovereain Lord King Jaymes owethe [i.e. owns] this booke'. In the Cambridge University Library is another MS. that belonged to Roscarrock, Hoccleve's *De Regimine Principum*, with Roscarrock's signature on the first and last pages, and on f. 68b. the arms of the family, a chevron between two roses in chief and a fish in base (actually, according to Carew, a sea-tench nageant proper).

Lastly, Lord William brought together a library, chief solace of the two old friends: it was strong in works of Catholic devotion and apologetics, mainly in Latin, and

12. *Surtees Soc., The Household Books of Lord William Howard.*

in medieval chronicles; nothing Anglican: just what one would expect. Lord William's study, in the solitude at the top of his tower, with the stream sounding pleasantly as it tumbles through its gully under the green foliage far below, survived unchanged up to our own time: it remained for us to disperse that.

From the *Household Books of Lord William Howard* we derive a charming impression of the life of that hospitable great house, the cautious Catholicism, the ordered days. There are the payments to men bringing salmons from the rivers round about, oysters from the coast, larks and moorcocks from the fells, the fat capons and geese, occasionally a swan or a fawn; to the maids bringing cherries, plums, pears, cowslips; cakes are brought from Penrith, sugar candy for the children. The tailor is paid for shapening my lady's waistcoat. Strolling players perform within the castle, or a play is acted at Brampton; dancers, minstrels, pipers at the gate, sometimes a blind harper, singing no doubt the ballads of the Border. A picture of St. Francis is purchased; painted glass for the chapel. Books are frequently bought: the *History of the Queen of Scots* (Con's Latin life published at Rome) – of acute interest in such a circle, which had shared the experience of persecution, and the secrets; Bellarmine's *Works*; Attorney Doddridge's book on the Duchy of Cornwall, of particular appeal to Roscarrock. There are payments for stringing and binding the books, skins for parchment; and with increasing frequency in this so bookish a house, money laid out for spectacles, horn for spectacles and silver frames. Along with this went the careful management of the estates; Lord William was able to bring not only order into his wife's neglected and much challenged inheritance, but greatly to increase its revenues and in the end to purchase further estates in the country round him. There was always, unobtrusively, a priest in the house. They did not do so badly.

In this busy household, with its wide spaces for silence, prayer and study, Roscarrock made an independent figure. Earlier, he may have given a hand with the tuition of the sons; we find him making some small payments for the expenses of the house; four gallons of sack in a rundlet are bought for him. In 1622 his brother Trevennor pays Naworth a visit; for he is given 10s. to bestow in Cornish diamonds – I suppose, quartz stones. What is obvious from the accounts, and rather surprising, is that Nicholas was quite well off. He seems to have received an annuity of £200 from Lord Arundel, presumably Lord William's nephew, the great connoisseur and patron of the arts. We find entries like the following in 1620: 'Received of Mr. Dix for Mr. Roscarrock, part of the money due by my Lord Arundel £100, ultra £100, before charged'. Again, the same year: 'Received of Mr. Dix by my Lord's appointment, 26 Nov., £100 in payment of Mr. Roscarrock's debt, taken into my Lord's hands, and another £100 which my Lord doth allow, which my Lord borrowed of Mr. Dix and my Lord hath taken to pay Mr. Roscarrock £100'. And then, in November 1633, shortly before his death, 'Received of Nicholas Roscarrock, being part of £400 paid in to him by Mr. Henry Lawson, £100'.

The upshot was that so far from being a dependent of the house, Roscarrock had an independent status as a friend of the family, a room of his own, sack of his own, and was a convenient source of ready money when anybody – usually my Lady – was short. Among the steward's accounts we read: 'Delivered my lady, borrowed of Mr. Roscarrock, £5'. Or, 'Borrowed of Mr. Roscarrock and delivered my lady, £5'. 'To Mr. Howard, by my lady's commandment, going to Malton, which was borrowed of Mr. Roscarrock and paid by me, £3'. Upon his death it is not surprising, therefore, to find: 'More to Sir Francis Howard which he laid out for buying a ring for Mr. William Howard, more than the legacy

Mr. Rocarrock gave, 20s'. Then, 'Given as legacies to several servants at Naworth from Nicholas Roscarrock, which my lady was owing him, £20'. Lastly, 'To Sir Francis Howard, money owing to Nicholas Roscarrock esquire, late deceased, by my Lord and to be disposed by Sir Francis Howard according to Mr. Roscarrock's appointment, £300'.

One relic of Lord William and Roscarrock's friendship remains to us, something unique: a gold rosary: no other medieval English rosary has survived.[13] It consists of fifty small oval beads, six lozenges and a large knop at the bottom. But two of the beads are not originals: they are late sixteenth-century additions. On one of these Roscarrock's patron saint, Endelient, is represented with her ox, a palm and a cauldron; at the back, St. William of Norwich. On another bead, there are two more St. Williams. It looks like having been Lord William's rosary, with him sharing Roscarrock's cult of St. Endelient. Or perhaps it was Roscarrock's? – for the arrangement of two saints on each head is dictated by the occurrence of their festivals in the Calendar, which was a primary interest of Roscarrock's. Perhaps it belonged to them both and they shared the rosary, as they did the faith: a touching memento of their friendship.

Such was the background to the last quarter of a century of Roscarrock's long life. (If he supplicated for his B.A. in 1568 he would have been born about 1550; he died towards the end of 1633). Naworth gave him the security and the peace for what was, next religion, nearest his heart: his antiquarian studies; the Lives of the Saints brought these two together. But it was getting late to bring them to a point.

Roscarrock was settled at Naworth by August 1607,

13. Now in the Victoria and Albert Museum.

and probably had been for some time before, to judge from a letter he wrote to Camden in that month: it gives us a pleasant insight into the kindly relations subsisting among those antiquaries and friends.

Understanding (good Mr. Clarenceulx) that your *Britain* is at this present in printing and ready to come forth, I thought fit (in a small show of our ancient love) to give you notice of two escapes in the last edition. The one in Cornwall (f. 156), where you make St. Columbanus, a man, to give name unto St. Columb: whereas, in truth, it taketh name of Columba, a woman-saint, who was a virgin and martyr, whose Life I have in my hands translated out of Cornish; besides, the day of her Feast differeth from the Feast of St. Columbanus, or St. Columba, the Scottish or Irish.

In his next edition Camden duly made the correction. Roscarrock went on to correct Camden's description of an inscribed stone which he had seen at Thoresby:

My Lord William, who hath it now with a great many more in his garden-wall at Naworth, where he would be glad to see you to read them, hath made it shorter [i.e. in measurement]; as also for the lines and letters which I have sent you here enclosed, drawn out by our good lord's own hands; and would have sent you some more, but that we think it too late, and that you mean not to overcharge your book with too many of that kind. I also send you here an inscription which my lord found out in a cross in a green before the abbey-church of Lanercost; which, though it be since the Conquest, yet it is (for the rareness) not to be contemned . . . And now if you would give me leave from crosses to fall across you, I beseech consider whether you in Staffordshire (p. 519), or Capgrave in the Life of St. Bertelm, be more extreme: you in terming him *minorum gentium Divum*, and he in making a king's son so great a saint and miracle-worker. In this kind, I could be longer, but it needeth not for that you out of your love and friendship will, I hope, pardon me and make use of it. Commend me, I beseech, most heartily to your good self, and remember my service to the good knight Sir Robert Cotton, when you chance to see him; and request him to conceive no unkindness of my boldness, upon his own offer, to take his Capgrave, Jocelyn, and other of his written books of that argument with me unto Naworth. If he would have them, I will most willingly send them whensoever he pleaseth. If you chance to see our old friend Mr. Henry Ferrers, I beseech you tell him that I live, remember and love him.

Meanwhile, at home in Cornwall, another of the antiquarian circle, Richard Carew, friend of Camden and Cotton, in describing Roscarrock in his *Survey of Cornwall*, had paid a compliment to Nicholas.

Roscarrock in Cornish meaneth a flower[14] and a rock in English. Roses are his arms and the north rocky cliffs, which bound his desmesnes, perhaps added the rest. The heir hath issue by the daughter of Trevanion. His father married the sole inheritrix to Pentire, whose dwelling, Pentewan, is seated on the south sea, so as he might make use of either climate for his residence. The family is populous, but of them two brothers, Hugh for his civil carriage and kind hospitality, and Nicholas for his industrious delight in matters of history and antiquity, do merit a commending remembrance.

14. It does not – Carew did not know Cornish; it means promontory or heath. Hence Roscarrock means the rocky promontory.

Nothing of all the past: it is pleasant that the love of antiquities should sometimes transcend religious difference.

Fourteen years after Roscarrock's letter to Camden, Lord William writes to Sir Robert Cotton in August 1621:

> Brother, your old friend and mine, Mr. Roscarrock, understanding that you have a manuscript of Johannes Anglicus, is very desirous to borrow the same; that, though he cannot take a view thereof, yet he much longeth to lend his ear to hearken to the reading of the same; and if it please you to send it down by this bearer it shall be safely, by God's blessing, returned to you again with all convenient speed, after he hath satisfied himself therewith.

There we have the explanation of Roscarrock's uncompleted work; it was now too late: he was blind.

There is no sign of this in the portrait that exists of him at Corby Castle: out of which he looks at us with dark, lively eyes undimmed. This portrait of him would have been painted in the early years of his residence at Naworth: it is of a man in his late fifties, already bald and with a careful, brushed white beard. Nothing to show what he had been through – except perhaps the questioning lines on the forehead, the quizzically sad expression about the eyes. For the rest, a long, slightly bulbous nose, the high domed forehead of the scholar: it is the honest, sober face of a countryman, with something of that indefinable air of a lived inner life.

All the same, with his experiences – the early days in Cornwall, the good friends there and at Oxford, the exciting underground life of militant Catholics in London, the visits to Douai and Rome, the private communications with Jesuits, Cresswell, Robert Parsons, Crichton, imprisonment and the rack, spies, the secrets he kept, the confidences never divulged, the friends he knew, so many of them torn limb from limb, traitors in a time of extreme danger – if only, one feels, he had written an Autobiography, instead of Lives of the Saints!

However, his Lives of the Saints are not without an autobiographical interest.

From the careful form of Roscarrock's book it seems clear that he meant it for publication. As the MS now stands it numbers some 402 leaves; a previous deleted numbering gives 479 leaves. There are small fragments of a considerable number of missing leaves at the end: the MS. is now incomplete, breaking off in the middle of an account of Simon of Sudbury – what followed on alphabetically from that point being now wanting. A letter from one Ff. Webbe, inserted at f. 313, gives us some information. It refers to Trevennor Roscarrock's having come across in an Oxford library the story of the 'children of Brechan' – the group of some twenty-odd saints who came from Brechan's country in S.E. Wales to found churches in North and East Cornwall: 'the story at large Mr. Roscarrock wrote and, keeping no copy of it, sent it to his brother Mr. Nicholas Roscarrock, who lived and died at my Lord William Howard's house in the North. Now some worthy Catholics of Cornwall being desirous to understand the full story, to the end they may the better honour these saints of their country, besought me to write into the North about this and to get out of Mr. Nicholas Roscarrock's writings this story, they knowing that he was wont to compile together such monuments for future memory.' Mr. Webbe had heard that Sir William Howard, Lord William's son, 'had Mr. Nicholas Roscarrock's book and papers, and that he could give me some light of it'. One sees that the group of Cornish Catholics, which was quite strong in the early seventeenth century, knew of Roscarrock's work; but knowledge of it faded as they petered out later in that century, to become practically extinct in the eighteenth century.

The MS. is almost wholly in Roscarrock's hand; but there are later interpolations in one or, at most, two other hands – of which we now know the explanation.

Roscarrock's title-page describes his work as 'A Brief Register: or Alphabetical Catalogue of such saints [and saint-like persons – has been added] as the Collector hath taken notice of to have graced our island of Great Britain, Ireland and other British islands bordering about it, with their births, deaths, presence, preachings or relics'. This is followed by 'A Sonnet. To the Courteous and well-minded reader, showing the Collector's resolution', which I give as a specimen of Roscarrock's original spelling:

> If this my labour serve but for a foyle
> to lend a luster to som learned quill
> to perfect this my undertaken toyle
> I have my wishe although I want my will
> depriv'de of helps and destitute of skill.
> whoe wholy in this work applied my penn
> to honnor God and not to humor men.
>
> If he be pleas'd I have my harts desyre
> wishing good mynds in doubts to deame the best
> and for my paines I seek noe better hyre
> of such as are with scorne and spleene possest
> but base contempt wth wch content I rest
> Beleive well, and live well, and hope well for Bliss
> farewell, and wish well, to him that wrote this.

On the next page there follow more verses – 'A friendly warning to the reader, wishing him to have due respect and reverence of saints and not to reject the true writers of their lives, many of them being also saints'. We thus early come upon the defensive note which is heard again and again in the course of the fabulous stories Roscarrock has to relate, and is not the least interesting feature of his book as a revelation of an Elizabethan mind.

As for the rest which sensuall drown'd in sense
so sensles are as nothing will beleive
but self conceipt, and self wills false pretence
It recks not much what Censure they do give
For sunn and starrs they scarsely will esteeme
of greater circuitt then there sense dothe deeme.

There follows a short preface on the moral utility of saints' lives, assuring himself that those who 'take a just view of them cannot but find all the commendable parts of an history in them, in which they may see how infidelity hath been supplanted and true religion advanced', etc.

Before the title-page there are some twenty-three leaves of preliminary matter, beginning with 'A Brief Discourse. How saints may be esteemed so. Secondly of their canonisation and the truest, infalliblest manner of discerning them, and what course the Collector of this Alphabet of Saints hath observed in this his Collection.' He cites Scripture to show that it is the will of God that we should honour saints – 'their miracles deserving it and our necessities requiring it, we are to receive benefits by praying unto them, which we could not do safely were we not in a sort warranted by the Church's canonisation of them to pray unto them or to adore them'. This consideration has moved not only Catholics, but the very heretics themselves, 'imitating therein, saith St. Augustine, (like apes) the Catholics, have reverenced their false and counterfeit martyrs and professors as saints: yea, Luther himself was not afraid to canonise in a sort John Huss the heretic by the name of a saint and a prophet, whom he maketh a goose to prove himself to be a swan'. And so with the veneration of Luther himself.

> But what need I go into Germany for examples when we may find so many of this sort in John Foxe's huge heap of saints and martyrs of his own making, whereof some were long after living, as How and Marbecke, who played long after merrily on the organs at Windsor, some that were never in being, as Sir Roger Only; some never put to death, nor as much as imprisoned, as Wyclif, a condemned heretic; others justly imprisoned as Cambridge, likewise condemned and burned in Oxford for heresy, who could not endure the name of Christ in the Bible; Acton executed for treason; Joan-of-the-eye for witchcraft; Trudgeover for felony; Debnam and others for sacrilege and thievery, and others for other like villainies.

All the same we may point out, as Protestants did not cease to point out at the time, that Mary did burn nearly 300 people for heresy in the course of three years. This was the greatest propaganda-point of Elizabeth's new deal: the burnings shocked the English people; and Foxe's Book of Martyrs proved most effective propaganda for Elizabeth's government. No wonder Catholics were so raw on the subject: they could not get round him; Roscarrock abuses once and again 'that huge and vain volume of his Monuments, which in truth doth rather serve the title of Miniments'. We note the mutual exclusiveness of men's absurd opinions, for which they kill or for which they die.

Roscarrock quotes Bellarmine's statement, *De Sanctis*, that there are many saints not canonized by the Pope who are venerated by the Church: saints in ancient time were not so much reverenced by any law or order, as by custom. He does not scruple therefore to include in his

Catalogue many ancient saints, especially of the Britons, who were not canonized, but have altars, churches, dedications and feasts observed, without contradiction of prelates or Pope: 'which connivency seemeth to be a privy consent . . . though of many such I cannot find their feast days, hoping others will effect what is not thoroughly performed'. It is indeed this heavy list in the direction of the Celtic saints that gives Roscarrock's book its special interest; for the rest, he relies on the known authorities, but for these he has some sources of his own: manuscript lives of such saints as Petrock, Nectan, Brechan, Perran and Samson, which he had collected; and, for their observances and festivals, his memories of Cornwall.

Roscarrock's basic authority throughout his book is the work that goes under the name of Capgrave, *Nova Legenda Anglie*, but is essentially the work of John of Tynemouth or Johannes Anglicus – we have seen Lord William Howard asking Cotton to lend his MS. of this for Roscarrock's use as late as 1621, when he was blind. But we are struck by the range of reading that has gone into Roscarrock's Lives: not only Capgrave, but almost the whole of medieval English chronicles – Bede, Ordericus Vitalis, William of Malmesbury, Giraldus Cambrensis, Matthew Paris, Matthew of Westminster, Thomas Walsingham, John Rous. He is equally well-read in recent chroniclers and antiquaries – Polydore Vergil, Leland, Bale, Dr. Caius, Camden, Speed, Carew. He has the advantage of a Catholic's more cosmopolitan reading over these last nationally-minded writers: Roscarrock has read widely in continental chronicles of the Middle Ages: Ado and Aimoin's *Historica Francorum*, Molinet and the voluminous works of Sigebert. When writing of the foundation of Mont-St.-Michel, he refers to the pamphlet of Dr. Francis Feuardent, printed at Constance [Coutances] in 1610. There were the works of his co-religionists, Nicholas

Harpsfield, J.W.'s *English Martyrologe*, published in 1608, and others in MS. to which he refers, like the MSS. collected by a Welsh priest, Edward Powell alias Hughes, or by Father John Whitford. Uniquely he had some Cornish sources; their disappearance is a matter for regret to those interested in the old language, students of which would have preferred him to devote his time to it. When we consider the immensity of the task, its encyclopaedic character – something comparable to Camden in his sphere, or Holinshed, or Stow – we may say that it was, in the spirit of the endeavour, if not in the subject it tackled, a true expression of the age.

For the Cornish interest of his book, we might begin with the legend of St. Endelient, the patron saint of his native parish.

She lived in a place in Cornwall called Trentinny: [This was where Trevennor Roscarrock's property lay], where I remember there stood a chapel dedicated (as I take it to her), which at this day is decayed, and the place in which it stood is yet called the chapel-close and lieth on the south-west of the parish church. Here she lived a very austere course of life. That with the milk of a cow only, which cow the lord of Trentinny killed as she strayed into his grounds, as old people speaking by tradition do report. She had a great man to her godfather, which they also say was King Arthurs who took the killing of the cow in such sort as he killed or caused the man to be slain, whom she miraculously revived. And when she perceived the day of her death draw near, she entreated her friends after her death to lay her dead body on a sled and to bury her there where certain young stots, bullocks or calves of a year old should of their own accord draw her. Which being done, they brought her to a place which at that time was a miry waste ground and a great quagmire at the top of an hill; where in time

167

after there was a church builded on her and dedicated
to her, which since proved a fine firm and fruitful plot
of ground, where her feast was accustomed to be yearly
remembered the 29 of April. And I have heard it
credibly reported that the chapel in Lundy was likewise dedicated unto her and bare her name. Yet my
good friend, Mr. Camden, saith the chapel was
dedicated unto St. Helen; but under correction,
except he have better warrant than bare conjecture, I
still hold the former report more likely, because her
brother St. Nectan had a church dedicated at Hartland point over against it, but fourteen miles from it
. . . whereof it is not improbable that she did also
sometimes dwell in that island.[15] For many of St.
Brechan's children planted themselves near one
another. As this St. Endelient, St. Memfry or St.
Minver, St. Mabyn, St. Tudy, etc.

Roscarrock follows this with verses in honour of his
patroness, the fourth stanza of which runs:

> For in that church a Christian I became
>> And of Christ's church a member first to be
> And also was confirmèd in the same
>> For which I thank my God and pray to thee
> This work to further in thy church begun
> With prayers that I my race may rightly run.

In the parish two holy wells bore her name, but the
tradition was that the one farther away from the church
was that frequented by her in her lifetime. 'Her tomb was
defaced in King Henry VIII's time and afterwards placed
upon one Mr. Batten in Chenduit's aisle, where it
standeth at this present . . . the table whereof is of

15. The tower of St. Endellion church is built of Lundy Island
    granite.

polished stone like black marble.' In our time it has been re-erected as an altar in that same aisle.

Within the parish was a chapel and a holy well dedicated to St. Illick, whose feast was solemnly held on the Saturday after Epiphany.

And the inhabitants used to say by tradition that she came miraculously out of Ireland on a harrow or hurdle, and that she lived there in the time of St. Endelient, which by guess we may think to be about the year 550. And the path whereon they used to walk or pass one to the other is noted by the inhabitants to be greener than any other part, especially after tillage. There was a tree over her well, which those that attempted to cut down had ever harm, so as they gave over to cut it. Till one more bold than the rest did cut it down, who hurting himself was noted to die shortly after. This happened in our time.

Old conservatives have often consoled themselves with this sort of reflection, never more than over the losses from the Dissolution and Reformation.

A neighbouring parish bears the name of St. Mabyn, 'the church of which being new builded about the year 1500, there was, as I have heard from the report of such as lived there at that time, a song or hymn sung of her signifying that she had twenty-three brothers and sisters'. Roscarrock finds this confirmed in the Life of St. Nectan and St. Brechan, yet her name is not in the Book of Llandaff nor in Edward Powell's Welsh pedigree. The twenty-four children of Brechan probably formed a missionary group from the country which took its name from Brechan and they founded churches, probably in the sixth century as Roscarrock says, along the north coast of Cornwall and Devon, particularly in the district he knew best.

St. Minver, the eponymous saint of the next parish, was another of them: a fair church was builded over her half a mile from the place where she was said to live, today called Tredrizzick, 'where in my time there stood a chapel also dedicated to her, less than two miles from where St. Endelient lived'. All memory of this chapel, like that of St. Illick in St. Endellion, seems to have gone. How thick with chapels and holy wells pre-Reformation Cornwall must have been, and how fascinating to the antiquary their cults and observances! No wonder Roscarrock had such a nostalgia for the irrecoverable past; his book gives us a sense of it and lets us, as few things do, into the mind of the medieval Cornish. He tells us the pretty legend of St. Minver's well, 'where the ghostly Adversary coming to molest her as she was combing her hair by the well, she flinging her comb at him enforced him to fly, who left a note behind him at a place called at this day Topalundy; where, at the top of a round high hill, there is a strange deep hole then made by the Devil in avoiding St. Minver'.

There follows a revealing defensive comment:

In report of which I shall, I fear me, as in many other parts of this my collection, be thought as simple as I may have just cause to think others irreverent in writing of this and other saints. For I do sincerely, in the testimony of my conscience, write that which I find, not daring to correct that which I know not how to control. Assuring myself with the prophet that God is wonderful in his saints; not caring to be scorned with him by any the followers of Micholl in the service of God, how basely soever men conceive of me for it. I wish to God we had some more intelligence than we have of our British saints; and particularly such as have churches dedicated unto them in Cornwall; for I am persuaded there are as many churches builded in honour of such saints as lived

170

there (whereof most were British and Irish) as there is in any one shire in England. And could wish that Mr. Carew (if he do again set forth his Cornish Survey) would be a little more large, as he would not be irreverent in discoursing of them: in which, in respect of my love to his person and parts, wish that he would rather imitate our good friend Mr. Camden in his *Britain*, than Mr. Lambarde in his *Kent*. For the first, being better advised in his later editions, hath discreetly retracted some faults, as I would he had done in all which he had formerly written. As namely of St. Nectan, whom he resembled to Neptune; St. Bartholin, whose pattens he played with, as Mr. Carew doth of St. Meneg and St. Issey; and as Mr. Lambarde doth generally, where occasion is offered, to show himself a censurer of saints. . . . Of which good meaning of mine, if Mr. Carew consider well, he will omit his poem on St. Keyne's well in his irreligious scorning, and that also at St. Nun's well. For, in truth, otherwise his work will be disgraced in the judgment of many that are no fools. For in these matters of saints, when we can say nothing that is good, we should in reason forbear to write that which is ill; being bound in all doubtful things to think the best.

That gives us Roscarrock's point of view, politely put like the gentleman he was. But he is sometimes hard put to it, as in the account he has to give of the miracles of St. Perran, patron of tin-miners, whose friend, St. Brendan, 'turned water into milk by blessing it, showing thereby he had no use of a cow, when St. Perran by blessing the said milk turned it again into water'. After these useful operations, St. Perran performed many strange miracles, raising from death his mother's handmaid Brunetta and seven musicians, making a stork to sing, causing a snow, going on the water dry-footed, procuring fire, turning water into wine and cold water into warm. He lived to be two hundred.

I doubt not but the curious will think many things incredible in this Life of St. Perran and other Britain saints, and censure me of simplicity and too too much credulousness. But I had rather be censured without cause than presume with some to censure such as report it, except I were justly able to control them, finding that which I relate here in Capgrave, a man neither childish nor vain, but grave and learned. The length of his life, besides his miracles is, I confess, not easily to be believed, and so the age of Johannes de Temporibus, and the long living of one in our time in the Indies, to wit, three hundred years, as Mapheus and Torquemada report, may seem as incredible. Yea, of many other saints, as of St. Patrick who lived 122 years and St. David 146, St. Kentigern 185, and St. Modwen whose life must be very long, if that which is written of her be true; which, whether it be God knows, no man's salvation dependeth upon the believing or not believing of it.

This shows how acutely aware Roscarrock was of the difficulties made for him by his chosen subject in the full consciousness of the Jacobean age. To the medievals these legends presented no such difficulties: they lived within the cocoon of faith, so certain that they could afford to take them even humorously: these legends were their fireside tales told on long winter nights in the remote parishes where they belong, attaching to the familiar places where, ages before, the eponymous characters had lived by well or stream, in frequented spots or by the sea-shore, or journeying round that southern Celtic world from Wales or Ireland to Cornwall and on to Brittany. Humour was not a part of Roscarrock's composition; but the Protestants who scoffed at the nonsense he believed had little idea that the things they believed were no less so. Roscorrock's mind is not uncharacteristic of the age he lived in, in its combination of credulity and criticality. We find him scrupulous in regard to his sources; but once his source is accepted he does not criticise. Is that very different from those today who are 'born to believe'? Protestantism was one step towards rationality: impossible to arrest it there. It was a challenge: the medievals could be poetic and humorous, but with the Protestant challenge to the cocoon of faith, these things had to be taken seriously. They had either to be believed or not believed. Roscarrock was in a bit of a fix.

His life of St. Modwen is a long one full of incident and impossible stories, collected mostly out of Capgrave. But he had seen two other manuscripts, 'one of which I had of my learned friend, Mr. Thomas Allen of Oxford'. Allen was one of a group of Catholics who lurked in Gloucester Hall: a mathematician and astrologer, who had the reputation with the vulgar of being a conjurer. John Aubrey tells us that his servitor used to impose on them by telling them that sometimes he would meet the spirits coming up Allen's stairs like bees. Here is Roscarrock's dilemma.

In this and many other lives I look to be freely censured by such as use to measure the wonderful works of God with the silly and shallow capacity of man, though I write nothing but what I find written before me by such as I have cited. But I resolve to bear it, choosing rather in the honour of God and his faith to subdue human reason to divine grace. But whereas I find some difficulties in the time in which St. Modwen lived, I thought needful to note to others, though I can hardly reform it, for I cannot see how she could live in the time of St. Patrick the Apostle of Ireland sent thither by Pope Celestinus about the year 431.

He concludes that there must have been another Patrick with whom she lived, c. 870. Dates are not a matter of belief; the miraculous events are. We see Roscarrock, the miraculous accepted, struggling scrupulously to get the historical framework accurate.

St. Nona, mother of St. David, was a religious woman, 'but not as Bale, the vowed enemy of virgins, babbleth a Vestal virgin, but a Christian nun'. She was ravished and got with child, who became a virtuous bishop, St. David. She afterwards lived a life of penance and was reputed a saint, 'no way to be scorned at by Bale, who had been much more happy had he made the like satisfaction for his apostasy and vow-breach'. (John Bale, a former friar, became a Protestant bishop.) St. Nona's ravisher was a king of Cardigan, which Capgrave maketh N. Wales, Leland S. Wales and Camden W. Wales, which by a favourable interpretation must be made good and that perhaps in respect of divers situations; for that which is north in respect of one place may be south in respect of another'. (One is reminded of Newman's famous piece of obscurantism, about the Bible telling us that the sun moves round the earth, science that the earth moves round the sun, and never shall we know which is right until we know what motion is.) In fact the Protestants were geographically right about Cardigan.

Roscarrock continues with the practice of 'bowsening' the demented at St. Nun's pool in Altarnun parish, of which Carew gives an amused, sceptical account: how the patients were thrown into the water and afterwards brought to the altar, where prayers were offered and masses said for them, 'by which it was thought that some have been dispossessed and others cured of their frenzy, howsoever it pleaseth some to make themselves merry with it. It is likely that this saint, which giveth name to this church, well and pool, lived there, but I dare not assure myself of it, till I find more warrant than a bare conjecture.' Meticulous Roscarrock, straining at a gnat: there is no reason to doubt that she once lived there.

So, too, with St. Perran's miracle of carrying a live coal in his bare hands to warm St. Rodanus, 'by which I gather the stone was coal such as they call sea-coal, for had it been a flint it had been no marvel, much less a miracle, to get fire out of it or to carry it in his naked hands without hurt'. Poor Roscarrock, what a time he had, struggling to make sense of these medieval stories in a post-Reformation world which had shattered the Middle Ages!

He is happier remembering for us, centuries later, the familiar places and the old observances attaching to them. Roscarrock criticizes his co-religionist, J.W. of *The English Martyrologe*, for making St. Perran's relics to have been preserved at Padstow:

Methinks the records of Padstow should hardly err so grossly in a thing so apparent, as every fisherboy in the town knoweth that St. Perran and Padstow are two distinct places and are twelve or thirteen miles asunder . . . I, who was born within three miles of Padstow and not far from St. Perran, remember his relics were wont to be carried up and down in the country upon occasion and have seen them so carried in the time of Queen Mary . . . There was a chapel not far from Padstow bearing his name but his relics were (I take it) always reserved in St. Perran's . . . where he was buried, being called St. Perran's-in-the-Sand; which chapel hath been overblown with the sands, though there standeth one at this day near that place.

At St. Breward, 'there was a tree growing in our memory in the place of his martyrdom, which was much regarded and reverenced, and thought to have continued there ever since his death'. At the feast of St. Petrock on 4 June, the priests of Padstow, Bodmin and Little

Petherick used to meet at St. Breock's beacon with their crosses and banners at a sermon and collation. In the parish of Newlyn East there was a chapel dedicated to St. Nighton with a yard belonging; within was a little mount with four stones where the crosses and relics of St. Perran, Crantock, Cubert and Newlyn were wont to be placed in Rogation week, at which time a sermon was made to the people. 'And the last was preached by parson Crane in Queen Mary's time, as I have been credibly informed by a priest who had been an eye-witness.' One of these four stones was taken and turned into a cheese-press by Mistress Borlase about the year 1580; but later one night it was 'carried back by one, willed so by her after her death or by something assuming her personage, and remaineth still where it did. And this I have from report of such as were of her kinsfolks and friends, who have cause to know it.' It has the makings of a Cornish ghost-story.

It is clear how much alive for the ageing man so far away at Naworth were the memories of the religion of his childhood in Cornwall: some part of his heart – as with so many Cornishmen living away from home – was anchored there. We note how narrow and restricted his experience of the county naturally was: he knew well only the parishes in the immediate neighbourhood of his home. He had once made the pilgrimage to St. Michael's Mount, 'sometime a religious house, now a place of strength'; for

in the main rock of that Mount there was a seat which I have seen, neither easy to climb unto nor to sit in, which is called St. Michael's Chair, where they say he hath made his apparition, which caused it to be frequented as a great pilgrimage. The true story of his apparition not fully known to me, I forbear to write more of it, referring you if your fortune be to see it, to Mr. Johnson's Ecclesiastical History, lib. 5, cap. 20.

When Roscarrock did not know, he took trouble to inform himself, as we can see from the case of the patron saint of my native parish, St. Austell. Roscarrock, writes, 'there was usually a feast kept in memory of that saint the Thursday in Whitsun week'. Feast-week at St. Austell is still that week; and when Bishop Bronescombe re-dedicated the church in the thirteenth century, by a title known to the Roman Calendar, he chose the Holy Trinity as falling nearest the feast-day of the Celtic saint, so as not to disturb the age-long custom. Roscarrock continues: 'I should be apt to think that this St. Austell and the Doctor of the Church or our Apostle should be one, but that their feasts do differ; which perhaps may grow of that the one is the day of his death, the other of the dedication of the church. The reason moving me to think so is the statue of a bishop or abbot, which standeth in the wall of the said church. More I cannot say, but wish others would inquire, both of that and many other saints in these parts and in Wales whereof by the injury of time we are ignorant.'

A different hand has added: 'And yet they hold by tradition there that this St. Austell and St. Mewan were great friends, whose parishes join. And enjoy some privileges together, and that they lived there together.' A third hand adds further: 'The feast of which St. Mewan is November 19'. This information is correct: in his blindness, Roscarrock's inquiries had been answered.

The folklore of a people has a creative vitality continuing beyond the ages of faith. Perhaps it would not greatly surprise Roscarrock to know that many of these observances – rogations, processions, pilgrimages to holy wells, masses in the churches of his beloved saints – have come back, after long sleep, in our time; for what is founded on the rock of the irrational in human beings has undying strength.

The Turbulent Career of
Sir Henry Bodrugan

Two years after Edward IV had successfully re-established himself upon the throne with the victories of Barnet and Tewkesbury, his enemies found a last focus of resistance in Cornwall. The Earl of Oxford, who had escaped from the field of Barnet with his companion, Viscount Beaumont, and had since been abroad in the Channel looking for an opportunity for a descent upon the coast, suddenly made for St. Michael's Mount. He had some eighty men with him, including his three brothers and Beaumont; such a small force could hardly be dangerous, but they were welcomed and, according to Warkworth, 'had right good cheer of the commons, etc.'[1] They took possession of the Mount on the morrow of Michaelmas 1473, at the very time when Edward was occupied by his brother Clarence's disloyalty. On 27 October he issued a commission to Sir John Arundell [of Trerice] and a large body of the Cornish gentry, among whom Henry Bodrugan was a leading figure, to array the county and if necessary the adjoining counties, and reduce the Mount.[2]

But the siege did not go according to plan. We learn from Carew a century later that Sir John Arundell was killed in a skirmish on the sands; and he tells a characteristic Cornish story which came down in the

1. *Warkworth's Chronicle* (Camden Society), 26.
2. *Cal. Pat. Rolls, 1467–77*, 399.

family from that time. 'It is received by tradition that Sir John Arundell was forewarned by a wot not what calker how he should be slain on the sands. For avoiding which encounter he always shunned Efford and dwelt at Trerice, another of his houses. But as the proverb saith, *Fata viam invenient,* and as experience teacheth men's curiosity, *Fato viam sternit.* It happened that what time the Earl of Oxford surprised St. Michael's Mount by policy, and kept the same by strong hand, this Sir John Arundell was sheriff of Cornwall, wherethrough upon duty of his office and commandment from the Prince, he marched thither with *posse comitatus* to besiege it. And there in a skirmish on the sands, which divide the Mount from the continent, he fulfilled the effect of the prophecy with the loss of his life, and in the said Mount's chapel lieth buried.'[3]

After this untoward event the command devolved upon Bodrugan, who proceeded to play a curious independent game. It was said afterwards that he used the King's commission to 'assess the people of the shire to great notable sums' and converted them to his own use.[4] Certainly he does not appear to have been anxious to bring the siege, profitable as it was to himself, to an end. There were skirmishes in which Oxford took a few prisoners, and one in which he was wounded in the face by an arrow; still more there were parleys – perhaps Bodrugan had a tacit understanding with the Earl, for he allowed him to revictual the Mount and gather in an abundance of supplies. A whole month passed and the siege advanced no farther. The King issued a new commission granting power to offer pardon to every man in the Mount, except the Earl, his brothers and Beaumont; and transferred the command to the new sheriff, John Fortescue, though he did not leave out

---

3. Carew, Survey of Cornwall (ed. 1769), 118–119.
4. *Rolls Parliament,* vi, 133 foll.

Bodrugan.[5] There ensued 'great divisions' between these two: but the siege was pressed, various encounters were followed by truces, in which Fortescue made much use of the royal offer of pardon among Oxford's men. At the same time the King ordered reinforcements of men and ordnance, and commissioned several ships, the *Garce*, the *Garican*, the *Christopher* and the *Mary* of Calais to transport the men and cut off the Mount by sea. Oxford was looking for aid to the King of France, to whom he had dispatched his brother, Richard de Vere, under Bodrugan's nose.

From 23 December the siege began in earnest. Oxford would have been able to hold out longer if it had not been for the power of pardon with which Fortescue was armed. As help from abroad failed to arrive, one by one, Oxford's men were secretly won over, until there remained only eight or nine whom he could rely on. It was impossible to fight in such conditions, and Oxford sued for pardon. It was granted him, and all others in the Mount except Beaumont and Richard Lanarth; and on 15 February he surrendered, though Fortescue found, on entering, that the defenders, far from being reduced to extremity, had 'victual enough till Midsummer after.'[6] According to tradition, Edward attributed the dilatoriness of the siege to the disloyalty of the Cornish, and was wont to say that he looked upon Cornwall as 'the back-door of rebellion.'[7]

Just at this time the career of Henry Bodrugan reached a climax in a series of depredations and oppressions upon the smaller fry. We hear of an attack upon Polwhele and a threat to burn the house down, carried out under Bodrugan's orders by John Cardigan of Tregony, 'accompanied by divers rebels, late servants to John, Earl

5. *Cal. Pat. Rolls, 1467–77*, 418.
6. *Warkworth's Chronicle*, 27.
7. Blake, *Journal of the Royal Institution of Cornwall* (1915), 55.

of Oxford not yet reconciled to your grace.': which shows the terms Bodrugan was upon with some of the freebooters who held the Mount.[8] His career in Cornwall was so symptomatic of what was going on elsewhere with greater personages that it is worth investigating; the more so since there is no account of him in the *Dictionary of National Biography*.

Bodrugan was the last of his line. The family had been a leading one in mid-Cornwall throughout the Middle Ages. The young Henry succeeded to his estates, after a minority in which they were in the hands of the Crown's grantees, in 1447.[9] A few years later we find his name frequently upon commissions to investigate piracy cases, usually in connection with Fowey, which was so much to the fore in this respect, upon commissions of array, to muster archers – in short, he was taking an increasing part in the affairs of the county. In June 1460 order was sent by the Council to arrest him and bring him before them to answer certain charges.[10] Whatever they were, he was rehabilitated upon Edward IVs accession; for in March 1461 he was appointed to a commission to arrest John Arundell, John Trevelyan and other Lancastrians in insurrection in the county.[11] He was appointed on several further piracy commissions; and then in 1465 was himself charged with laying an ambush at Lostwithiel for Richard Tomyow, a tin merchant, and carrying off 100 pieces of white tin.[12] We learn next that his wife's son John, who went by the name of Beaumont, her first husband, was proved a bastard.[13] He was, in fact, Bodrugan's son; he was brought up at Bodrugan, his estate on the cliffs between Mevagissey and the

8. *Rolls. Parlt.*, vi, 133 foll.
9. *Cal. Pat. Rolls, 1446–77*, 126.
10. *Ibid., 1452–1461*, 609.
11. *Ibid., 1461–1467*, 28.
12. *Ibid.*, 488.
13. *Cal. Pat. Rolls, 1461–1467*, 539.

Dodman, and became a partner in his father's later misdeeds. In October 1467 Bodrugan received a general pardon for his offences.[14]

During Edward IV's exile and the period of Warwick's rule, 1470–1, Bodrugan was not named in the commissions of the peace; he was a Yorkist, and with Edward's return to power he reappears in local administration. Next, in 1472, he was in the Fleet for a debt owed to Anne, Lady Neville, and for denying two recognisances of his to Alfred Cornburgh; two Cornish friends, John Penlyne and Richard Bonython, went bail for him, and he was pardoned of his outlawry.[15] From now on he went wild, and there is a whole series of charges laid against him and his retainers, accomplices and servants.

Thomas Nevill complained that he had spent £100 in working a mine called the Cleker and wrought it to a depth of twelve fathoms before coming to its 'proper beam, which found and the likelihood of the avail thereof being perceived by Henry Bodrugan, esquire, and Richard Bonython, gentleman,' they seized the work by force, parted the ore between them and their companions, and took £40 worth of tin stuff.[16] Nevill petitioned Parliament that he could obtain no remedy at common law, 'for if any person would sue the law against the said Henry and Richard, or against any of their servants, anon they should be murdered and slain, and utterly robbed and despoiled of all their goods, so that no man dare sue, nor any man pass against the said Henry and Richard or their servants within the said county, whereby the said county is as lawless and like to be utterly destroyed'.

James Trefusis complained that on the Feast of Pentecost, in this same year 1473, Bodrugan had made a

14. *Ibid.*, 526.
15. *Ibid.*, 1467–77, 362.
16. *Rolls Parlt.* vi, 133 foll.

forcible entry into his house, and taken away goods, chattels and horses to the value of £40; and that on 20 June he had entered a ship of Trefusis's, the *Bride* of Feock, and taken 40 marks worth of stuff thence, while the latter dare not attempt any suit against Bodrugan 'for doubt of death.' A memorandum is appended to the petition, of the goods taken, three horses, sixteen kine, a bull and two calves, two coarse girdles, harnessed with silver and gilt, a pair of beads of coral, gauds of silver and gilt, five gold rings, brass pots and pans; all suggesting the economy of a small country gentleman's household of the late fifteenth century.

John Arundell, John Penpons, William Carnsew, Otis Philip, had similar complaints to make of their houses forcibly entered and goods carried off. They cited a piratical exploit in addition, stating that on the vigil of Holy Trinity, Bodrugan had set to sea two carvels, the *Mary Bodrugan* and the *Barbara* of Fowey. They met a Breton carvel of 50 tons, chased her into St. Ives, and there spoiled her of wine and cloth worth 300 marks, slew one of the Bretons and kept the rest in prison. At various dates he had broken into the houses of the complainants, who annexed schedules of their goods taken: feather beds, counterpanes of arras, pillows and bolsters, wheat and hay, silver cups, spoons, girdles. At Polwhele, Otis Philip complained, Bodrugan's servants had environed the house with fire and threatened to burn it with him in it. Further, they petitioned Parliament, 'it is openly known in the said shire that the said Henry Bodrugan, not doubting God, nor the dreadful censures of the Church, without any authority spiritual . . . taketh upon him to prove testaments of the people there, both of people of great substance of goods and others, to change their last wills damnably, take yearly great sums of goods and also to commit the administration of like persons dying testate and intestate at his pleasure, and seizeth and taketh by colour thereof all goods and chattels of such persons so dying, and then to his own use taketh and converteth to the worst example that may be.'

On these various accounts proclamation against Bodrugan was made by the Sheriff at Launceston; but he appeared neither there nor at Westminster to answer the indictments against him. So, by default, for his felony his lands were declared forfeit for life; and he was attainted. A commission was sent down for his and his servants' arrest. Next year, January 1475, a petition was exhibited in Parliament on behalf of him and Bonython.[17] Their case was plausibly put in the matter of Nevill's mine; they said that they had only intermeddled as J.P.s at the request of certain poor men, tenants of the Duchy, who 'at their cost first digged the mine from the grass root till they had found the proper beam thereof'; and that they were only restoring these men to their rights. They besought Parliament to consider that by the Act of Attainder they and their heirs were disabled; that Bodrugan's wife (his second), Margaret Viscountess Lisle, 'which is a great estate of this realm,' had by the Act lost her dower both of Bodrugan's and of her own lands, and had nothing to live by. The attainder was reversed; and on 18 April, on the creation of Prince Edward as Prince of Wales, Bodrugan was knighted.[18]

Next year he was in trouble again. On 1 May 1476 he received a pardon of outlawry for not appearing to answer a debt of £150 18s. 7d., to Nicholas Mills, citizen and tailor of London.[19] It was a large sum in the currency of the time; no doubt it meant that Bodrugan and his wife made a brave show in London at the time of his being knighted. He was in debt again two years later to Sir Philip Courtenay for £200; to which he had not answered, was outlawed and again pardoned.[20] It would

17. *Rolls Parlt.* vi, 133 foll.
18. Shaw, *Knights of England*, I, 136.
19. *Cal. Pat. Rolls, 1467–77*, 576.
20. *Ibid.*, 1476–85, 81.

seem that much of Bodrugan's troubles – and it was characteristic of the time – was due to over-spending himself, in ostentation, over-hospitable living, keeping a band of dependents and retainers. Meanwhile, in 1477, John Beaumont received a general pardon.[21] In June 1480 Sir Henry was granted a general pardon for all offences committed up to 6 July last;[22] two years later he successfully petitioned for the exemplification of his letters patent of pardon, the originals having been, characteristically, lost.[23]

During the remainder of Edward IV's and Richard III's reigns, Bodrugan had things very much his own way in Cornwall. He was a tried Yorkist, and that is a sufficient explanation of his having been let off so lightly. He was during these years the most powerful person in the county; his name appears at the head of all the commissions directed to inquire into piracy cases, commissions of array, to assess subsidies and appoint collectors; he was in all the commissions of peace from 1477 to 1484.[24] Sir Henry went on his way as before. We find new evidences of his little ways among the petitions to the Prince's Council.[25] Philip Wise of St. Austell, a tenant of the Duchy manor of Tewington, complained that Sir Henry pretended a title to his holding, and distrained upon him for a relief which he said was due to him; Wise also complained that he had a mine-work with thirty persons working upon it, but that they dare not occupy it for fear of bodily hurt from Bodrugan and his servants.[26] Bodrugan's defence was that the disputed claim was a matter determinable at common law. In all his disputes Bodrugan showed a not unnatural affection

21. *Ibid.*, 48.
22. *Ibid.*, 280.
23. *Ibid.*, 314.
24. *Cal. Pat. Rolls, 1476–85*, 556.
25. *Ancient Petitions*, Addenda: Special Collections 6 (P.R.O.).
26. *Ibid.*, File 344, E 1278.

for the processes of common law: he had the twelve men of the jury perhaps under his thumb. It gives one the background to the passing of Henry VII's Star Chamber Act, with its summary way of dealing with over-mighty subjects like Bodrugan. There may have been something in his defence that he was interposing on behalf of poor men, as against middle men, their employers and the small gentry. That was rather the Yorkist line, as against the Lancastrian; and it was the success of the Tudors that they continued the Yorkist tradition of effective government, and the protection of small people, rather than the Lancastrian. It has to be remembered, too, that Bodrugan left a popular memory behind him in Cornish tradition.

There were, however, other petitions against him from Duchy tenants. Nicholas Roche charged Bodrugan with entering his holding, 'accompanied by a great company of people arrayed in manner of war, with bows, bills, swords,' etc., and carrying away sixty beasts, and thereafter took the rents and profits, with all toll tin, for the past two years.[27] Bodrugan claimed that the lands were part of his father's inheritance, but asked for time to prepare his defence. Another petitioner claimed that Bodrugan had distrained upon him for more rent than was due, and then put him out of his holding, making him forfeit the lease.[28] There was another petition from Bodrugan himself regarding the manors of Restronguet, Tremodret and Trevylyn which he held of the Duchy.[29] He claimed that he held them by six and a half knights' services, not fifteen, as the Duchy officials said, who wanted him to pay a large relief upon his resettling these manors on his marriage to Viscountess Lisle. Since the Sheriff would make no deliverance of the manors

27. *Ibid.*, E 1279.
28. *Ibid.*, E 1280.
29. *Ibid.*, E 1281.

contrary to the command of the Chancellor of the Duchy, and Sir Henry felt that his 'refusal would encourage others to repugn', he had bound himself to pay £50 relief, and now appealed to the Council to discharge him of payment. Finance was at the bottom of Bodrugan's troubles, as of many other great personages in this period; though there must have been other factors in his turbulence – his character, the early death of his father leaving him a minor, the failure of either of his marriages to produce an heir, the disorder of the time.

Bodrugan's career comes to an end in a haze of picturesque stories as they have come down in Cornish tradition, from which it is now possible to disentangle the facts.[30] Moreover, there is usually something in tradition: in this case, in the part which Edgcumbe and Trevanion had in bringing him down. The older Cornish histories speak of Bodrugan fighting on the side of Richard III at Bosworth field, and of his escaping afterwards into Cornwall.[31] There is no evidence of this. He is more likely to have lain low in Cornwall; for after Henry's accession, in February 1486, he was named, along with the Earl of Devon, Sir Robert Willoughby, Sir John Halliwell, Sir John Treffry and other triumphant Lancastrians, to serve on yet another Fowey case of piracy.[32] But it was his last. Sir Henry had been too closely associated with Yorkish rule, and too well rewarded by it, to feel comfortable under that of Henry VII, with his former enemies now in the ascendant. The tradition is that at the time of Buckingham's conspiracy against Richard III, Bodrugan had taken the lead in the pursuit of Richard Edgcumbe. Carew tells the story which had come down in the Edgcumbe family, how

30. The following paragraphs are based on my *Tudor Cornwall*.
31. *Cf.* Davies Gilbert, founded on Hals and Tonkin MSS. histories, *Parochial History of Cornwall*, II, 108.
32. *Cal. Pat. Rolls, 1485–94*, 105.

Edgcumbe was driven to hide in the thick woods at Cotehele overlooking the gorge of the Tamar; 'which extremity taught him a sudden policy, to put a stone in his cap and tumble the same into the water, while these rangers were fast at his heels, who looking down after the noise and seeing his cap swimming thereon, supposed that he had desperately drowned himself, gave over their further hunting and left him liberty to shift away and ship over into Brittany.'[33] From which he returned with Henry. For his services to Richard III, Bodrugan was rewarded with the manors of Trelawne and Tywardreath.[34]

When Henry VII came to rule, it was then Edgcumbe's turn, who was in a powerful position, one of the chief agents in executing the King's policy. By 1487 Bodrugan's discontent with the new régime had betrayed itself. There is no evidence that he was with the Earl of Lincoln at the battle of Stoke, as has been said;[35] nor is he charged with having been there in his subsequent attainder. But on 8 February 1487 a commission was granted to Sir Richard Edgcumbe to arrest Bodrugan and Beaumont and other rebels, 'who have withdrawn themselves into private places in the counties of Devon and Cornwall and stir up sedition.'[36] Edgcumbe must have leaped at the chance of getting his own back. The story is that Bodrugan slipped away out of his house to the cliffs nearby, where there was a boat waiting for him: 'as soon therefore as he came to the cliff above an hundred feet high, he leaped down into the sea upon a little grassy island there without much hurt or damage, where instantly a boat which he had prepared in the cove attended him there, which transported him to a ship

33. Carew 114.
34. Harleian MS. 433, 1616.
35. Cf. Blake, *Journal of the Royal Institution of Cornwall* (1915), 64.
36. *Cal. Pat. Rolls*, 1485–94, 179.

that carried him into France, which astonishing fact and place is to this day well known and remembered by the name of Henry Bodrugan's leap or jump.'[37]

However that may be, Bodrugan and his son certainly left the country; and that may well have been their manner of leaving. They went to Ireland; on 9 November 1487 an Act of attainder was passed against them and their lands were declared forfeit.[38] In the Act they were charged with imagining and compassing the death of the King, in company with the Earl of Lincoln there. But in a Star-Chamber case of the next reign, John Reskymer and Richard Antron, heirs to the Bodrugan inheritance, state that Sir Henry 'departed into Ireland to a kinsman of his when he soon afterwards there deceased'; but that he 'was never in company with the said Earl, nor never spake with him, nor never sent him message by writing, nor none otherwise, nor never committed treason.'[39]

It is a likely enough story. Perhaps the old man – he must have been over sixty – had had enough. His wife, Viscountess Lisle, had died before him. Early in 1486 he had tried to put himself right with Sir Robert Willoughby, a leading supporter of Henry VII in the west, by granting him his manor of Trethewe after his death.[40] Upon his attainder the Willoughbys took the rents and profits of it, and afterwards bought it outright.[41] It was a good time for those on the right side. Trevanion, for his part, got the manors of Restronguet and Newham.[42] After various payments made to Hugh Oldham, Walter Smert, citizen and skinner of London,

37. Davies Gilbert, *op. cit.*, 108.
38. *Rolls Parlt*, vi, 397; for Beaumont inheritance, v. Maclean, *Trigg Minor*, I, 552–3.
39. Star Chamber Proc. Henry VIII 23/305.
40. *Cal. Inq. post mortem*, Henry VII, II 872.
41. *Cal. Pat. Rolls*, 1494–1509, 503.
42. *Ibid.*, 350.

and others to whom Bodrugan was in debt,[43] the bulk of
his manors, Bodrugan, Tregrehan, Tremodret and many
others, were granted on 26 April 1488 to Sir Richard
Edgcumbe.[44] A junior branch of the Edgcumbes came to
inhabit Sir Henry's house out on the cliffs near Chapel
Point, and were buried in his parish church at St.
Goran. It is through the inquisition taken on the death
of Sir Richard Edgcumbe that we learn the details of the
economy of Bodrugan as it was in Sir Henry's time, his
reeve's accounts: the forty-one kine, eighteen oxen, the
calves and heifers, the dutiful payments for blessed wax,
to the brethren of St. John of Rhodes or St. John of
Acre, which suggest those last, lingering days of the
middle ages.[45]

43. *Rolls Parlt*, vi, 400.
44. *Cal. Pat. Rolls, 1485–94*, p. 224. There was an annuity charged
    upon them to Sir Thomas Lovell; this was later extinguished
    and the Edgecumbes entered into entire possession.
45. Henderson MS., xxv., R.I.C., Truro.

Henry Trecarrell of Tudor Days

Henry Trecarrell must have been well known in the Cornwall of his time – getting on for 500 years ago – but little is known of him today.[1] However, he did great things for his neighbourhood, for Linkinhorne church and Launceston parish church in particular, besides leaving the finest medieval house in Cornwall, though unfinished – except for Cotehele. With the aura of Plymouth for ever encroaching, now is the time to emphasise that East Cornwall is as Cornish as the rest of it. We recognise that the Cornishry of West Cornwall is more concentrated in essence – you can hear it in the intonation of the dialect: I always think of St. Ives as a kind of Cornish Caernarvon, where the Celtic essence is at its most intense.

In Linkinhorne, at the other end of our little land – for it is not a mere county, let alone English – its Celtic character is no less evident. Take the meaning of the name. The first element *Lin* is really the familiar *lan*, meaning sacred enclosure, the area surrounding a church. Kinhorne is the name of a Celtic chieftain, in Welsh Cynharne, meaning 'iron chief'. This name appears in two other places, Polkinghorne in the parishes of Gwinear and Perran-ar-worthal. It may have been a not uncommon name for a Celtic chief; but certainly a memorable one of the name must have lived in the neighbourhood, for this parish to have taken its

1. A Commemoration Address in Linkinhorne church, East Cornwall.

name from him. When I notice that a Dark Ages camp is not far to the north of the churchtown, we need hardly doubt that that was where he lived.

I wish I could tell you the meanings of the names of this beautiful parish: the most urgent need for Cornish studies is a dictionary of our Place-Names; next, a short guide to our Surnames. To Cornish folk in general Linkinhorne is best known for its tall church-tower, and for its ring of bells cast by the admirable Penningtons of Stoke Climsland in the year of Trafalgar.

Henry Trecarrell's connection with Linkinhorne was close since he owned the manor of Trefrize. This had come to him by inheritance, so that the family was connected with the parish for some time, back into the slumber of the Middle Ages – when we were all speaking Cornish – before the modern world broke in upon us with the Reformation. Trecarrell recognised his obligations as a leading landowner more than generously; for he not only largely built the remarkably sculpted church at Launceston – more like a church in Brittany – but also the north aisle and tower at Linkinhorne.

Around the town-place (i.e. farm-yard) at Trecarrell one can still see shaped and moulded stones lying about, as they have lain waiting to be used for over four hundred years. A touching sight it is to anyone who knows their story and responds to their mute appeal. Yet in our time, after the lapse of all those years, they have found a voice in our poet, Charles Causley, and the lively ballad he has dedicated to the story. Some people think that, since there is no monument to Trecarrell, we do not know where he is buried – though it is a fair certainty that he would be buried in his own parish church at Lezant. For a monument there, his three daughters and co-heiresses failed him – perhaps they considered that he had already spent too much of their inheritance on the church.

Henry Trecarrell's life spanned the transition from the inefficient hugger-mugger of the medieval world to the beginnings of the modern state. He lived to see the end of the medieval order, with the dissolution of the monasteries that had been a familiar feature of the land-scape for centuries – at Launceston, Bodmin, Tavistock, St. Germans, round about him; at Tywardreath, Truro, Penryn, St. Michael's Mount further west. He died on the threshold of a religious revolution that he could never have envisaged, let alone the destruction that went along with the renewal of the nation's life on a more secular basis.

Trecarrell can hardly have expected the ruin of the medieval Church, the revolution that a desirable measure of reform let loose. He died in 1544, three years before the terrifying old tyrant, Henry VIII, died and revolution was unleashed. The backward elements in remote Cornwall reacted against the new deal, with the Rebellion against the new Prayer Book in 1549. The Cornish – or their clerical leaders – said that they didn't like the new service in English, which seemed to them more like a Christmas mumming: they preferred the old ways, and the Latin Mass. To which Archbishop Cranmer replied very pertinently: how many of them understood Latin better than they did English? All the same, what a pity it was that the Prayer Book, and the Bible, were not translated into Cornish – as they were, providentially, into Welsh.

Half a century before, in 1497 – when Trecarrell was in his twenties – there had been two rebellions in Cornwall, starting from the revolutionary parish of St. Keverne. The first rising was on account of the extra taxation imposed by the government to pay for a war on the Scottish Border: the Cornish said that this was nothing to do with them, was not of their making, and refused to pay.

Why should this remote parish near the Lizard have sent forth so many rebels in both 1497 and again in 1549? The answer is – because the parish was a sanctuary, and hence the population contained a number of criminals, thieves, robbers and outlaws.

What kind of picture of the Cornwall of that remote time do we have in our minds?

Many evidences remain: enough for a portrait of our little land in my book, *Tudor Cornwall*. There are a few new strokes to add from William Worcester's *Itineraries* recently published at Oxford. William was a Bristol man, secretary and man of affairs to Sir John Fastolf (from whom Shakespeare adapted the name Falstaff). Worcester was also an observant antiquary, who travelled the length of Cornwall in 1478, when Trecarrell was but a child.

From his diary we get a precious glimpse into the simple culture of that time, when so much is silence. He stopped a night at Launceston priory, enjoying the hospitality of the canons, who showed him their chief treasure: the head of the martyred St. Gennys. Next day, September 14, which was that of the Exaltation of the Holy Cross, he rode across the Moor – where his horse stumbled and fell – to Bodmin. Here he put up at the 'George', and had converse with a number of people. There were the canons of the priory: Dom William John, who had knowledge in physic and showed him several ancient medical books; so had the sacristan, Dom John Stevens, with whom he had a drink. We see that the monks must have acted as doctors in the community.

Worcester inspected the Calendar of Saints' days they observed, and here a number of our Celtic saints appear, not all recognised by Rome. But we recognise a good many of them: St. Constantine, king and martyr, St. Perran, patron saint of miners, Saints Petroc, Crantoc, Cadoc, Nectan; but *not*, I regret to say, St. Melor, patron saint of Linkinhorne. Worcester inspected the Register of the Franciscans, under the guidance of Brother Mohun. He met the Bodmin lawyer, Benedict

Bernard, to whom he gave a book, a romance of Troy, and a paper book, a supposed tract of Aristotle, in French. He was much impressed at talking with Thomas Limbery, a gentleman who lived on the north coast at Padstow, and also with Richard Kendall, a lawyer, who lived at Duloe on the south coast. These are all names we have with us still.

So he went on to Truro, where he stayed the night with Otys Philip (or Polwhele), one of the King's Grooms, a leading figure in the administration of the Duchy under Edward IV, and viewed the Martyrology treasured by the Dominicans. Thence to St. Michael's Mount, where he heard Mass on St. Lambert's day, and viewed the Calendar of Saints kept there. Next day back to Penryn, where he stopped probably with the canons of Glasney, and returned to Bodmin. Whence he made a visit to Fowey, to spend a night as Bodinnick with Robert Bracy, who showed him various books of chronicles, and gave him information about the Cornish saints buried in the neighbouring churches – St. Manacus at Lanreath, St. Sirus (or Cyric?) at St. Cadix, the little cell in St. Veep, now occupied by my friend Raleigh Trevelyan.

William Worcester returned via Liskeard and across a ferry, thus to Tavistock abbey. Everywhere he visited he measured the churches, took down their obits and made notes of matters of interest. Simple and taciturn as these people appear to us they were not unlettered: they had their culture, essentially bound up with the church.

It was the churches that were the chief things to see – naturally enough, for the surplus wealth of the community went, with parish pride, into the building and furnishing of their churches. This was the richest period of church-building in Cornwall, and this must testify to increasing returns from the land, source of wealth and subsistence. The tallest church-towers were going up – Linkinhorne, St. Cleer, Fowey, Probus,

St. Austell in just these years. The furnishing of the churches was giving widespread employment to numbers of admirable craftsmen, carving the woodwork, pews and bench-ends, images of the saints, the elaborate rood screens with their figures. Painters were decorating the walls with their frescoes, the glass makers filling the windows with such treasures as we still see at St. Neot. The churches were ablaze with colour, rich with carving and decoration.

They were at their apogee when the blow fell, and the Reformation proceeded to destroy. The images and figures were smashed, the paintings white-washed over, the rood-lofts with their figures pulled down, most of the rood screens followed. Then, in the next century, with the odious Civil War and the victory of the Puritans – dreadful Philistines – the stained glass windows were largely destroyed. The churches were left as bare as barns: a revolution had passed through.

Once more, the sickening thing is that people cannot put through a desirable measure of reform without destroying things. I attach more importance to the admirable works of men's hands than to the nonsense they think. I found recently that Queen Elizabeth I was much opposed to pulling down the rood-lofts, with their roods, but simply could not prevail against the Protestant bishops and Parliament. She was a cultivated and intelligent woman. Why make the unoffending works of men's hands suffer for the nonsense they suppose themselves to think?

For the last century we have been trying to repair the damage: putting in much less good woodwork, filling the windows with inferior stained glass – with some exceptions, such as the excellent glass at Cardinham. We have an example of what the churches lost in the beautiful Renaissance pulpit at Launceston, with its exquisitely painted designs. After centuries of coats of paint and varnish, it has been restored to its pristine glory, as it was put up there on the eve of the Reformation, by the discerning taste of Norman Colville of Penheale.

We have examples of what all Cornish churches should look like in Blisland, Lanreath, St. Crantock, St. Columb Major, Little Petherick. The work in this last is that of a genius among church decorators, Sir Ninian Comper. The grand lost opportunity in Cornwall is that Truro cathedral – finest of Victorian churches – was being decorated and furnished throughout his long life without once calling him in.

On the political side, a great change occurred in Cornwall, along with the rest of the country, as the result of the battle of Bosworth in 1485, and the restoration of the Lancastrian line in the person of Henry Tudor, as Henry VII. The Lancastrian royal house would never have failed, but for the imbecility of poor king Henry VI. But the West Country remained loyal to, and suffered along with, the unfortunate royal line. However, after the deplorable episode of Richard III and the brief rule of a gang of ruffians – in Cornwall Sir Henry Bodrugan, who was no exception, bore sway – things came round again with Bosworth, and the West Country came into its own. John Trevelyan many years before had been a personal favourite with Henry VI, who made his fortune for him; he lived long enough as an old man to see the triumph of the cause with Henry VII. Sir Richard Edgcumbe became one of the closest advisers of the new king, employed on the most important missions: to receive the submission of Ireland, to Scotland to arrange a marriage-treaty – it is to the marriage of Henry's daughter, Margaret, to the Scots king that the present Queen owes her throne. Another of Henry's friends, Lord Willoughby de Broke, ran the Duchy for him: we see him on his fine, but much defaced, Renaissance tomb in Callington church. From this time forward we find the Cornish gentry to the fore at Court, in the swim of things.

Henry Trecarrell in his time turned the tragedy in his family life, the end of his name, to the service of the community and of religion. People still set store by the continuance of their old family name in the male line. In Tudor times a male heir was even more important, for only that providence kept the family estates together: among daughters they were divided up, so that the family lost not only its name but the cohesion of the estate, bits of which whizzed off to recruit other planetary systems, other families.

This was what happened to the Trecarrells. They did not belong to the greater gentry of Norman descent, Courtenays, Arundells, Grenvilles, St. Aubyns; they belonged to the lesser indigenous gentry of Cornish stock, Trevelyans, Tremaynes, Treffrys. In the fifteenth century Cornish surnames were not yet settled, and this family went by the name of Esse. Henry, or his father, seems to have settled for their chief place of residence, Trecarrell, which may mean the place, or house, of Charles. By this time the Trecarrells had built up a good clutch of properties in this area, in the usual manner, I suppose, by marrying heiresses – Trefrize, in Link-inhorne parish, would have come to them this way. Henry Trecarrell was a man of some mark who was all set to carry the family a stage further forward: he too had married a small heiress, Margaret, daughter of John Kelway or Kellaway whose arms we see sculpted upon the remarkable exterior of St. Mary Magdalen at Launceston. Early Tudor people are still medievals and apt to be disappointingly anonymous; so that we have little information about Trecarrell.

Throughout the 1520s and 1530s he was chief steward of the borough of Launceston; thus he was the most important person in the town's affairs and would receive a fee as its regular officer. Twice he served as mayor of the town: in 1536, the year when the lesser monasteries were dissolved; again, a second time, in 1543, the year before his death. By then all the monasteries had fallen, their lands and goods confiscated, the monks dispersed. The internal landscape of Launceston already looked different with the ruin of the priory that had stood so long at the foot of the hill, the buildings robbed of their lead and allowed to fall into ruin – we see part of the fabric in the fine Norman door of Polyphant stone brought up the hill to form the entrance to the 'White Hart'.

We do not know what Trecarrell thought of these changes, and he never served in the Reformation Parliament that confirmed them. He confined himself to local service as Justice of the Peace; a commissioner of sewers for the waters of the Tamar and the marshes thereabouts; and regularly one of the commissioners of gaol-delivery for Launceston Castle, i.e. for assizes, in the 1530s along with better known names like Sir Peter Edgcumbe, Sir John Arundell of Lanherne, and Sir Richard Grenville, grandfather of the hero of the *Revenge*.

Historical researchers often come up with something disagreeable to surprise one: I cannot find, and I do not think, that Henry Trecarrell was ever knighted, that in fact he was not *Sir* Henry. But isn't that, in a way, more interesting? Popular tradition, the instinct of the people, may have knighted him for his good works.

We know the familiar story. Everybody in those days believed in astrology – and not a few in our enlightened days. Trecarrell consulted the stars upon the impending birth of a hoped-for son and heir. But they portended a most unfavourable conjunction, a short life for the boy and an accidental death. The traditional account says that he 'begged the midwife to delay the birth, if possible, by an hour, but nature and fate both conspiring against his wishes, a son came to light immediately, to the joy of all present, excepting the father'.

At about the same time the famous astrologer, Cardan, cast the horoscope for Henry VIII's little son, the prince who became Edward VI. The astrologer forecast for him a prosperous and a long life: the poor boy died at sixteen.

But, true it is, that Henry Trecarrell's boy, in spite of all the care taken of him, drowned in his bath. And this it was, according to tradition, that led him, disconsolate, never to finish his fine house. The hall, with its mullioned windows and splendidly arched and braced roof, must have been built in rivalry with Cotehele, inspired by it, possibly by the same craftsmen or the next generation carrying on the admirable tradition. The useful Pevsner says that 'it could become one of the major medieval monuments of Cornwall'. But it already is – and yet very few people in Cornwall know it: everybody should make a pilgrimage to see it.

Fortunately everyone knows the virtually unique, but again unfinished, parish church at Launceston, the decorated exterior, practically every stone sculpted, granite too, encrusted with emblems, figures, Latin inscriptions from the medieval faith soon to be discarded: *Ave Maria Gracia Plena Dominus Tecum*. At the east end a recumbent figure of the Magdalen with her vase of ointment, angels attending her. I suspect that Trecarrell must have contributed to the building over a longer period than is realised; for the front of the porch, displaying his arms with his wife's, is dated 1511 and he did not die till 1544. Perhaps the work was halted by the Reformation as much as by his death – though fortunately that at Linkinhorne was carried to completion.

Though the family came to an end with three daughters, co-heiresses among whom the estate was broken up, they married into local families – another

Kelway, a Devon Kelly and a Harris – so that there may be people in these parts descended from the Trecarrells. The house itself has a later memory, from the time of the Civil War, when it belonged to Ambrose Manaton, a Royalist like most of the Cornish gentry. In 1644, the centenary of Trecarrell's death, Charles I entered Cornwall pursuing the Parliamentarian army under Essex to its surrender at Lostwithiel. The King spent the night of August 1 at Trecarrell, while his army lay about the fields around the house, a fine sight.

It is right and proper that a good man should be commemorated and that, half a thousand years afterwards, when he is only a name to us, while the stones themselves still remain, they should find their interpreter.

The Elizabethan Plymouth Pilchard Fishery

Fish was a subject near to the hearts of the members of the Privy Council under Elizabeth. Apart from the large part it played in their diets, to judge from records of their meals, concerned with the necessity of maintaining the fisheries as an important factor in national power. It was an aim as much political as economic, if indeed it is not false to distinguish between the two, so closely were they interwoven in Elizabethan minds. They desired to encourage the fisheries as a training-ground for mariners and a school of seamanship, no less than as a source of food-supply for the home market and for export abroad.

With this policy Cecil was closely identified; as early as 1553, he had inquired into the condition of the industry and the reason for the decline in the number of boats employed in the various fisheries.[1] The fishmongers replied that there was a lack of sale for fish, owing to the non-observance of fish-days. The moment Cecil became Secretary of State, we find among the considerations to be presented to the Parliament of 1559: 'Let the old course of fishing be maintained by the straitest observation of fish-days, for policy' sake; so the sea-coasts shall be strong with men and habitations and the fleet flourish more than ever.'[2] It was followed up by a more stringent enforcement of the Act of Edward VI appointing Fridays

1. *Cal. State Papers Dom.*, Edw. VI, Vol. IV, 56.
2. *Hist. Mss. Com.*, *Salisbury* 1, 165.

and Saturdays to be observed as fish-days; by an Act of 1564 adding Wednesdays to them; and by an active policy of stimulating the home industry, by restricting imports, while at the same time attempting to interpose with measures of control in the interest of the consumer.

The difficulties encountered in imposing order upon changing economic conditions and in reconciling conflicting interests, are nowhere better illustrated than in the disputes that arose in and around Plymouth concerning the pilchard fishery towards the middle of the reign.

Certain technical developments in the method of fishing on the coast were upsetting the old arrangements. Seine-fishing was becoming prevalent; this led to cutting out smaller people, since the size of the seine demanded three or four boats to the net, each boat carrying about six men apiece. Hence the domination of the market by the merchants, dealing on a larger scale and chiefly for the export market. The needs of the export market brought about a change in the manner of curing the fish: instead of being smoked singly, they were finned and packed into hogsheads 'made purposely leaky, which afterwards they press with great weights, to the end the train may soak from them into a vessel placed in the ground to receive it.'[3] The price of fish went up and complaints were made that there was a scarcity among the inhabitants, while the merchants engrossed the profits. The trade began to be concentrated away from the inner harbour at Plymouth, and to move to Cawsand at the mouth of the bay, where the merchants and seiners set up their cellars, so that the trade in the town began to decline. As soon as Plymouth was affected by this development, the Council began to take serious notice; for the changing conditions in the fishery could not be allowed to detract from the convenience of

3. R. Carew, *Survey of Cornwall*, 1602 (edition of 1811), 102.

Plymouth, the key to maritime power in the west. The Council were in a dilemma; and though they hesitated for a time, they ultimately chose on considerations of national power to hold in check the new economic tendency.

These points emerge in the evidence; but is by no means easy to piece together or to make out with certainty. Let us take first that of Richard Carew of Antony, as the most direct, for he was a contemporary witness of the changes and had some part in the controversy. He says of the pilchard-fishing: 'This commodity at first carried a very low price, and served for the inhabitants cheapest provision; but of late times, the dear sale beyond the seas hath so increased the number of takers, and the takers jarring and brawling one with another, and foreclosing the fishes taking their kind within harbour, so decreased the number of the taken, as the price daily extendeth to a higher rate, equalling the proportion of other fish: a matter which yet I reckon not prejudicial to the commonwealth, seeing there is store sufficient of other victuals, and that of these a twentieth part will serve the country's need, and the other nineteen pass into foreign realms with a gainful utterance.'[4] Carew was no blind advocate of the merchants' interest, but he was inclined in favour of the seiners who were taking the risks. 'The seiner's profit in this trade is uncertain, as depending upon the sea's fortune, which he long attendeth and often with a bootless travail; but the pilchard merchant may reap a speedy, large and assured benefit, by dispatching the buying, saving and selling to the transporters, within little more than three months' space. Howbeit, divers of them, snatching at wealth over-hastily, take money beforehand, and bind themselves for the same, to deliver pilchards ready saved to the transporter, at an under-rate, and so cut their fingers'.

4. R. Carew, *Survey of Cornwall*, 1602 (edition of 1811), 104.

The case against the merchants, on behalf of the smaller fishermen and the inhabitants of Devon and Cornwall, was put in a petition to the Queen about 1578.[5] Their complaint was that the inhabitants and common people 'cannot as they have done buy any of the said fishes for their relish and sustenance, by the reason of the greedy merchants which are the transporters, without great and excessive prices; and the fishermen themselves hath for their travail but low prices for the same, which is for every xii *d.* that they have the transporter gets v *d.* in consideration thereof. If that shall please your Majesty to grant to your poor servants a general restraint to be had from those two counties Devon and Cornwall during the term of – years, they will pay unto your Majesty xxxx marks by the year during the said term of years and all other customs thereunto belonging heretofore paid for the same'. The fact that a sum of money was offered for the restraint, shows that the petition had a group, not without resources, behind it; it is probable that it came from some interest in the town of Plymouth which was antagonistic to the Cornish merchants at Cawsand.

Meanwhile, within Plymouth, there were arising with regard to forestalling and engrossing difficulties of the same nature as Carew describes. In 1581, the Mayor (who was in that year Sir Francis Drake) and the town council adopted an order 'that if any person or persons inhabiting within this borough, do make or save any quantity of pilchards, whereby shall grow that he or they have either sold or promised the said pilchards before they be saved, or that have received any money beforehand of any person or persons not inhabiting within the town directly or indirectly to make the same pilchards; then he shall be called before the Mayor . . . to answer the same, and if he refuse to answer it, he shall

5. S.P. Dom., Eliz., vol. 127, f. 62. (Public Record Office.)

be for that year barred to make any pilchards. And that no woman, either wife of widow, or man-servant shall at any time hereafter sell or make price for or upon any pilchards brought to this town upon pain to incur such a fine or punishment as by the direction of Mr. Mayor and his brethren shall be thought good.'[6] This Order was clearly aimed at those people in the town who were aiding the merchants to engross the supply, and particularly those who were hand-in-hand with the Cawsand merchants.

The Mayor and his brethren could not break the link between them. In 1584 there followed a second order directed specially against women setting a price for or upon any pilchards brought into the town; evidently they had been the means by which the first order had been evaded, and a fine of ten shillings was fixed.[7] There followed further orders against the fish-wives; one of them specially saying that women were allowed to make provision for any household; but that 'persons bringing hake to the town were to sell to every freeman equally some indifferent portion'. The freemen of the borough were the protagonists in the struggle, and anyway determined to be supplied first.

In 1584 the trouble came to the notice of the Privy Council, which sent down instructions for it to be dealt with by the leading gentlemen of the district. Neither the Council's letters nor the efforts of the leading gentlemen were effective, and the matter came up again in 1586. The inhabitants of Plymouth, we learn[8] had complained 'two years since or thereabouts of certain cellars and store-houses built of late on the cliffs and sea-coast for the storage of pilchards, to the great

---

6. The White Book of the Corporation quoted by J.E. Risk in *Transactions Devon Association*, vol. 32, 515.
7. Cf. R.N. Worth, *Cal. Plymouth Municipal Records*, 52.
8. *Acts of the Privy Council, 1586-7*, 217–18.

hindrance of that haven town, that chiefly doth stand by that trade, and forestalling of the markets'. The gentlemen appointed by the Council had then met and set down 'an indifferent Order by general agreement'; but the owners of the cellars at Cawsand had not obeyed the Order, and when asked to appear for breaking it, they appealed to the Council with their case 'and the letters from some of the commissioners in their behalf'. In short, the Commissioners had divided on the issue, 'some of them favouring the townsmen, others taking part with those that have the cellars on the sea-coast'. There was a clear conflict of interest and it could not be compromised.

This became clearer two years later, when, there being no improvement in the situation, the Council had to consider both sides of the case. They wrote on September 21, 1588, to Sir John Gilbert and other justices, first, saying that since the abuse was not reformed but rather increased, they were to see that the owners of the cellars were not permitted to engross or forestall the pilchards, 'but that they be brought to Plymouth as they were accustomed.'⁹ This must have been followed by a protest on the part of the Cornish merchants, for on November 18, the Council heard the case between the towns of Plymouth, Millbrook, Stonehouse and Saltash on the one side, and the merchants on the other. The argument on behalf of the towns followed the usual lines; but 'the merchants of Cornwall alleged in their behalf that they ought not to be compelled to bring the said fish, taken by their labour and industry, to the said port of Plymouth, and to lose the benefit of serving the county of Cornwall therewithal, and venting the same to their best commodity, which they might more conveniently do by bringing their fish to the cellars in the same Cawsand

9.   A.P.C., 1588, 283.

Bay than to come to the foresaid towns.'[10]

The Council, still insisting on its 'indifferent course,' laid down a compromise in which most of the sacrifices were made by the merchants. They were to build no more cellars at Cawsand, convenient rendezvous as it was for the fishermen, lying at the entrance to the haven. And 'always hereafter of such store of pilchards as the said Cornishmen and seiners shall take, of three parts thereof they shall bring two parts presently to the town of Plymouth and to the other foresaid towns within the haven of Plymouth, and the other third part they shall dispose of as heretofore they have done in the old cellars'. Their lordships added that they 'thought it very reasonable to have regard especially to the trade in the said town and port of Plymouth, being a principal haven town, that it should be maintained with the dressing and venting of as much of the said commodity as might conveniently be had.' Moreover, from henceforth no Londoners or merchants dwelling in remote parts from Devon and Cornwall should have any cellars at Cawsand Bay. Lastly, there was to be a restraint for the present and for a year to follow, on the export of the pilchards. The Council may have had good reasons for the restraint in the Armada year 1588–9; but this is precisely what the petition of 1578 had asked for, and it points again to the townsmen of Plymouth as its originators. The merchants had got nothing out of the compromise, except that the existing cellars were left undisturbed.

These were years of general restrictions on trade, with the war with Spain at its height. Their effect upon commerce in the west may be seen from the Council's instructions to Sir Francis Godolphin of December 31, 1588.[11] Two ships had been stayed at St. Michael's Mount and at Falmouth, in accordance with the

10. *Ib.*, 348–50.
11. *A.P.C.*, *1588*, 421–2.

embargo on trade with Spain. The Council ordered that if they or their lading did not belong to any of the King of Spain's subjects, they were to be released and to continue on their voyage. The Council's aim was not to hinder the course of ships bound eastwards for France or any countries in perfect amity with the Queen, even if they came from Spain, unless the ship or part of the lading belonged to any inhabitant of the King of Spain's dominions; but that no ships of what place soever might be permitted to pass with their commodities that way towards Spain or any other country under the government of the King. This embargo did not apply to the Queen's subjects who had in respect of their losses obtained letters of lawful reprisal.

In spite of the Order of 1588 and the restraint on the export of pilchards, the merchants at Cawsand did not remain inactive; they took the opportunity afforded by leaving them their cellars, to extend their accommodation. In the summer of 1590, the Council learned from the local justices, that the Order was not obeyed, and that 'the seiners and owners of the cellars do not only continue the forestalling and engrossing of pilchards, not contented with the third part allowed unto them by that Order, but do erect a new kind of store-house called lymryds . . . which must needs increase the forestalling and decay of a haven town for the enriching of certain private persons.'[12] Sir John Gilbert and Drake were directed to join with the other Commissioners to inquire into the breach of the Order and to bind over such as broke it to appear before the Council to answer their contempt; and in the meanwhile to stay the building of new cellars, palaces[13] and lymrids.

---

12. *A.P.C.*, 1590, 422–3.
13. This word has continued in use up to modern times in Cornwall to denote cellars for storing fish. I do not know what lymrid means, unless it is lime-rid, or lime-pit.

On December 8 of the same year, four of the owners of
the cellars, John Whitford, William Skawn, Anthony
Ingram of Millbrook, and Stephen Nicholas of Rame,
were called before the Council as transgressors of the
Order. It was argued on their behalf 'that neither in law
nor reason they were to be enforced to bring their fish
taken by their travail and charge to Plymouth rather
than to any other place, but that they ought to be left at
their own choice for selling the same at such places
where they might have most for it'. On this argument,
the Council decided 'to take a new hearing of the whole
matter touching this point in the presence of both
parties and of their counsel learned on each side.'[14]

On December 20 the Council, having heard the case
argued anew, reaffirmed the Order of 1588, with certain
additions and explanatory clauses.[15] The sheds and
pent-houses erected since the Order were to be plucked
down by the owners. No person was to make any
bargains or agree beforehand with the takers of pilchards
for any merchants or for any other person to the intent
to be carried beyond the seas; but it was permitted to the
inhabitants to buy for their own household provision at
Cawsand Bay. The third clause ordered that out of the
two parts of the fish brought into Plymouth, the townspeople were to buy for their own houses, and the rest to
be sold to the people of the country districts adjacent
who came into the town to buy. But if the bringers of the
pilchards had not a ready sale at reasonable prices within
the space of four tides after the pilchards had been
brought in on land, then the seiners and bringers might
carry them away for sale to any other place within the
same counties, but not beyond the seas. Neither at
Cawsand nor Plymouth nor anywhere else were the
pilchards to be dressed by finning them, 'a matter of late

14. A.P.C., 1590–1, 107–8.
15. Ib., 137–42.

years used to make them meet to be carried out of the realm.' It was thought 'convenient that the town of Plymouth took order in the said town that a convenient number of men should dispose themselves to be fishermen, as in Millbrook and other towns within that haven are known to be.' No pilchards should be converted into train (*i.e.* oil) 'from driving of the fish from the coast but to be to increase the said fish observed for meat'; and drift-nets should only draw within the points of land two days in the week, Tuesdays and Thursdays.

The Council expresses 'the principal intention of all these foresaid Orders' to be 'to preserve the use of this kind of fish called pilchards being taken afore or in the sound or haven of Plymouth to serve for the food of the leige people of the said counties, and particularly to continue the vent thereof at Plymouth, Millbrook and other towns within the same haven of Plymouth as hath been accustomed, and not to be for private gain carried out of the realm to strangers and to defraud the natural inhabitants of their profitable food.' But the Order goes on to provide that if at any time 'it shall please God to grant increase of the same kind of fish in those parts as may be found more than sufficient to serve the necessity of the natural people of the realm,' then there shall be licence given upon application to the Council for the export of such a proportion as may be spared from the necessary food of the people of Devonshire and Cornwall. In case of export, then the fish may be finned for more surety of carriage; and as usual certificates must be given that the place to which they are to be exported is in league and amity with England and that they are to be carried in English vessels and not in foreign bottoms. Six Commissioners were appointed: for Devon, Sir John Gilbert, Sir Francis Drake and Christopher Harris; for Cornwall, Richard Carew of Antony, Anthony Rouse and John Wray. They were to meet in the time of fishing, *alternibus vicibus* at Plymouth and Mt. Edgecumbe, to see the Orders impartially executed.

It was only to be expected that the Council would in the end come down on this side, though the fact that they ordered a new hearing of the case first, shows that they were not unappreciative of the point of view represented by the seiners and the merchants, the growing tendency of the market. The forces of conservation were too strong for them; the Council's view was dominated by the desire to regulate the supply in the interest of provisioning the population; and also not to let any trade be diverted from a haven town like Plymouth. It does not appear whether they realised that the trade might be even more profitable for the country if the restrictions on export were relaxed and the merchants left to decide for themselves which was the best depôt for distribution. The idea of subordinating private gain to considerations of national power was still in full strength with the Council; yet we have seen that Richard Carew for one, writing while the Order was still in force and himself one of the justices responsible for executing it, regarded the free export of pilchards as 'not prejudicial to the commonwealth'.

The Tudor conception of government in this case, as in innumerable other cases, was bent on opposing the economic currents of the time. The difficulties inherent in the attempt to reverse the trend, or at least to check it, are plain on the surface of the Order. It is clear what scope for disputes was afforded by the provision that if the bringers had not a ready sale for their fish at reasonable prices within four tides, they might carry them elsewhere. Moreover, it would be interesting to know what effect was given to the recommendation that the town of Plymouth should take order that a convenient number of men should dispose themselves to be fishermen; for the fact was that in these years Plymouth was going up in the world, and as it became more prosperous and important, its inhabitants were likely to find more remunerative occupations than fishing. The war with Spain was making of Plymouth a great port; in these years water was brought to the town from the River Meavy, seventeen miles away, and it was strongly fortified and garrisoned from 1591 onwards. The war doubtless made it more possible for the government to maintain its policy of control and restriction than it would otherwise have been.

There is no evidence that the Council's efforts met with success in the case of the pilchard fishery, and some evidence that the trouble continued. In 1591, the Council wrote[16] that four of the Commissioners, of whom Sir Francis Drake was to be always one, might assemble themselves to see to the observing of the Orders. A month later, having received information that the disorder had increased, the Council wrote to the Commissioners to put all points of the Orders effectually into execution.[17] At the end of the year, Sir Francis Drake had made stay of the export of pilchards and other fish 'in respect of the proclamation inhibiting transportation of all manner of victuals'; but the Council was anxious that as soon as 'the country should be served, we think it not amiss for the better encouragement of the mariners and fishermen that both the pilchards and the other fish may be carried forth of the realm,' with the usual sureties given.[18]

From 1592 onwards both the Council and the town of Plymouth had a motive for not discouraging the export trade in pilchards. At the request of Plymouth itself, the town was being fortified on a more elaborate scale; and to meet the charges of the works, the Queen granted, besides an annuity out of the customs of Devon and

16. *A.P.C., 1591*, 377.
17. *Ib.*, 432.
18. *Ib.*, *1591–2*, 78.

Cornwall, 'a certain impost upon every hogshead of pilchards that shall be transported out of the realm.'[19] The impost was to be at the rate of 1s. 6d. on every hogshead transported by strangers, and 1s. a hogshead for Englishmen.[20] By 1595, a total sum of £1,327 4s. 6d. had been raised, of which by far the larger part, £877 4s. 6d., came from the impost on pilchards.[21] It is impossible to tell from this figure what the exact volume of the trade was, but we may not be far wrong in estimating the average export of pilchards in these years as about 6,000 hogsheads a year, of which not all, however, were sent from Plymouth.

During these years, when the town was mainly occupied with the bringing of the water and making the fortifications, and later a good deal taken up with quarrelling with successive commanders of the fort, the arrangement seems to have worked. As long as the impost lasted, it was to the town's benefit not to oppose the export. And all the while there was considerable danger, and still greater expectation, of an attack from Spain. Within the town, in 1597, there was a further Order adopted by the town council for the regulation of the fish-wives; there were to be fourteen only, whose names were given in a schedule. But as soon as the external pressure was relaxed a bit, the townsmen returned to the charge, with a petition to Richard Carew and the Commissioners that they would see to exact compliance with the Order in Council as regards the Cawsand fishery.[22] This was in 1602. By 1606 the Mayor and his brethren were petitioning the Council again, who responded by appointing a body of Commissioners as before, who were to see to the execution of the

19. *Ib.*, 524.
20. *Cal. Plymouth Municipal Records*, 2.
21. C.S.P. Dom., 1595–7, 366.
22. Worth, *Cal. Plymouth Mun. Records*, 199.

Elizabethan Orders. But government under the Stuarts was in a much weaker position to enforce restrictions, however much it wished to perpetuate the old order; nor had it the same case in urgent political necessity, to oppose the natural course of trade and the primacy of the market.

The St. Stephens-in-Brannel Story

Every parish has its story. But what is the story of St. Stephens-in-Brannel? I had never heard. The next but one to my native parish of St. Austell, only some four or five miles away from the town, it might be in the wilderness – perhaps that was what the mysterious word 'Brannel' meant? – so far as we were concerned. It was not till I went there for the parish feast in the Rectory field one windy, rainy summer that I learned that it had a story, and what it was.

Nothing stands out about St. Stephens parish, nothing dramatic in its history to compel the attention, only the minor irritant about its name. A recent rector devoted the whole of his long ministry to his pet hobby of insisting that it should 'properly' be called St. Stephen, without the 's': this was the bee that buzzed in his bonnet for nearly forty years. With the result that it now appears on maps and in the illiterate local newspaper as 'St. Stephen'. Quite incorrectly: the only 'proper' usage in these matters is the ancient local usage, as it appears on the signposts, in the old histories and documents – and on the tongues of all the inhabitants of the parish, when not bemused by their spiritual (not archaeological) pastor.

Perhaps the reason why this St. Stephens – there are three of them in Cornwall, St. Stephens-by-Saltash and St. Stephens-by-Launceston in addition to this 'in Brannel' – has made so little impression in the books is that it is so usual a Cornish country parish. Nothing exceptional, it is divided between the good farming soil

216

of the southern half, between the valley of the upper Fal river on the west and a little tributary stream on the south, and the bare china-clay uplands towards the heights of St. Dennis, now much the richer and more populous half.

Throughout the Middle Ages those were barren windswept wastes: not much of consequence up there, except the rounds and camps and barrows of the prehistoric people. The medieval life and wealth of the parish were lower down 'in Brannel' – which means the cultivated tilth appreciated by the crows, from the Cornish word 'bran', meaning crow. Here were the medieval farms and habitations: Brannel itself; Hendra, the old homestead; Gwindra, the white homestead; Langerth, the garden enclosure; Bodinnick, the dwelling by the little camp; Tolgarrick, the rocky hillock. The eastern side of the Fal valley is dominated by a high stretch of land that is yet fair farming land, Resugga, the upland heath. This comes to a point at Resugga Castle, a formidable prehistoric earthwork dominating both the valleys of the Fal and its tributary stream.

The parish church lies on the boundary between the good lands and the upland wastes where Cookworthy found the best china-clay in the world and the great Josiah Wedgwood came down to lease it from old Thomas Trethewey of Treneague, an ancient indigenous gentleman. Nothing remarkable about the church, except its upstanding tower of grey granite extending its protection to the church-town nestling round. Throughout the Middle Ages the church, along with more isolated St. Dennis on its hill, had a dependent chapelry in little St. Michael Caerhays on the coast.[1]

The big manor of Brannel, which contained most of the parish, was held by Brismar the Saxon in the year in which King Edward the Confessor was alive and dead.

1. Cf. my *The Byrons and Trevanions*.

At the Norman Conquest – little did the Cornish care whether Saxons or Normans were their overlords – William the Conqueror granted the manor, along with a score of others in Cornwall, to his treacherous half-brother, Robert Earl of Mortain. By his treason it escheated to the Crown; and King John granted it to his son Richard, Earl of Cornwall and titular King of the Romans – for his wealth, coming from Cornish tin, enabled him to purchase his election as Holy Roman Emperor. Richard granted it to his natural son by Joan Valletort, Richard of Cornwall.

Of the numerous children of this illicit union – the Cornwalls – several were provided for by the Church. Godfrey of Cornwall, born here at Court, the manor-house of Brannel, was a Carmelite friar, of whose learning some fragments remain in a manuscript of his Quodlibets at Merton College, Oxford. His brother, William of Cornwall, also born at Court, became prior of Beaulieu, then abbot of Newenham in Devon; another brother, Nicholas, a monk of Beaulieu followed William to Newenham.

The Cornwalls came to an end at Court – not unnaturally, with all these monks. Though they have long disappeared from hereabouts they have left some memorial of themselves in the Anglo-French name they gave to the place, which stands alone among the Celtic names of the farms and hamlets of the parish. Court was the head-place of the manor, at which suit of court was made. And so Court passed through various families, Hendowers or Henders and Tregarthens, until it came into the hands of the Tanners, with whom my story is concerned.

The Tanners were not Cornish folk, as indeed their name betokens: they originated in Somerset, moved westward into Devon, where George Tanner of Cullompton married a daughter and co-heiress of the last Tregarthen at Court. Their son Anthony Tanner lived and died at Court in the reign of Queen Elizabeth, dying some five years before the Armada alert upon our coasts. Their son John married a Roscarrock. By this time the Tanners were armigerous gentlefolk, with a coat of arms: *Argent, on a chief Sable, three men's heads Or.*

The head of the family in the next generation was Bernard Tanner, who married Julian, daughter of Sir Richard Buller of Shillingham, that Parliamentarian family of East Cornwall. Of this Bernard we have the will, made 1st October 1640; he died five days later, not long before the outbreak of the Civil War, a cruel experience for Cornwall. He willed that his 'truly loving wife' should have for life all his estate in the barton of Court, also Bodinnick and all his goods both indoors and out. Bernard was only forty-six when he died, leaving his wife with young children; he willed that she be advised by Sir Richard Buller, her brother Francis, and the Tanner brothers. He left £5 for the poor of the five adjoining parishes. £5 for 'the building of the almshouses by Carwensack Gate in the wastes of Brannel', and 20s. to each of his servants. He had in hand a tenement called Trevellick in the parish of Creed, made over to him by his 'brother' (perhaps foster-brother), Hugh Boscawen, for £100 which Boscawen owed him. This was all: a small estate, evidently not prosperous.

In one or two generations Tanners had married in the Pye family, who were Parliamentarians. The old Tory, William Hals, a kind of Cornish Aubrey of the *Brief Lives*, tells us that the Tanners had bought Bodinnick of the Pyes – 'some of which family afterwards, in the interregnum of Cromwell, turned decimators and sequestrators with the Sprys upon the lands and revenues of the Royal laity and clergy of this county: to that degree of hurt and damage that it occasioned the making of that short litany not yet forgotten in Cornwall:

From the Pyes and the Sprys,
  – Good Lord deliver us.'

When Bernard Tanner died his son and heir, young John, was only twelve and the estate he inherited was nothing much – not enough to ensure a well-endowed bride for himself, or at least to persuade such a young lady's father on the look-out for a good match. Hence the story Hals tells of his matrimonial fortunes.

'To refresh the tired reader,' he says in his endearing way, 'I will recount a story of the unfortunate amours of John Tanner aforesaid, with his lady, Madam Wyndham, to whom he made his first addresses of marriage and after some time of good liking fell deeply into each other's affection. But the conditions of marriage proposed by Mr. Tanner not being hastily agreed upon by her father, Mr. Wyndham gave opportunity to Charles Speccot, Esq., a gentleman of much greater estate than Mr. Tanner had, to make an overture of marriage to the lady aforesaid, together with a larger settlement in jointure than Mr. Tanner was able to grant or perform. Which proposals were forthwith accepted by Mr. Wyndham, so that he constrained his daughter, notwithstanding what amours had passed between her and Mr. Tanner, to marry Mr. Speccot.'

Poor young Mr. Tanner! – like Martin Luther on another occasion, he 'could no other': he had no more to offer.

Hals continues: 'At the news of which cross accident Mr. Tanner, her former inamorato, was so discontented and perplexed in mind that, in order to quiet his disturbed soul and to obliterate and extinguish the memory of this beautiful woman – for such she was – he forsook this land and travelled into France.

In brief Tanner, having been eighteen months in France, notwithstanding the variety of faces and company he met with, grew there also discontented with himself, and a continued impulse lay upon his spirit, which he could not suppress, that he must return back again into England. But for what reason he knew not. Whereupon at length he went on board a ship and came safe into the port of London. Where he had not remained scarce ten days before he heard the news of Mr. Speccot's death within that time. Upon which intelligence he forthwith posted from London to Thornbury in Devon, where she then resided in a mourning state, who received him in such a joyful and welcome manner that, soon after, the marriage was concluded betwixt them: by whom he had a great estate as aforesaid.'

All's well that ends well. But can we altogether trust Hals' information, who loved to round off a good story upon his tongue and pen? We must check it from the documents.

The Tanner pedigree confirms that John married his Katherine Speccot, and that they had a son and three daughters, the daughters born at their mother's house of Thornbury in 1657, 1660 and 1661 – in the last year of Cromwell's rule, and the first two of the restored Charles II, in glad Maytime when the younger girls were born. We do not know when, or where, the son, another John, first drew breath. And we can check the greatly improved estate and prosperity of lucky John Tanner, the father, from his will a quarter of a century later. After all his wife would have brought him not only her considerable dowry, but she would enjoy all her days her jointure – her widow's third of the estate of her first husband, the unlucky Speccot.

So it was that, when John Tanner came to make his will on 30th October 1683, it was a very different affair from the small estate of his father. He was now described as John Tanner the elder, of St. Stephens in Brannel, and to his only son, John the younger, and his heirs for ever he devised all his manors and lands in the counties of Devon – this would have included Thornbury – and Cornwall or elsewhere in England. To his daughter Katherine he left the not inconsiderable fortune, for that time, of £1,500 – £40 a year till half were paid, then £50 a year until the rest were. Evidently the two other daughters had died young: no expense. His mother was still alive – he himself was a man of only fifty-five when he made his will – and she was to be sent 'fit and convenient mourning for my funeral according to her quality.' The same was to be provided for his daughter, and for his sister, Mary Westlake. Each of his two brothers, Bernard and George, was to have £10 for mourning; another £10 for the poor of St. Stephens.

Nothing whatever is said of his wife, by whom the wealth came; she must have died before him. He himself died next year, 1684; nor did the son live long, dying some nine years later in the early summer of 1693. A debilitating strain seems to have entered into the stock, for the young man can have been only in his thirties and in that short time had run the estate into difficulties and burdened it with debt. It devolved upon his trustees to sell what was necessary of the estate to cover his debts. It is from the Act of Parliament empowering them to do so, I George I, cap. 22, that we learn something of its extent: besides the estates in Devon there were the manor of Brannel, the barton of Bodinnick, the grist-mills and tin-mills called Brannel Mills in St. Stephens, other lands and tenements in the parishes of Creed and Cuby (Tregony), along with the advowson of the churches of St. Michael Caerhays, St. Stephens and St. Dennis.

That fat living, combining both rectorial and vicarial tithes undivided, fell very conveniently for uncle George in 1676; he held it, enjoying the fruits, for twenty-eight years until he died in 1704 – the year of Blenheim – choosing to be buried in the family vault at

St. Stephens. It fell to uncle Bernard to probate the will of his brother John the elder – the younger John, who had run down the estate, having left no will. What was left of it came to a cousin, Anthony Tanner of Carvinack in St. Enoder, and he, poor man, had only daughters – six co-heiresses. That was enough to finish the Tanners at Court: their long reign in the parish of St. Stephens came to an end when the famous Governor Pitt, grandfather of the great Earl of Chatham, bought the mortgage on the manor with a fraction of the proceeds of the sale of the Pitt Diamond. And so his ultimate heirs the fortunate Fortescues came to reign in Brannel up to our ruinous time.

Before I left the Rectory field that day I learned an interesting piece of parish lore. In the Tanner vault in the church, now sealed up, there are four coffins of extraordinary size, one of them approaching seven feet in length. Evidently those last Tanners were very tall fellows, rather too elongated, perhaps somewhat etiolated. Who were they? I wondered as I went my way back to the church-town, past the grey tower under whose shadow they lie. Certainly lucky John who married his love, Katherine Speccot, after all; certainly his clerical brother George, as we know; perhaps the third brother Bernard, who held out for a while at Court after the mischief wrought by his ne'er-do-well nephew, and perhaps the nephew as to whose demise we know nothing.

When the parish feast was well away – wireless, loudspeaker, stalls, skittles, raffles, pony-riding, tea in a marquee – I went off to explore the (to me) unknown lower end of the parish, the deep, ferny lanes towards St. Stephens Combe. Here was lushness, luxuriant vegetation, medieval meadows with plenty of feed for cattle – here were their successors, rich gold, steaming together at a gate. Glints of honey-coloured light hardly got through the thick over-arching trees; the hedges were a tousled mass of long grasses, bracken, tall delicate cow-parsley with flowers of white lace, honey-suckle, little red trumpets of bugloss punctuating the greenery.

On my way back I went off the road and down a broad stony lane, farm implements and tractors lying about, to find Court. There it lay in the fold of its own little valley looking south, the high upland of the Resugga country sheltering it from the west. The old manor-house of the Tanners had long ago gone, but there were its stones in this stony place: a high wall enclosing the garden of the decent old farmhouse, ancient trees that might go back to the Tanners, oak, sycamore and ash.

I approached warily, expecting to be intercepted as a trespasser, to ask my questions, or at least arouse a farm-dog. Not a soul about; not a sound, not even the noises of cattle. I peered through the gate into the enclosure – the usual vegetation of a Cornish garden, rhododendron, hydrangeas, fuchsias in flower.

The family must be away at the feast.

Where below in the Combe there was a sense of summer, here there was already a touch of autumn in the trees. The sun had gone behind the great shoulder of Resugga; the landscape was grey and cold. How to describe the indescribable sense of autumn? – the chill upon the look of the landscape, the touch of weariness, flower and fruit and harvest over, the reflective mood of melancholy, the land withdrawing into itself, becoming remote, folding up for winter. A young poet has written: 'It is quite impossible to write about the feeling of autumn; and, in any case, everyone knows it'.

No one came to the door; no one was about; the house was alone with its memories, behind its high stone-wall, looking a little sideways and southward down the valley. The sense of absence laid a cold finger on the heart, of a place waiting for someone to come home.

Saddened, with a strange impression of desertedness and desolation, yet corroborated rather than surprised, I withdrew in the grey of evening up the stony lane those generations had often ridden or walked to church or market, till at length they were carried up it to the sealed vault in the shadow of the church-tower.

Jan Tregagle in Legend and in History

It is sad to think that the life is going out of the old Cornish legends and folk-lore. I was just in time to catch the last echoes of the traditional tales that filled the minds of our forebears: tales that had been told for generations by winter firelight while the gales blew in from the sea and roared in the chimney. On the lips of my parents only fragments of this traditional culture remained in snatches of song, in verses and phrases. All the same, it was just not too late for me, while the present generation has hardly even heard of Tregagle, the leading figure in the Cornish mythology of the past three centuries as King Arthur was in the Middle Ages. The ill-omened name means the place of the dunghill.

What was characteristic of Tregagle was his howling or roaring, like the wind. 'That's Jan Tregagle,' my mother would say to me as a child when the wind roared down the funnel of our cobble-stoned court. When I asked who he was my mother couldn't tell me; she would laugh, as if she didn't much believe in him. Once she got as far as to say that he was the spirit of a bad man, who was being punished for his sins. More than that she did not know; belief in him was dying out.

Still people would say of a crying child, that he was crying like Tregagle, or that the child was a Tregagle. A fellow clay-worker said to my father, proud of his daughter's accomplishment on the harmonium he had bought her: 'She d'maak 'n roar like a g'eat Tregaglon.'

Polwhele, writing in the year 1803 when belief in Tregagle was in full flower, tells us:

'Amidst all the wonders that work upon a Cornish imagination, the acts of Tregagle have surely a right to the pre-eminence. If nature appear in forms that are fantastic, or strike by uncommon occurrences, Tregagle is at once called in, to solve the difficulty: he is the being to create or conduct the machinery. The pool of Dozmary is, in the vulgar opinion, unfathomable. The idea is preserved in the task to which he is condemned: to empty it with a limpet-shell, with a hole in the bottom of it. On the rising of an easterly wind, the devil used to chase him three times round the pool; when he would make his escape to Roche Rock; where putting his head into one of the chapel windows, he was safe. That, before the existence of the Loe-bar, Helston was a port, is more than a notion of the lower classes. This persuasion also, is proved and illustrated by the giant Tregagle's dropping his sack of sand between Helston and the sea: his sack of sand was the Bar. If the echoes of the Loe hills be heard in the storm, they are the howlings of Tregagle. So extensive, indeed, is his fame or his infamy, that if there be a high wind in Cornwall, it is "Tregagle roars"'

Polwhele appends a note that reveals some uncertainty.

'The exact crisis of Tregagle's entry into being is enveloped in darkness. But I think that he is a personage hoary with age; and that he was known to our remote progenitors, notwithstanding the familiarity of "Jan Tregagle" now current amongst us. The story is, that he by some means got within his grasp the heir to a considerable property, murdered the father and mother, and seized the estate of their orphan child'.

Davies Gilbert, with the scientific spirit of a President of the Royal Society, takes us a step further. In his *Parochial History of Cornwall*, some thirty-five years after

Polwhele, he writes: 'Tregagle is the name of a family not long extinct. Mr. Lysons says Tregagle, of Trevorder, in St. Breoke; arms, argent, three bucks passant Or. One of this family having, for some reason, become unpopular, the traditions respecting a mythological personage have been applied to him. The object of these tales of unknown antiquity was, like Orestes, continually pursued by an avenging being, from whom he could find refuge only from time to time, by flying to the cell or chapel on Roche Rock; till at last his fate was changed into the performance of a task, to exhaust the water from Dozmary, with an implement less adapted, if possible, for its appropriate work than were the colanders given to the daughters of Danaus . . . Tregagle is provided simply with a limpet shell, having a hole bored through it, and with this he is said to labour without intermission; in dry seasons, flattering himself that he has made some progress towards the end of his work; but when rain commences and the *omnis effusus labor* becomes apparent, he is believed to roar so loudly, in utter despair, as to be heard from Dartmoor Forest to the Land's End'.

These activities of Tregagle relate mostly to the area from Roche Rock across St. Breock Downs to Dozmary Pool on Bodmin Moor: a Mid- and East-Cornwall *locale*. Later in the century William Bottrell, in *Traditions and Hearthside Stories of West Cornwall*, adds a few bits to our knowledge from further west. He tells us that the unscrupulous lawyer made a compact with the Devil to have his wishes for a number of years. For this his punishment after death, in addition to dipping out Dozmary, was to make a truss of sand from Gwenvor Cove, bound with ropes of sand, and carry it up to Carn Olva. One frosty night, by taking fresh water from Velandreath brook, he managed to freeze the sand together and carry it to the Carn. After that, he was bound not to use any fresh water again, and remains still toiling at his endless task.

In West Cornish tradition Tregagle is a mischievous spirit, who swept all the sand out of Nanjizel bay and around Pedn-penwith into Porthcurno, or who does it as a task imposed on him – a spirit not without pathos in his penance without end. But in West Cornwall, too, Bottrell notes that as a boy at St. Levan the weather-wise old men would say, taking a look at the weather, 'Tregagle is roaring, there'll be a northerly gale tomorrow'.

It would seem that Tregagle was in origin a weather-spirit, a spirit, in especial, of the wind. All kinds of recognisable elements enter into his legend: the compact with the Devil, the punishments inflicted, the eternity of his torment and toil, the association with water and sand. We are faced with something more primitive than any historic figure, and with legends that crop up in the folklore of many European countries.

What is fascinating is that something so general in character and so remote in time, going right back into antiquity, should have become attached in the unconscious memory of the Cornish to a definite historical figure from a comparatively recent period. It is the connexion of the two that is so fascinating. And the problem is: how did it come about?

Jan Tregagle was a seventeenth century person whose career has been made out for us.[1] The family came from the vicinity of Truro, where they made their way up along with the tin-mining magnates, the family of Robartes, (i.e. Roberts), the maker of whose vast fortune is to be seen on his alabaster tomb in the north transept of the cathedral. His son – an immensely tall man, to judge from his coffin in the vault at Lanhydrock – moved thither, built his large Jacobean house and purchased his peerage from Charles I's favourite, the Duke of Buckingham.

1. v. B.C. Spooner, *John Tregagle of Trevorder*.

The eldest son of the new peer, John Robartes, was fostered along with the young John Tregagle and, as was often the case in Celtic societies like Wales and Ireland, fostering created a strong bond between the foster-brothers. When Tregagle grew up and acquired the useful training of an attorney, he became chief steward of the second Lord. The Robartes estates were widely scattered in small bits and pieces all over Cornwall, having fallen in from usury and mortgages: no doubt John Tregagle became a familiar figure, in his lordship's service, in many parts of the county.

No portrait of Tregagle exists. But there are several of his foster-brother, the Puritan peer, at Lanhydrock: a long-visaged, sour-faced type in black with Bible in hand, looking down upon his library of theological works, the divines who were his sole amusement, it would appear. He was a man of ability, stern and uncompromising, the leading figure on the side of Parliament.

At the outbreak of the Civil War, Cornwall was mostly rallied to the side of King and Church by the Grenvilles, Godolphins, Arundells, Trevanions, Killigrews. The Parliamentarians were a minority, and among them Lord Robartes had the ascendancy by his wealth, his title and his ability. He insisted on Parliament sending the army under its general, the Earl of Essex, into Cornwall to extinguish the King's hold there. This led to a disaster for Essex's army: it was cooped up within the narrow peninsula, the King followed fast upon its heels and the Parliamentarian army was forced to surrender.

The Cornish foot, under its own leaders, fought its way up through the West, winning victories from Stratton to Lansdown and Roundway Down and on to the siege of Bristol. But it suffered terrible losses: by the end its ranks were grievously thinned and its leaders had been killed, Bevil Grenville, Sidney Godolphin, Slanning and Trevanion, 'the four wheels of Charles's wain'. In 1644 the little land suffered the depredations and pillage of two armies marching through it and living off it: Cornwall was exhausted, drained of food and money, its only independent source of wealth, its tin, pledged abroad for the King, many of its young men killed in battle, especially in the desperate struggle for Bristol. The blithe spirit had gone out of the war; when the disarmed bands of Essex's soldiery straggled out of the county, the peasants turned on them and cut off any they could. In spite of the sacrifices and the heavy burden for a poor county, all was unavailing: the superior resources of Parliament were bound to win in the end.

Lord Robartes and his foster-brother were refugees in London, but their turn was now to come. In 1645 the King's cause was cracking up: the rule of the Saints was to begin. In that year comes the first of Tregagle's transactions, by which he got the lands of people in distress by the troubles of the time into his hands. The parish of St. Breock, that upheaved country running from the high pre-historic Downs to the Arthurian estuary of the Camel on the north, is the area to which the historical John Tregagle attached his name and which he had his eye on. Next to Trevorder, which became his home, are two bartons on the way to Wadebridge, Treneague and Trevanion. The owners, a family called Carter, also refugees in these disturbed times with Tregagle in London, had not wherewithal to live. Tregagle advanced them £100 for a 500-year lease of the properties at a low rent. This was taking advantage of their necessity with a vengeance; but Tregagle proceeded to interpret as an outright sale what the Carters had meant as a mortgage to get their property back on tendering the money.

With the Parliament's victory, Lord Robartes and his steward became leading powers in Cornwall; Tregagle was made a Justice of the Peace, very active in all kinds of works. The Carters made every effort to redeem their property; but Tregagle always stuck to the strict word of the bond. He had driven an unconscionable bargain.

After various lawsuits, when the Carters tendered the money for redemption, Tregagle refused it; and in 1652, in the full flood-tide of the Commonwealth, the Puritan Justice appeared at Launceston assizes and secured the ejectment of the Carters' tenants from their farms.

Three years before, in 1649 – the year of the King's execution at Whitehall – Tregagle had been able to buy, for £1,500, one of the largest bartons in the parish, Trevorder itself, a little further back along the side of the wooded valley from Treneague; and there he seated himself. With these three properties the newcomer was the leading landowner in the parish; he had built up a fair domain which, if all had gone well with the family, would have constituted park and pleasance, regular classic house with portico and drive in Georgian days.

All this brought people's hatred upon his head: Cornish folk did not forgive this flagrant injustice at a time when they were going through misery and want. And then Tregagle took a step that crossed the deepest instincts of the people, that went counter to their unconscious life, and challenged their primordial beliefs.

This disturbance of the time gave rein to the disordered fancies of a number of people who imagined themselves endowed with gifts of prophecy and healing. In Cornwall a young woman became well-known, Anne Jefferies, whose epileptic fits left her with a power of healing. She spoke and danced with the fairies; she fasted for long intervals and could make herself invisible; she cured people. Stories of her cures spread, and 'people of all distempers, sicknesses, sores and agues came not only so far off as the Land's End, but also from London, and were cured by her. She took no monies of them, nor any reward; yet had she monies at all times, sufficient to supply her wants. She neither made nor bought any medicines or salves, yet wanted them not, as she had occasion'.

Tregagle, whose Puritanism represented some advance in rationality, did not hesitate to challenge the most primitive force in human nature, the unconscious, the irrational. He became the young woman's chief persecutor, had her arrested, tried and put in gaol. After her release, he kept her confined in his house: she had pretended to be able to do without food, very well, let her go without food. It was on a par with the Republican attitude towards the Divine Right of Kings: no arguing with people who believed in the sacrosanctity of a king: cut his head off and let them see. Unfortunately this no more persuades human irrationals than rational arguments: it incurs only hatred. And this is what happened to Tregagle. All the sympathies of a defeated people, who had fought and sacrificed their lives for the King, were with the harmless young woman whose powers of healing they believed in, whose ways of devotion and fasting were those of the proscribed Church and the martyred King, against the upstart lawyer who had gained his estate out of other people's necessity.

This must be the point at which the historical person of John Tregagle, Justice of the Peace, squire of Trevorder, fuses with the supernatural, the unconscious memory of a people: he becomes Jan Tregagle. The explanation of the fusion is to be found in the circumstances of the time, that particular moment in history. Those were black years for Cornwall: so many hundreds dead in the war, the countryside eaten up by armies passing and repassing, its resources exploited for others' benefit, ruinous fines imposed upon the Royalists (who were the great majority) – to be defeated at the end of it all, and ruled by such people as Tregagle.

Tregagle did not live long to enjoy his prosperity; nor can he have been old when he died. In the summer of 1655 he made his will. He was well-off, and he had lands in several parishes from Hartland to St. Columb minor and Luxulyan, where he must have been known and seen

233

in his life-time. The first sentence of his will reads: 'First I give and bequeath my soul unto God the Lord who gave it me.' On October 3 it was fetched away.

Nor did his attempt to found a county family, on the estate he had got together, prosper. At the time of his death his son, another John, was a minor. He had not his father's business capacity; he seems to have grown up feckless and extravagant. Unlike the father he was generous. In the days of the Restoration he contributed handsomely to building an aisle on to the church at St. Breock: the aisle on the south side, for himself, his family and servants to sit in. When only thirty-four he died, leaving small sums to the poor of the parish, but chiefly an inextricable tangle of debt in connection with his office as Receiver-General of Cornwall. He left a boy of six to succeed him – the third John Tregagle. When he grew up this Tregagle had nothing but a losing battle with the mounting tide of debt. He died at the same age as his father, intestate: there was nothing for it but to sell the estates to meet the debt. And that was the end of the Tregagles at Trevorder, as if there was a curse upon them there.

It was not long after the end of the family that the tradition begins to take shape: the historic John Tregagle, whom we have forgotten, becomes the Jan Tregagle of the collective folk-memory. 'An unscrupulous lawyer of low estate, who married and murdered heiresses; who murdered his children; who forged documents; who seized the estate of an orphan whose parents he had murdered; who sold his soul to the Devil in exchange for the fulfilment of his wishes during his life-time'[2] And so 'he goes through the yard at Bokelly in St. Kew every Saturday night, and some say he's black; he walks like a giant, eats hugely, shouts like a giant, throws like one; a menhir at St. Austell is

2. Spooner, 34–5.

Tregagle's Walking Stick;[3] it was Giant Tregagle who groaned in the oven at Trevorder. He got drunk with the Devil at Lanlivery, and the two went to Helman Tor and threw quoits to Quoit: there are two stones still at Quoit. He flung a boulder at Egloshayle Church from St. Breock Downs, and missed; but the boulder is still at Clapper, where it fell, carrying the imprint of his fingers to bear witness. He would roar his commands to men working on Pendevy and his Egloshayle lands from Trig-the-Wheel hill in St. Breock, and walk from St. Breock to Launceston in a single hour in order to sit on the bench as sheriff, eating a whole sheep on arrival. He was obliged, after death, to supply Lanhydrock House with water from Dozmary. This he did by means of a swing-drum chain. He would swing the drum round and round by the chain and send it hurtling through the air to the nearest toll-house. The toll-house keeper would repeat the performance and so on till it reached Lanhydrock; for the toll-house keepers were in league with Tregagle. All untoward night-happenings in St. Cleer are "Tregagle". He was at Launceston castle when word came that the Devil himself was at Polson Bridge, seeking entry into Cornwall: would Tregagle deal with the situation? He did. He told the Devil that in Cornwall all Things were made into pasties, all Men into saints. The Devil took no risks: he left Cornwall. The sea-cave under Carne, in Veryan, was called "Tregagle's hold". It is he that sweeps the sand from Nanjizel Bay. He is the crying of the storm on the Goss and the Bodmin Moors and down the whole length of the coast of Cornwall from Helston to Padstow'.

One winter's day some years ago I set out to track Tregagle, the historic person, down in the haunts that had known him in life – Trevorder barton and St. Breock

3.   This, in the field next to my former house at Polmear Mine, is the subject of 'The Stone that Liked Company' in *Cornish Stories*.

church near Wadebridge. Up and across the high china-clay country of mid-Cornwall, an unparalleled landscape – I went to bare St. Breock Downs, pre-historic country with its tumuli and longstones. Coming down off the moor I asked the way of a friendly farmer. He was amused at my pursuit of Jan Tregagle – but he at least knew about him. 'You see him up on Hustyn Down, chasing over the downs at night with his white dog.' (Should it not be a black dog?) 'Mind you, I haven't seen him myself,' he added, 'I haven't got the right kind of sight'.

At the end of a long lane hard-bitten by the wind, the old farmhouse stands solid behind its fence of gravestones from some churchyard. The original house must have been larger: this looks rebuilt on a smaller scale for a farm in the eighteenth century; the big oven of the tradition was left a ruin in the farm-yard; the front door was used again with its date 1652 – the year that Tregagle fore-closed on the Carters of Trevanion and Treneague and took possession.[4]

It is a bare, wind-swept place, built up on the side of the living rock. The farmer's wife told me what she knew of its story – of a previous farmer and his wife a century ago, having gone to market, leaving no one in the house. On their return at dusk they saw the house lighted up, the shutters closed: within, a scene of revelry around the long table. The farmer placed his key in the lock; at once every light went out, the cries and howls dropped into silence as still as the grave. I asked the farmer's wife of today if she ever heard anything. 'Well, sometimes at night, when we're gone to bed, we do hear noises behind the panelling; but no doubt it's the wind.'

It seems that, a long time ago, a service of exorcism was held to lay the unquiet spirit, binding it first to the horse-block, then driving it into the oven, finally

4. My friend, Donald Carter of Fowey, still remembers family tradition how they were done out of their property.

banishing it over the moor to Dozmary to its endless task.

In pursuit of the body's last resting-place I made my way to St. Breock church, at the bottom of a precipitous descent, with slate tombs and headstones terraced down the side, amid beeches, cypresses and yews. Within the darkened church there was enough light to make one's way up to the aisle that John Tregagle II built to hold himself, his family and servants, and to house his dead. Here is his slate-grey memorial: 'Here lieth buried John Tregagle, of Trevorder, Esq., and Elizabeth his wife, who was the daughter of Sr William Hooker, Alderman of London, ye said Elizabeth was buryed the 19th daye of Maye, 1679; and the said John Tregagle was buried ye 7th of February, Anno Dom. 1679.' (i.e. 1680). Next, on the north wall is a tablet to the wife of John Tregagle III: 'Near this place lyeth ye body of Jane ye wife of John Tregagle, Esq., of Trevorder, and daughter of Sir Paull Whichcote, Knt. and Barronet, of Quy Hall, in Cambridgeshire, who departed this life ye 19th day of March, 1708; in ye 28th year of her age.' When her husband came to die, only four years later, there was no money for a memorial stone.

But as to the whereabouts of the body of John Tregagle himself, that unquiet spirit, no one knows where in the church he lies.

The Slate Figures of Cornwall

A part of the charm and richness of the past is in the local diversity of its arts and crafts. If one looks at a modern town there is not so much difference whether one is in Coventry or Rotterdam, Plymouth or Marseilles, or Cleveland, Ohio. Modern architecture, if it has any style at all, has an international idiom. In earlier centuries, building and its allied arts rose directly out of their soil: in East Anglia, where there was little stone, fine red brick; in the eastern Midlands the splendid stone of Barnack and Ketton; in Somerset the snuff-coloured Ham Hill stone, in Dorset the silvery-grey of chalky stone, in Devon red sandstone, in Cornwall granite and slate.

Slate monuments with figures carved on them are a speciality of Cornwall, practically unique. Even so they are to be found mostly in the east and north of the country, where the slate lay – in particular, the famous Delabole quarry, with its beautiful blue slate. There are a few such monuments in West Devon, an outlier of the area; and on the eastern rim of Penwith in West Cornwall, where there is an outcrop of slate.

Altogether, there are over sixty of these figured monuments in nearly fifty churches. The craft was at its peak from Elizabeth's reign to the Civil War – though, with Cornwall's remoteness, it is remarkable how long the traditional idiom continues. In the middle of the eighteenth century we find one monument, at Callington, with a woman kneeling at a prayer-desk with lighted candle, that might almost be Elizabethan.

These charming and idiosyncratic monuments have at

last been studied with the care and attention they merit. Mrs. Bizley has devoted fifteen years to studying and drawing them – for it is impossible to photograph them satisfactorily. Many of the monuments were evidently painted, red, green, gold, and on some of them colouring has survived or been renewed. This could hardly be reproduced, so faithful line-drawings were the best choice. With all the information gathered about the carvers no less than the persons commemorated – we have a guide not only to the monuments but to the social life of Cornwall during the period.[1]

It is, on the whole, the lesser gentry and middling people – or lesser members of the grander families – who are portrayed. Grandees are apt to have grander monuments. Richard Robartes, for example, founder of the immense Robartes fortune, lies on a sumptuous tomb at Truro that was ordered from Gerard Johnson's workshop at Southwark, Corinthian pillars and all; the Arundells of Lanherne lie under their brasses at St. Columb major. Nevertheless, the slate figures often portray interesting people in themselves: they come alive as we look at them in their armour or kirtles, their headdress and accoutrements, with their family records around them in prose or verse,

L'art personnel, les âmes singulières.

One can give only a sample of this small, rustic, idiosyncratic society. Richard Carew remarks on it in his *Survey of Cornwall:*

'This angle, which so shutteth them in, hath wrought many interchangeable matches with each other's stock and given beginning to the proverb that 'all Cornish gentlemen are cousins'.[2]

1. A.C. Bizley, *The Slate Figures of Cornwall.*
2. Richard Carew, *Survey of Cornwall* (ed. 1811), 179.

This was true of most counties – people married mainly within the county, except in and around London and the Court – but it was particularly noticeable in the remoter regions, little worlds sufficient to themselves. The results were sometimes amusing. Here is Ann Smith at Duloe, for instance, who by a second marriage became aunt to her own daughter.

Ann was born a Coffin of Portledge in Devon, of that family which goes on in the male line in New England. She married one of the Tremayne sons of Collacombe, several of whom won fame in Elizabeth's reign – Edmund was Clerk to the Privy Council – and all are depicted on the monument in Lamerton Church. Ann came into Cornwall for her second husband. Marrying widows was a feature of the age: it was highly advantageous since they already had their widows' thirds – their jointure from their previous husband's estate – and were less likely to breed numerous children to support. (Those celebrated women, Bess of Hardwick, Lettice Knollys and Frances Walsingham, were each married four times.) A popular outcry occurred on the subject; even petitions to Parliament for legislation.

Ann Coffin Tremayne Smith, as the Americans would call her, died in 1592 and is depicted in a high-crowned hat and ruff of the period, a richly diapered dress with puff sleeves, holding gloves and prayer-book. This is clearly the work of Peter Crocker the slate-carver, who was active in the 1580s and early 1590s. He was the best craftsman of them all; nothing is known of him except that he came from Plymouth and carved other slate-figures at Talland, Lansallos, St. Martin's-by-Looe and Pelynt.

The finest of his monuments is that at Talland to John Bevill, 1579, and this he proudly signed: 'Peter Crocker made this worke'. Many will know that church above its cove, the detached bell-tower built into the rock, the view over the shoulder of the hill to the sea and, within, the carved bench-ends. The monument is a tomb-chest, complete with backplate with elaborate achievement of arms, panels with verses and coats of arms; on the chest the full figure of a man in patterned armour cut in bold relief; on the end panel a powerful bull passant, crest of the family.

In the floor of the same church at the chancel step is set a very different monument of half a century later. This is an incised slab with a woman in bed, holding a baby and resting against an embroidered bolster. A Jacobean bedpost is sculpted with part of the frilled canopy, realistic in its detail. We are told: Heere lieth Jone Mellow and her little Sonne. Greate traveill she indured by ye birth of him. But beinge delivered God did soe decree That she and her sonne together shold dy.

This slab is not Peter Crocker's work, but there are other examples of his craft in the neighbourhood. At St. Martin's-by-Looe there is a recumbent figure of a man, Philip Mayow, in the long gown and sleeves of a merchant, 1590. Of a Looe family, he was a member of the Merchant Adventurers Company and made money in trade, so that the Mayows moved out into the country. In the next century they produced a physiologist of mark in John Mayow, Fellow of All Souls and of the Royal Society, who made important discoveries about the process of respiration; he wrote about rickets, muscular action and the chemistry of combustion, but died when under forty in 1679.

At Lansallos is a coffin-shaped slab of 1579 to Margery Budockshide, of the same type as that to Ann Smith thirteen years later, and this is signed between the feet, 'Per Peteur Croker fecit'. Margery's second husband, Philip Budockshide, was a restless fighting young man who went abroad with Richard Grenville to fight against the Turks in Hungary in 1566, and with the youthful Walter Ralegh in France in 1570, when he died.[3] In a

3. Cf. my *Sir Richard Grenville*, 62–3.

few years the Budockshides – they were pronounced Butshead – came to an end and a painted slate tomb-chest was put up to them in St. Budeaux church, near Plymouth.

Pelynt has a fine Crocker figure – evidently the top of a tomb-chest – to William Achym of 1589: a robust figure of a man in armour, lying on a helmet, long sword and dagger with girdle on hips, gauntlets clasped in prayer, patterned trunk-hose and small shields with arms. This church also has a tomb-chest, tall backplate, pediment and all, with figures, of Francis Buller of Tregarrick, 1616. Tregarrick was really the inheritance of the Winslades; but John Winslade forfeited it for his part in the Prayer Book Rebellion of 1549. He had made it over to his wife; but after his execution, her second husband, John Trevanion of Caerhays, cheated the Winslades out of their inheritance. By remaining Catholics they lost everything, except, of course, their faith.

It is possible that the grand, elongated Vyell monument at St. Breock, 1598, is by the same hand though of a different design. Apart from the figures the emphasis is on the heraldic shields and all their quarterings. These give one the family connections, with Grenvilles, Arundells of Lanherne, Bevills, Prideaux, Devon Risdons and Dennises. The Vyells lived at Trevorder at this time – afterwards occupied by the sinister Jan Tregagle, to whose family there are slate monuments in the church, but with no figures, appropriately for a Commonwealth Puritan family.

A monument to two Wreys, 1595 and 1597 – formerly in the church of St. Ive near Liskeard – has figures similar to the Vyell monument in drawing and treatment, and considerable traces of colour likewise remain. As recently as 1924, this was removed to Tawstock – fancy anybody letting it go, even to the finest collection of monuments in Devon!

Sometimes the inscriptions or coats of arms correct the printed pedigrees or present a problem. At Helland is a much-worn figure of Humphrey Calwodely, a leader of the Cornish rebellion of 1497, who was attainted of high treason. Was he not then executed – Henry VII was humane in his treatment of the rebels – or was the tomb erected before Humphrey's death? The attainder was reversed in 1506 and the estates restored in 1508. But this did not teach the family a lesson: Humphrey's grandson, Humphrey Arundell, was a leader of the Prayer Book Rebellion of 1549, for which he certainly was hanged at Tyburn.

The fine church of St. Neot, with its windows still filled with pre-Reformation glass, has a tomb-chest complete with backplate, with long inscription to William Bere. The name gives a chance for punning, of which Elizabethans were inordinately fond:

Here lyeth Bere whom Angelles to heaven beare . . .

This man is noted as skilful in the law, which land-owners in that litigious age needed to be. Edward Trelawny of Bake is described on his monument at Pelynt:

Heere lyes an honest lawyer, wot you what-a thing for all the world to wonder at.

The monument is of good design and retains most of its colourings of red, gold, green and blue; its date is 1632 and it is signed by Robert Wills.

Anthony Colly signed work at Pelynt in 1634 and at Lamorran in 1666. A whole generation has passed between the first and the second, and the difference of style is so great that 'one would scarcely credit them as the work of one man were it not for his signature'. There remains the possibility that there were two Collys, father and son, for the craft of stone-carving often was thus handed on. Robert Oliver, whose excellent lettering is to be found on nineteenth-century headstones in North Cornwall, mainly around the Camel valley, was the son of a carver at St. Minver.

Michael Chuke of Kilkhampton was the son of a mason there. At Kilkhampton is a slate carving of his, 1727, and another at Poughill, 1739. Eight of the monuments in Kilkhampton church are attributed to him, and in 1724 he was painting pulpit and pews. I suspect that these carvers put their hand to other work than slate-carving – perhaps, for example, to the grand plaster coats of royal arms which are a feature in this vicinity. Michael Chuke left a snug little fortune, amounting to near £600. His slate headstone in the churchyard, 1742, describes him:

> Here lieth the Body of Mr Michael Chuke of Heardacut in this Parish Carver.

Of all the Cornish slate-carvers the most eminent was the Victorian, Nevil Northey Burnard, son of a stonemason at Altarnun. Here, in the churchyard, the boy of fourteen sculpted an eagle in flight against the rays of the sun; over the Wesleyan chapel is a strong profile portrait of John Wesley. Burnard was sent up to London to become a pupil of Chantrey and for some years had great success: busts of his exist in St. Paul's and in the royal palaces. Success was more than this large shambling fellow could stand. He took to drink and the roads; became a tramp, and came home to Cornwall to die a pauper.

His work is out of bounds. But within the bounds of this book we see what a little world of its own Cornwall is. It gives one a wry amusement to reflect how little is really known of it by the thousands of ignorant tourists who invade it every summer.

Here commemorated on their monuments are the people who made a stir in their day – Grenvilles, Killigrews, Godolphins, Edgcumbes. It is rather endearing as one goes by the grey granite churches to reflect that one knows who lies within. As I pass by Lanivet church tower, I remember Richard Courtney figured on his slate monument, and his careful provision for his widow in his son's house: 'the chamber that I doe now lie in and the chamber over the little buttery to her proper use during her life with free ingress and egress for herself and her assigns'. Or at Mevagissey there are all the little Darts kneeling behind their parents, eight of them:

Death shoots sometimes as archers doe
one darte to find another
But now by shooting 't hath found foure
and all layd hear together.

This was evidently a commonplace of the time, much given to archery, as we find it in Shakespeare:

In my schooldays, when I had lost one shaft,
I shot his fellow of the self-same flight
The self-same way with more advisèd watch
To find the other forth . . .

To have these things to think of as we go about the country, to know the lives of the people in the churches and the old houses and farms where they lived, to reflect that at the end of every leafy lane or over the hillside or down in the sounding valley, there will be something or someone to engage our interest adds a dimension to life.

For what should we know beyond our own memory without history? History is the extension of our memory into all other memories of which we have record. This historical knowledge is in a sense the foundation of all knowledge.

Robert Stephen Hawker of Morwenstow

It is good that Hawker of Morwenstow should be remembered by centenary celebrations – 'I would not be forgotten in this land', he wrote. And, in fact, he never has been forgotten in Cornwall; Morwenstow is a place of pilgrimage because of him. But he is remembered more widely, and has several claims upon our attention and affection. He is one of the best of the lesser Victorian poets, known to everyone who knows anything of English literature or history for his famous ballad with the folk-refrain, 'And shall Trelawny die?'
Sir Walter Scott's quotation of this made the ballad better known than its author, but Hawker was a fine writer of ballads, a rather rare genre.

Besides his writings, in prose as well as verse, Hawker's life of devotion claims our remembrance: his care for his parish, on which he poured out his money and time, building a school, caring for the poor. He was well-known to sailors and the maritime community for his passionate concern for the ship-wrecked on that coast and burying their dead. In Church history he was the initiator of harvest festivals – something good in itself to remember him by – and, of more clerical concern, of ruri-decanal synods. He was the patron-saint of the endearing community of eccentric Cornish clerics, with their good lives and their good deeds.

Of the various kinds of countryside there are within the bounds of Cornwall – the casual passer-through has no idea of its diversity – that from Bude to the Devonshire border, the country of Hawker of Morwenstow, is the most striking. There the cliffs rise to a height of six and seven hundred feet: it is a terrible coast with shale strata twisted and up-ended into jagged rocks and there is always an undertow off the shore. It is not a coast for boats; there are hardly any beaches and no harbours – only a few crevices in the cliffs, like Boscastle, Bude, Hartland Quay. In the nineteenth century it was one of the worst stretches in the whole country for wrecks, especially in the last days of sailing ships when the westerly gales drove them in relentlessly upon those rocks. During the half century in which Hawker lived there, from 1824 to 1874, there were some eighty wrecks in the neighbourhood of Bude.

Inland, the country is a high plateau, cut with deep, narrow V-shaped coombes, each with a stream running down to the cliffs and usually ending in a waterfall. There in spring the primroses and violets are biggest, the honeysuckle, red campion and valerian most luxuriant in high summer. It still is rather inaccessible, and so has preserved its character, its aloof atmosphere so hard to lay hold of, the loneliness and grandeur of those cliffs. In the nineteenth century its remoteness was extreme; there was something cut off and folded in upon itself about that region, when even coaches had ceased to pass and the railway had advanced no further than Launceston, and only the daily post, which a benevolent Postmaster-General had specially allowed as a solace to Hawker in his solitude, served to connect him, as he used to say, with Europe.

Such is the country associated with the name of Robert Stephen Hawker of Morwenstow, for he was a remarkable man: one of those men of original personality who impress themselves upon a place in such a way that one cannot think of it without thinking of the man, any more than one could think of Grasmere without Wordsworth, Dorchester without Hardy, or Fowey without Q. Hawker's claim upon our memory is strong enough for this vicar of an obscure Cornish parish, who for forty years hardly set foot across its boundaries, never to have been forgotten. He is remembered as a lovable eccentric, patron of the race of eccentric clergymen in which Cornwall is so prolific. He has his niche in English literature as a poet, if on a small scale and in rather a fugitive way, author of one famous ballad – *And shall Trelawny die?* He was a religious mystic, and something of a saint. He is no less interesting to study as a figure in complete reaction to all the dominant trends of the nineteenth century than those more famous figures who similarly found themselves going counter to it, such men as Newman, or Ruskin, or William Morris – or Pio Nono himself.

Hawker was not born there, but at Plymouth, in 1803. He came of a respectable Devonshire family, most of whose members were either parsons or doctors. His grandfather was well-known in his day as Vicar of Charles Church, Plymouth, an Evangelical divine of the reign of George III, a popular preacher and author, who wrote *The Poor Man's Morning and Evening Portion.* Robert was brought up mostly by his grandfather, whose generous and open-handed charity had their influence upon the ways of the grandson. As a boy he was remembered for his odd turns of humour, his pranks and practical jokes. He had an invincible dislike of Dissenters, and one day when walking with a friend through Stratton, where his father was vicar, the friend said, 'Look! Someone has written "Satan" on the door of the Wesleyan chapel.' 'No doubt he did it himself', said Robert, 'It is no uncommon thing for a gentleman to put his name on his own front door'.

At Oxford Hawker did nothing surprising, except to marry while still an undergraduate. He was nineteen, good-looking, a persuasive and original talker; his bride was forty-one, an heiress in a small way, whose family lived at Efford, the old manor-house of the Arundells of Trerice, practically on the sands at Bude. This extraordinary marriage turned out very happily. Their honeymoon was spent at Tintagel, where Hawker's interest in the legend of the Holy Grail was first awakened. This interest was to bear fruit forty years later, in the melancholy months after his wife's death, when Hawker wrote his longest poem *The Quest of the Sangraal*. There is a curious similarity to Hardy here, in whose mind Tintagel, where he courted his wife, had a place apart and to which he returned after her death, to write those *Poems of 1912–13*.

On his return to Oxford Hawker had to migrate, on account of his marriage, from Pembroke to Magdalen Hall. It may be surmised that he was not much of an exact scholar; his curious mind was following its own idiosyncrasy in desultory reading among the early Fathers in the Bodleian. Then in 1827 he won the Newdigate with a poem on 'Pompeii', the subject on which Macaulay wrote his prize poem at Cambridge a few years previously. Hawker entertained a lifelong devotion to Oxford, which he was hardly ever again to see after his undergraduate days: 'In my time it was the abode beyond all others of the unchangeable'. When he was up, the University had not yet been disturbed from its slumbers by the Oxford Movement; but once it was under way he, like a good many other parsons in the country, followed it with sympathy and some excitement, from his fastness in the West Country. In later years, when the boundary between fact and fancy, between what had happened and what might have happened, became dim in his mind, like George IV about Waterloo, he imagined that he had been present at its initiation, that he remembered the discussions in the common-room of an evening, the very faces and words of Newman, Pusey and Ward.

It was while on vacation from Oxford, staying at Coombe Cottage, deep in the wooded valley beneath the Grenvilles' Stowe, that Hawker wrote the poem by which he is known to the world:

A good sword and a trusty hand!
　　A merry heart and true!
King James's men shall understand
　　What Cornish lads can do!

And have they fixed the where and when?
　　And shall Trelawny die?
Here's twenty thousand Cornishmen
　　Will know the reason why!

Hawker tells us that he wrote the ballad under a stag-horned oak in Sir Bevil's walk in Stowe Wood. He also says that the history of the ballad and its reception was suggestive of his whole life: his sense of neglect in later years was summed up by what happened over it. The poem became famous all over the English-speaking world; its author remained 'unnoted and unknown'. This was understandable in a way. Hawker printed the poem anonymously in a local newspaper, *The Royal Devonport Telegraph and Plymouth Chronicle*. The sharp eyes of Davies Gilbert, President of the Royal Society, noticed it, and he contributed it to the *Gentleman's Magazine* as a find of his own, taking it to be an ancient traditional ballad. Walter Scott made benevolent reference to the poem; Macaulay accepted it as genuine and quoted it in his *History*; Dickens reprinted it in *Household Words*. That was fame indeed; but the poet remained without a name:

All these years the Song has been bought and sold, set to music and applauded, while I have lived on among these far away rocks, unprofited, unpraised and unknown.

Though partly Hawker's own fault, for he was utterly unpractical, it was even more owing to circumstances: he lived out of the world, out of touch with men of like mind, or even – since there were very few of like mind to his – with anyone in the literary world. He would print a ballad on a broadsheet at his own expense and circulate it by post to his friends. Sometimes he would publish, again at his own expense, a little collection of poems in a booklet, and wonder that nobody ever noticed them. (These brochures of his are now rare and much sought after by collectors.) He grew discouraged. It was not until the last decade of his life, that, married a second time and with a family of small children, he tried to make contact with London periodicals, to publish his poems and stories and make something of them. He met with little encouragement: most came from *All the Year Round*, which published the stories afterwards collected under the title *Footprints of Former Men in Far Cornwall*. Odd poems appeared in such places as *Notes and Queries* and *Willis's Current Notes*. He once tried to publish poems in *Macmillan's Magazine*; they were rejected. He did not try again.

Yet no one now questions the quality of his ballads, such pieces as *The Silent Tower of Bottreaux*, *Sir Bevil – The Gate-Song of Stowe*, *Mawgan of Melhuach*, *Featherstone's Doom*, *A Croon on Hennacliff*. They have the note of simplicity, coming out of the past and expressing the life of a people, the way of an uncomplex society, as a ballad should. Hawker could write such ballads because his own nature was so closely akin to his people's, simple and believing, direct and unforced; he shared their memories and traditions, their beliefs and superstitions. He shared, if more intensely and imaginatively, the faith that upheld them and lapped them round from the cradle to the grave. It is this that inspires many of his poems – for example, *Datur Hora Quieti*. To the MS. of this poem is the following note: 'Why do you wish the burial to be

at five o'clock?' 'Because it was the time at which he used
to leave work'.

> 'At eve should be the time' they said.
> To close their brother's narrow bed:
> 'Tis at that pleasant hour of day
> The labourer treads his homeward way.
>
> His work was o'er, his toil was done,
> And therefore with the set of sun,
> To wait the wages of the dead,
> We laid our hireling in his bed.

Or such a poem as *Are They not all Ministering Spirits?*

> We see them not – we cannot hear
>   The music of their wing –
> Yet know we that they sojourn near,
>   The Angels of the spring!
>
> They glide along this lovely ground,
>   When the first violet grows;
> Their graceful hands have just unbound
>   The zone of yonder rose!
>
> I gather it for thy dear breast,
>   From stain and shadow free,
> That which an Angel's touch hath blest
>   Is meet, my love, for thee!

The realm of spiritual experience, of mystic belief
which was his own, made all the legends of the Church
real for him as for a medieval. Many of his poems are
on these subjects, like *Modryb Marya – Aunt Mary –*
so called from the old-fashioned Cornish way of pre-
fixing 'Uncle' or 'Aunt' to a name as a token of affection:

Now of all the trees by the king's highway.
Which do you love the best?
O! the one that is green upon Christmas Day,
    The bush with the bleeding breast.
Now the holly with her drops of blood for me:
For that is our dear Aunt Mary's tree.

There are poems on the sacraments, on the offices of the
church, on the symbolic meaning of its rites:

I climbed a poor and narrow stair,
    The prince's christening day;
I sought a cottage bed, for there
    A travail'd woman lay.

With covering thin, and scanty vest,
    Her babe was on her arm:
It was the strong love in her breast
    That kept that infant warm.

I came, a country minister
    A servant of the Lord;
To bless that mother's child for her,
    With Water and the Word.

The dim light struggling o'er the room
    Scarce reached the lowly bed:
And thus mid woe, and want, and gloom
    The Sacrament was shed.

All this faithfully reflects the life he lived as a parish
priest. It was George Herbert over again – the life of
Hawker's Morwenstow, as he was aware, not so very
different from that of the early seventeenth century.

He was a compassionate parish priest, single-minded,
devoted, charitable to the point of improvidence. The
formidable 'Henry of Exeter', Bishop Phillpots, with his

knowledge of men and the world, would have preferred to see Hawker in some place 'where access to congenial society would be easy to you, and where you would be justly appreciated'. But Hawker had always loved Morwenstow and opted for it on his marriage. The parish had been utterly neglected for a hundred years – no resident vicar during all that time; the vicarage was a ruin; Hawker's first care was a work of reclamation. He spent the whole of his wife's portion on building a vicarage, a much-needed bridge over the stream, and a school which he supported single-handed. He was under a financial handicap from the first, which his open-handed largesse to his parishioners did nothing to lessen. The vicarage was built on a considerable scale, as he thought things ought to be done, with chimneys designed recognizably after the towers of neighbouring churches. Over the door he set his inscription:

A House, a Glebe, a Pound a Day;
A Pleasant Place to Watch and Pray.
Be true to Church – Be Kind to Poor,
O Minister! for evermore.

So he settled down to his chosen lot, the forty years of pastoral work in that forgotten place, which is now remembered because of him.

He was a fine figure of a man, with a powerful voice that could be heard all over the glebe, and an imaginative preacher. He had natural taste, strong prejudices and a sense of humour. He was easily capable of turning the tables on those who thought him a joke. He could not bear the colour black; so he dressed at first in a brown cassock. Later he settle down to a habit of a fisherman's blue jersey, with a small red cross woven into the side to mark the entry of the centurion's spear, a long blue coat like a cassock, Hessian boots, various kinds of headgear, and a pastoral staff. Sometimes he was followed about the parish, like parson Herrick, by a favourite pig. 'I congratulate you', he said to a waggonette-load of clergy who thought his get-up odd, 'on the funereal appearance of your hearse.' His tastes, though simple, were expensive. His stationery, of rich yellow parchment, with faint ruled red lines, was specially made for him by De La Rue: he could write on no other; and they had to undertake not to supply the same to anybody else. For his tea he wrote direct to Twining's; he smoked pure Latakia. Even when hard-up he insisted on his stationery, his tea and tobacco, and would order crimson gauntlets or a Greek Orthodox hat to be specially made for him by the best hatters and glove-makers in London.

So he went about his work in the parish. He reclaimed his church, repaired it and made it staunch against wind and weather – not in the horrid spirit of 'restoration' which was then laying waste the Cornish churches, the movement that brought Thomas Hardy to work at St. Juliot a few miles away: work which Hardy in after years regretted. Instead of destroying the old carved bench-ends Hawker bought them up from other churches whence they were being thrown out and filled his with them. He restored the shingle roofs – at improvident expense. The chancel he used to strew with wormwood. He was one of the first to start Harvest Thanksgivings and Rural Synods. It is true that as he got older the services grew odder: often they consisted of the Vicar roaming about the chancel reading from Bible or Prayer Book or making his meditations. Or he would shout down the nave to the bell-ringer:

'Now, Tom, three for the Trinity, and one for the Blessed Virgin'.

The churchwarden's little niece, who handed the list of hymns through the rood-screen to the Vicar, would receive a piece of barley sugar. He did not mind the people not coming to his daily service; they were at work in the fields, 'and they know when I am praying for them, for I ring the bell'.

He was very well attuned to his parishioners, since he adopted all their folklore, was as firmly attached to it as they, and even more credulous. He always used the proper gesture of the fingers to avert the evil eye. His Notebooks are full of charms and invocations, for curing snake-bite, to make butter come, how to become a witch, for sleepy foot:

Foot, foot, foot is fast asleep:
Thumb, thumb, thumb, in spittle we steep,
Crosses three we make for to ease us,
Two for the thieves and one for Christ Jesus.

The sign of the cross was 'to be made, *me judice*, when we meet a heretic, or pass a conventicle, or hear of schism'. 'Peace be to this house', he would say when he came to a parishioner's door, blessing it. Notwithstanding his rooted dislike of Dissent, he was as generous to Dissenters as to the others: 'I like to give them a little comfort in this world', he said, 'for I know what discomfort awaits them in the next'. The world was full of signs and portents to him:

Davis (the Rector of Kilkhampton) had a Dinner party on Wednesday. Three Protestants, Clyde, Thomas and another, were overturned on their return at night.

Or there was a December storm of hail, wind and thunder during Sunday service, the church black with gloom and the faces of the congregation pale in contrast. It put the Vicar in mind of Bossuet's Advent Sermon and his breaking out with, 'What if this Roof were at this very instant to cleave asunder, and we saw through the rent the Son of Man coming in the clouds!' Church service at Morwenstow was not without its excitements. Meanwhile, though windows were smashed in various parts of the parish, 'not a pane was cracked in Vicarage or Church'. It was something to be under Divine protection.

The Vicar had a marvellous way with animals. He was often attended to church by all his cats and dogs; some stranger once looked into service and saw four or five cats grouped peaceably about the lectern. The glebe was a bird sanctuary. 'Did I tell you of a saying of, I think, St. Basil – *Ubi aves ibi angeli* – wheresoever there are birds there are angels?' His Notebooks record many such thoughts:

Birds: They were first seen in the soft Sunlight of the fifth day, and as they floated through the silent air with their silver plumage and feathers like Gold, the Angels said to one another, 'Behold what beautiful images of the Mind of God have come forth with wings'. There is piety in the domestic Wren and Religion in her Nest.

He heareth the grieving supplication wherewith they entreat for food, that low beseeching cry.

He regarded their depredations with entire good-humour:

Beans and Peas are interdicted by the Jackdaws. We have sown twice, and twice they have devoured them all. And a Scarecrow put up by my old Man, was so made up in my Hat and broken Cassock that they took it for me, and came around it looking up to be fed.

Hawker's heart went out to the poor; not that there was anything remarkable in that – so many Victorian clergymen did their duty devotedly, but there was something special in the quality of his feeling. He hated the inhumanity of the New Poor Law of 1834 – and in that links up with the benevolent sympathies of Anglican Tories like Southey and Coleridge, Fielden and Sadler – or indeed of Carlyle and Dickens. He loathed the new 'Poor Law Bastilles' as much as the poor themselves did; he thought that they should have cottages of their own and that it was the duty of their fellow-parishioners to provide for them when past work. To that end he instituted a weekly offertory – one of the first of the clergy to do so; and for his pains was singled out by name for an attack in *The Times*. *The Times* represented the new middle-class school of thought, the new economics, which held that any subvention in aid of wages would have the effect of depressing, not raising, their level. Hawker's protest was refused admission by *The Times*, whereupon he addressed an open letter to John Walter, which is a fine specimen of invective. The Christian duty of alms has, we are told, become obsolete:

As well might a man infer that any other religious excellence ceased to be obligatory, because it had been disused. The virtue of humility, for example, which has been so long in abeyance among certain of the laity, shall no longer, therefore, be a Christian grace! The blessing on the meek shall cease in 1844. . . . Voluntary kindness and alms have been rendered unnecessary by the compulsory payments enacted by the New Poor Law! As though the twenty-fifth chapter of St. Matthew had been repealed by Sir James Graham! As if one of the three conditions of our Christian convenant was to expire during the administration of Sir Robert Peel!

One sees what a pamphleteer was lost to the world by Hawker's being buried away at Morwenstow. The worldly

Phillpotts (who knew all about pamphleteering) was quite right: Hawker would have made his mark in his own time if he had been nearer the centre of affairs. But what was nearest to this man's heart may be seen from his Notebooks:

> What, I wonder, was the purpose of my life? Why was I rescued from the knees? All was done for the wisest and the best: of this be very sure. But still I wonder why – O may God grant that I may have bound up the wounds of at least one by the wayside! that I may have carried a cup of cold water in these hands to *one for whom Christ died.*

His deeds of charity were innumerable; but it is when one comes across his innermost thoughts that one reflects that he was much of a saint. In a letter he describes the burying of the first pauper that came to him from the workhouse:

> I had to send East and West till I had induced Four Men to come, and to bring the coffin to the Church, and thence to the Grave. No Mourners – No Parish Officer – none – by myself and casual Bearers.

He tells the story of this lonely old woman:

> Born an orphan – a solitary life – for she never married – and a very lonely Burial, as I can testify. If there were not a God to receive her Soul, what would life have been to her?

Hawker first became a name in the West Country for his devotion in burying the victims of the wrecks that piled up a grim record on that coast. He was a deeply sensitive, highly-strung man – a cross word from some one in his parish would sometimes make him sleepless for

259

a week; and these events rent him with anguish. His letters have many vivid descriptions of such scenes. One August dawn, in 1852, there came the cry at the vicarage of a stranded ship on the shore below. Hawker rushed down in cassock and slippers; he was the first on deck, to find the crew had been taken off.

> The cabin door was shut, and there was a noise within. I called – opened the door, the two little dogs, pets of the Sailors, leaped out and devoured me with caresses of joy.

More often the scene was like this – it is ten years later, in November:

> The Channel is full of wreck – Cargo – and among it corpses – thirteen came ashore at Bude at the time of the wreck, some lashed to the raft – these are buried all in one pit in Bude Churchyard. This I do not call Christian Burial. We have lived in continual horror ever since, i.e. in sad and solemn expectation of the Dead.

Sometimes the smell of the

> poor dissolving Carcase of Adam, seventeen days dead, has so filled the surrounding air that it is only by a strong effort of my own and by drenching my men with gin for Bearers, that I can fulfil that duty which must be done, but which nothing could sustain a man to perform but the remembrance that to bury the dead won Raphael to Tobit's house and is one of the Seven Corporal Acts of Mercy for a Christian Man. . . . And now with twelve bodies still unfound and the Set of the Current always urging on the Creeks or Morwenstow you will understand the nervous wretched state in which we listen all day and all night

for those thrilling knocks at the door which announce the advent of the dead. . . . The County gives 5/- for finding each corpse, and I give 5/- more. Therefore they are generally found and brought here to the Vicarage where the inquest and the attendant events nearly kill me.

As he grew older, he grew less able to stand the strain of the wrecks. He would get so agitated, riding up and down the coast on the dismal news, sometimes trying to get the Bude or Clovelly boat out in impossible seas, upbraiding the men, offering to go out himself, offering them money to attempt the hopeless. This is not the place to tell the stories of the loss of the *Bencoolen*, the wreck of the *Caledonia*, the *Phoenix*, the *Alonzo*, and many other good sailing ships of those days. He has told the story of some of them in his letters, in his *Reminiscences of a Cornish Vicar*, in poems like *The Figure-Head of the 'Caledonia' at her Captain's Grave:*

> We laid them in their lowly rest,
>   The strangers of a distant shore;
> We smoothed the green turf on their breast,
>   Mid baffled Ocean's angry roar;
> And there, the relique of the storm,
> We fixed fair Scotland's figured form.

Sometimes the Vicar had good fortune and rescued a man alive. Edward le Dain, a Jerseyman, the sole survivor of the *Caledonia*, stayed at the vicarage for six weeks; and ever afterwards, when the Vicar wanted to buy a Jersey cow, le Dain and his family ransacked the island to find for him "The sleekest, loveliest, best of that beautiful breed." But the effect it had on Hawker's nervous sensibility may be judged from his pathetic lament when an ageing man, in the winter of 1866, 'I hear in every gust of the gale a dying sailor's cry'.

Hawker had his reward in the affection of the simple people to whom he ministered: he became something of a legend in his own life-time. At Clovelly once, the farthest limit of his perambulations, there was a hold-up of fish on the quay, the men refusing to sell at the usual prices.

But there arose friends all around who cried – Parson Hawker the Sailor's Friend, He that buried so many poor drowned fellows at his own expense. Shame that he should want fish.

The Vicar got his fish, if nobody else did. When the vicarage caught fire all the men in the fields rushed to his aid:

They risked life and limb and the Dissenters were conspicuous among them all for vigour and zeal. . . . After their conduct I must never doubt the goodwill of my whole people. Their conduct was beyond all praise. I shall never forget it or cease to be grateful for it as long as I live. The delicacy too with which when the fire was stopped they went away, as if not to intrude even for praise, was very striking.

That instinctive delicacy of simple West Country folk is (or was) characteristic; one sees too that they must have loved him, and were proud of him. Already his photograph was on sale at a shop in Bude, and the Vicar heard, with an innocent pleasure, that it was a best-seller.

All the eminent who appeared in the neighbourhood came to pay their respects. By far the greatest occasion for Hawker was Tennyson's visit in 1848; he never forgot that blessed day. Matthew Arnold's brother, Edward Penrose, came to inspect his school. It was a pity that Arnold himself didn't come, since his Poems were among the most treasured of Hawker's few volumes. Lord Harrowby was fed on the Vicar's favourite bread and Cornish cream. Dean Liddell, of Christ Church, and his wife called, with their Court-gossip: the flunkeyism of the Liddells appears to perfection:

> they speak in the highest terms of the Prince of Wales. His disposition and temper are courteous to the extreme and his morals unexceptionable.

The heretic Gorham, who doubted the doctrine of Baptismal Regeneration and whose place in history is due to his having provided an occasion for Manning to go over to Rome, appeared at the vicarage and asked the name of some plant. It happened to be cudweed, and it gave the Vicar some pleasure to add that its Latin name was *Herba impia*. Gorham took the allusion; 'so the name now stands thus – *Herbia Impia Gorhamensis*'.

Hawker has his significance as a figure in complete reaction to the nineteenth century. Against its greed for gain, he placed the spirit of charity; against utilitarianism and conflicting class-interests, a life of devotion and selflessness; against the trend of scientific materialism, unquestioning faith in spiritual values; against its pretentiousness, simplicity; against its humbug, candour. He was content that he had never taken the impress of 'the smoothing iron of the nineteenth century'. 'The plain truth is', he wrote in 1851,

> that the whole Age is a Time of cowardly Negation, and, as Earl Derby so bitterly said, of compromise. Formerly there were *Men*, now there are nothing but *Votes*. Of Old, an insulted Gentleman damned his Adversary on the spot. Nowadays the Individual makes up a prim mouth and says, 'May the Lord in his judgment utterly take away every hope of thy final Salvation'.

It was an age of humbug: Hawker puts his finger on its characteristic expression. He could hardly be expected to feel at ease in the England of the Industrial Revolution:

Who is there to come down with succour? What angel could arrive with duties to perform for that large Blaspheming Smithery, once a great Nation, now a Forge for Railways?

Hawker understood very well where the intellectual trends of the age were leading and he had his own answer. In a time when the assumptions of faith were increasingly challenged, his reaction was to remove the whole basis of Christian teaching away from reason into the realm of faith. With him it was instinctive and natural, but in its way more effective than nineteenth-century attempts to compromise, which were bound to end in the supremacy of reason and the erosion of the historic tenets of the Faith. Hawker reacted as much as Newman into the world of faith, with its non-verifiable certainty. With him it was easy, for he was by nature a mystic and a poet who saw symbols of another world written upon the face of everything in this. His mind was possessed by the sense of the spiritual universe, of this world inhabited by ghostly beings just round the corner of the eye. In his Notebooks he writes:

The Earth is an Orb of Emblems – that and nothing more. God made this World for Man to see Him by. Every visible Thing is an embodied Thought of God. A Word that may be seen.

Every thought flows out of the Eternal Mind alive, and is forthwith a glorious angel or a lively scene, a shoreless sea of light, or it may be a star, for the thoughts of God must live since they be eternal, once formed they die no more.

The Seen World is but one vast Semblance. The
Reality is God.

The Natural World is the dream of God!

Creation: Myriads of Worlds spring up as the grass
of the Night.

In these jottings in his private Notebooks the
thoughts that sustained and occupied the life of his mind
are revealed: it might be Traherne or Vaughan or
Herbert. The two books upon which he rested his faith
were the Bible and St. Thomas Aquinas. (St. Thomas,
he once said, had been the means of rescuing him from
unbelief.) He took them literally and believed them
literally: they gave him an infinitely richer world than
our world of reason and sense. The world was full of
symbolism for him – everything was a symbol of the
spiritual powers that ruled, divine or demonic. The air
was thronged with spiritual beings, angels and demons.
The invention of the electric telegraph was no wonder to
him, who knew by constant experience the promptings
of the angels and the information they had to impart by
unseen channels. The answer to Darwin and Colenso
with their attack on the received time-scheme of
creation could be given by

> my little children at the School, who would teach
> them that whereas in Heaven Time does not exist
> there could be no such thing regarded as Dates or
> Periods or Years. . . . In Heaven with all their know-
> ledge they cannot tell you what hour it is on the clock
> or what day, month, or year.

Asked how he knew these things, Hawker would reply
that it was the angels who told him. There was no
getting round that. He had his own method of mystical
meditation:

This, which I practise in my Chancel—alone and often at night – is my most abundant source of instruction. There mysteries are made clear, doctrines illustrated, and tidings brought, which I firmly believe are the work of angelic ministry. Of course the angels of the altar are there, and the angel of my own baptism is never away.

In a letter of 1857 he says:

My own mode is to go into my own dim Chancel divided from the Nave by a Screen, there kneel, walk, or sit and meditate, close the eye and send out a Spiracle of Research from every pore. Gradually in such an atmosphere every fine fibre of the Soul brightens like the gossamer – St Mary's silk – upon the grass, and becomes a Ray – hence knowledge and reply.

It was not only his intellectual needs that were met in this way. Once five farmers made a concerted attempt to diminish the Church Rate. Hawker convened a vestry,

over which I read the Exorcistic Service of the Western church, in Latin of course. They knew not the meaning of the voice, but those who inhabited them did. The five fled from the Room howling, as my Deacon will attest, and my Rate was forthwith carried by a Majority of 24 to 1.

Still, it was usually intellectual aid which the Vicar received from his lonely meditations:

there is hardly a point of Doctrine which I am fain to know but I receive it in clear and beautiful Words as the lightning leaps from the dark cloud suddenly.

It was clearly, without Hawker's realizing it, the process of poetic inspiration.

In consequence of these habits there were all kinds of things the Vicar knew which other people did not. For one thing, 'angels have no wings: not a single feather'. He was very strong on this; it was heresy to think otherwise. The fish which filled the apostolic net in the Sea of Galilee were mullet; and he had a seal made which depicted the mullet, inscribed with various symbolic Greek letters. The pixies, who cut such a figure in Cornish folklore, are the souls of unbaptised children. When his little girl Morwenna was baptised 'she behaved most orthodoxly. She cried in the right place and was silent after Exorcism, as she should'. It is well known that the body of an unbaptised person is open to a demon always. On the other hand for those who were fortified by the rites of the Church there was the promise of bliss. There are several inscriptions in Morwenstow church-yard which testify to the beauty of Robert Hawker's mind, if nothing else.

To the memory of Richard Cann, of Lower Cory in this parish, Yeoman, whose Soul was carried by the Angels into Paradise on the 16 day of February in the year of the Church 1842. Aged 31 years. The Second Life which he received at the Font he cherished in the Chancel, insomuch that with the certainty of the One True Faith, through the Assurance of the Blessed Sacraments, and in the Safety of the Ancient and Apostolic Worship of Christ in this consecrated Sanctuary of God, he clave steadfastly unto the Lord until he was not, for God took him.

Since their Vicar was so sure, the people thought that he knew the answers to everything. Once when there was a pall of gloom over the whole parish for three days together, 'two or three farmers came to ask if I could tell the reason of such unnatural darkness'. Hawker consulted his glass, but his real opinion was that God was angry with the land.

To the influence of his lonely meditations there should be added the effect of taking opium, which increasingly blurred the distinction between fact and fancy, at the same time as it stimulated his imagination, as with Coleridge and De Quincey.

Nor was it all gain to be on such familiar terms with the spirit-world.

From my being the only Clergyman in the Diocese who exposes continually the existence and usages of the Demons I am especially obnoxious to them. I was actually saying in Church in a Sermon on Job, 'Touch not his life', when on the Fast Day the first Roof fell down, and now I had been denouncing them as the Authors of Storm and Tempest Fire and Hail when this second onslaught was made on me in the night.

A gale had blown the roof of his barn off.

Still there were compensatory excitements. It was interesting to know that the Superior Demons 'are distinguished by a more lurid glow around their faces than the rest'.

And Hawker was agog with anxiety to know:

Have you ever heard that there is at All Souls in the Library a Signature, or at least the Autograph, of the Enemy of Man . . . ? I have not one Friend left now in Oxford except the Vice-Chancellor, and he is too awful a person now to be written to on such a theme.

Hawker's curiosity was not to be allayed. He wrote again later:

Have you succeeded in your Search for the Demoniac Autograph? If you do, pray secure a tracing of it. I have heard or read somewhere that such signatures are scratched as it were with the claw of a cock on the Sand. . . . All this however will not reveal the writing which exists I am persuaded in Oxford, howsoever reluctant the members of a College may be to avow their Founder's Kin.

I am bound to say that I have read a good many books in that library without ever coming upon the signature; but Hawker seems later to have transferred his suspicions from All Souls to Queen's.

Hawker is, above all, interesting to us as a man with whom the full panoply of medieval faith remained. Dr. Tillyard has shown us how much of that faith remained in the minds of the Elizabethans.[1] Hawker is a rare case of one with whom it remained in full, quite naturally and unquestioningly, among the Victorians. There was the whole medieval cosmology, which in his own way he brought up to date, to answer Darwin and the geologists, Colenso and the Biblical critics.

We perceive, being inspired, the realms of surrounding space peopled by immortal creatures of the air –

> Myriads of spiritual things that walk unseen,
> Both when we wake and when we sleep.

Behold the battalions of the Lord of Hosts! the workers of the sky! the faithful and intelligent vassals of God the Trinity! These are they that with a delegated office fulfil what their 'King Invisible' decrees. They mould the atom; they wield the force; and, as Newton rightly guessed, they rule the World of matter beneath the silent Omnipotence of God.

1. E.M.W. Tillyard, *The Elizabethan World-Picture*.

Myriads, Myriads, of intellectual Creatures, descended, and descend, in gradual attribute from God the bodiless to Adam the First Man.

There is stated, in so many words, the medieval doctrine of the Chain of Being, by which all creatures are linked. The lower creatures are not forgotten in the Notebooks.

Fish: Did they share the Fall? Not? Therefore fitter emblems of a second birth – of those who never die.

Tomorrow: The flowers put on their robes with loveliness each after their kind and are happy in the sun. They drink the dews of even and bend their brows in thanksgiving. Tomorrow they fade and die – die happy. They have served God's purpose with their beautiful array and adorned the world of God.

Why did God fill with fragrance the blue chalice of the violet and the ruddy censer of the rose?

Paradise: How lovely must its fields have been since even Earth, the land of our Exile, is so surpassingly fair.

Such thoughts expressed in his Notebooks and letters are the notes of a poet: only a poet could dare in modern days to be so blissfully medieval in his beliefs.

It was during the melancholy months after his wife's death that Hawker devoted himself to writing his most important poem, *The Quest of the Sangraal*. The inspiration of the poem went back to Tintagel forty years before – as with Hardy and his *Famous Tragedy of Iseult, Queen of Cornwall*. (It is curious to think what an impression that place has made in English literature from Geoffrey of Monmouth onwards.) Hawker says:

There we used to roam about and read all that could be found about those Old-World Histories, and often was this legend of the Sangraal talked of as fine Subject for Verse. Often I have said, 'If I could but throw myself back to King Arthur's time and write what he would have said and thought it would make a good Cornish Book'. The crest of Her Family was three Birds, the red-legged Chough, King Arthur's Bird, as the common people call it around the Castle.

Years before, on the memorable day's talk with Tennyson, Hawker had urged him to undertake this theme; now he was to compete with Tennyson on his own ground. He took a leaf out of Tennyson's book and set himself to write a few lines every day, going down to his hut out on the cliffs with its magnificent view, and writing there all the evening till late sunset. So he completed the first canto that summer, all that he wrote of the four or five he projected.

Devotees of Hawker are apt to say that his poem rivals, or even defeats Tennyson on his own ground. It is true that Hawker's poem has the quality of mystical belief that Tennyson has not (Hawker denoted him, rightly, a Maurician); one sees that Hawker believed the medieval legends and that his mind moved naturally and easily within that world of faith. All the same, as poetry it is less good. Nearly all Hawker's poems are in simple rhymed measures, and as a ballad-writer he was at his best. With blank verse he was less happy; his lines are too frequently end-stopped, and though he decorated them with alliteration, the effect is over-regular and monotonous. On its own ground and within its own terms the poem is effective and has some fine passages. The Cornish saints are described in lines that fit Hawker himself, their natural successor:

271

So they unrolled the volume of the Book,
And filled the fields of the Evangelist
With antique thoughts, that breathed of Paradise.

The poem is full, and appropriately, of Hawker's own
medieval lore:

Eastward! the source and spring of life and light!
Thence came and thither went, the rush of worlds,
When the great cone of space was sown with stars.
There rolled the gateway of the double dawn,
When the mere God shone down, a breathing man.

On the angels:

Myriads, in girded albs, for ever young,
Their stately semblance of embodied air,
Troop round the footstool of the Southern Cross,
That pentacle of stars: the very sign
That led the Wise Men towards the Awful Child,
Then came and stood to rule the peaceful sea.
So, too, Lord Jesu from His mighty tomb
Cast the dear shadow of his red right hand,
To soothe the happy South – the angels' home.

The poem speeds up towards the end, with the visions
that express what Hawker felt about the age he lived in:

Thus said pale Merlin to the listening King:
'What is thy glory in the world of stars?
To scorch and slay: to win demoniac fame,
In arts and arms; and then to flash and die!
Thou art the diamond of the demon-crown,
Smitten by Michael upon Abarim,
That fell; and glared, an island of the sea.
Ah! native England! wake thine ancient cry;
Ho! for the Sangraal! vanished Vase of Heaven,
That held, like Christ's own heart, an *hin* of blood!'

It was a pity that Hawker did not go on with the poem: the theme suited him and his handling of blank verse would have grown with practice. But the effort was too great. Like Robert Bridges with *The Testament of Beauty*, he came to his *magnum opus* too late. Hawker wanted concentration. As he grew old, he felt that he had not done justice to his faculties and gifts. There is a pathetic autobiographical passage which he puts into the mouth of King Arthur:

I have no Son, no daughter of my loins,
To breathe, mid future men, their father's name;
My blood will perish when these veins are dry;
Yet I am fain some deeds of mine should live –
I would not be forgotten in this land.

There were several other things that Hawker wanted besides concentration: for one thing, encouragement; for another, contact with men of equal powers and interests. *The Quest*, when published, as usual at his own expense, was hardly noticed. A reviewer in the *Church Review* said that Hawker had 'no originality' – the one thing of which he had, if anything, too much. Hawker, who, like Tennyson, could never support the obtuseness of the third-rate, was furious. 'I know that I am,' he replied innocently, 'dogmatic, proud, mysterious. But I am not a plagiarist, and I will give you or yours £10 to name a thought or a phrase or a word in my Poem that is copied from another Man.' He could not go on; and so what still remains his most considerable poem is a fragment. Nor, in the remaining years of his life, did he write much verse: he turned to prose.

To prose – and to marriage. The loneliness that descended upon him at Morwenstow after his wife's death, was absolute and unbearable. The surprising man who in his handsome teens had married a woman of forty-one, now in his sixties married a Polish girl of nineteen. Nothing that Robert Hawker did was quite like anybody else. He proceeded in a short time to incur a family of three children.

Family life brought him a measure of happiness; but it added to the financial worries of his last years. 'I had money once,' he wrote, 'but it is all gone, invested in Morwenstow for the benefit of the unborn'. He continued to be as charitable as ever, selling stock from the glebe to give all the poor of the parish a good Christmas dinner. He could not cut down on his necessary luxuries, stationery, tea, his ideas of clothing. The church was in disrepair again: he made a journey to London, for the second time in his life, to raise money for Morwenstow. On the way he lost his hat and sent for the station-master at Salisbury to buy a new one from that astonished official; 'Bless my soul! what a benighted place this is,' said the Vicar, equally surprised that the station-master didn't supply hats. Hawker wanted to go on with *The Quest of the Sangraal*, but he found his overdraft at the bank his greatest obstacle. To raise a little ready cash he wrote a number of prose sketches which appeared in these years in *All the Year Round*. His poems were collected and published under the title of *Cornish Ballads* in 1869; the prose sketches in the volume *Footprints of Former Men in Far Cornwall* in 1870. His work was complete.

Over his later years there was the growing tragedy of uncertainty – it was no less, for one who had been so certain. He had always been out of sympathy with the dominant trends of the age, and as time went on he found them gain the ascendant in his beloved Church. The redoubtable 'Harry of Exeter' who held the fort so long for orthodoxy (and so profitably for his family) was burnt in effigy at his own cathedral door. Worse still, when (at last) he died, he was succeeded by the heretical Temple, contributor to the notorious *Essays and Reviews*. Moreover, had Archbishop Tait ever been baptised? There was grave doubt on this point, and it gave Hawker anxious concern. Since the Archbishop never settled the point, a doubt rested upon all the orders he had conferred. Of Colenso and his tribe of Higher Critics, the Vicar wrote:

> That which makes me mad is that I see the Miracles and Wonders of Revelation received with reverent belief by such majestic intellects as St. Augustine and St. Jerome and then to be carped at by the unutterably debased minds of this XIXth Age, who are really and literally incompetent to criticise the Catechism of the Church.

There was at any rate certainty somewhere: Rome was unchanged and unchanging. The Vicar's syllabus of modern errors coincided with that of the Vicar of Christ, and like the Syllabus of 1867, it included railroads among them. Indeed the Vicar of Morwenstow went further, for he included the Great Exhibitions. More and more Hawker's mind turned to the mother of us all. He exchanged friendly letters with Catholic, indisputably Catholic, bishops, with Ullathorne of Birmingham, whom he venerated, with Grant of Southwark, with Wiseman himself. When the Cardinal died, Hawker wrote a fine poem, which may be compared with Francis Thompson's *On the Dead Cardinal at Westminster*:

> Hush! for a star is swallowed up in night!
>   A noble name hath set along the sea!
> An eye that flashed with heaven no more is bright,
>   The brow that ruled the islands – where is he?
>
> Where reigns he now? What throne is set for him
>   Amid the nine-fold armies of the sky,
> Waves he the burning sword of Seraphim?
>   Or dwells a calm Archangel, crowned on high?

In the end, he graduated to Newman and Manning. He sent his *Canticle for Christmas*, 1874 to them, and received very characteristic letters from them both. From Manning:

> I wish my Countrymen knew how I love England and Englishmen. If I ever seem to speak sharply it is only against the errors which mislead so many, and the miseries which make havoc of our beautiful land. I pray every day in the Holy Mass that the England of S. Edward both in popular liberty and in Catholic unity may return once more.

From Newman, that supple, insinuating spirit, there came the question beautifully put:

> Of course there is just one thought which rises in a Catholic's mind, which he finds it difficult to answer; and the more he discerns the grace and skill of the composition the more the question intrudes itself upon him. Do not think me ungrateful to you in thus speaking – I am constrained to do so, and the more pleasure I take in what you so kindly say of me, the more I am bound to recollect that in what I say to you I have to please Another, not myself.'

The question haunted Hawker's mind in his last years. He had long venerated the Sovereign Pontiff, and loathed such enemies as Garibaldi. He welcomed the promulgation of the dogma of the Immaculate Conception – indeed he had long held it; he wore a medal in honour of it, on one side Pio Nono, on the other the Immaculate Virgin. His last poem, *Psalmus Cantici*, was written on Manning's elevation to the purple:

Behold the ruddy Coif, the scarlet Vest,
   The sigilled Glove, red with symbolic Blood,

The placid brow above the thrilling Breast,
　Where throbs the pulse of an Ethereal Flood.

Shout, Happy England, for the sceptred Hand,
　The rod of Aaron and the barren stems,
The throne of Rock amid a quivering Land,
　The Brow to sway a thousand diadems.

As the Vicar's mind lost grip and he grew more fuddled, the boundaries between one thing and another, one Church and another, became somewhat blurred. Are we altogether to blame him if on his death-bed, in a state of semi-consciousness, he slipped over the boundary into the arms of Rome? Does it much matter?

We can have only one regret – that he does not lie buried at Morwenstow. Still his name is indissolubly linked with the place, the place with his memory. He thought that his life was a failure, that he would leave nothing but broken fragments behind him, nothing to remember him by. In fact, his was a recognisably original and idiosyncratic spirit; he has left a name and is remembered – better than many men who had far greater *réclame* in his day.

Truro as Cornish Capital

In the century since Truro was constituted a city, with a cathedral and a bishop ruling an independent Cornish diocese, it has asserted itself as a genuine county capital. Mediaeval Cornwall had its assize town on the border at Launceston, subsequently moved to Bodmin; but when the diocese was set up in 1877, followed by the County Council in the next decade, Truro was chosen as the centre. This westward shift followed the balance of population, tilting to the west with the development of tin-mining.

The founding of the diocese and the building of a cathedral, first in the country since the Reformation released an astonishing stream of Cornish patriotism, a renewal and reinforcement of Church life when it looked as if Methodism had taken over the county. The full story of the achievement has been told by Canon Miles Brown, in a book as full of information and research as it is human and lively.[1]

The building of the diocese and of the cathedral coincided with the disastrous decline of tin-mining and the fisheries. 'The population of St Agnes, for example, reached a peak of 7,757 in 1841; but in 1881 it had fallen to 4,627. A report made in 1896 commented: "In the last 40 years hundreds of cottages have gone down in rural parts – our miners go abroad".' Yet all this while the building of a splendid Victorian church went on,

1. A Century for Cornwall. The Diocese of Truro, 1877–1977. By H. Miles Brown.

278

until completed in 1910, in a small impecunious county
– while rich Liverpool had scarcely begun.

This was but the beginning. The first Bishop, Benson
(subsequently Archbishop of Canterbury), treated
Cornwall as a mission field; by 1884, 58 new mission
churches had been started, 44 parish churches restored,
8 new ones built, a flood of gifts of all kinds received for
furnishing cathedral and churches, schools and institutions for charitable and social purposes. Gifts, too,
came from Cornish folk overseas; we certainly have good
reason to celebrate this centenary.

It is marked, too, by a number of books, of which the
most opulent – full of eloquent illustrations, prints,
handbills, posters – is *The Book of Truro*, by H.L.
Douch, Curator of the admirable County Museum.[2] It is
a piece of work scholarly and appealing – not the less so
for its inflexion. One of R.H. Tawney's followers wrote
the other day, with some disapproval, that our history
had been mostly written from the point of view of the
upper classes. True enough; but then they are more
interesting and significant, intellectually and in every
way. Mr Douch does 'not write about famous men,
because they won their fame elsewhere and they have
their other monuments; rather I choose to put a little
flesh to the bones of some of those who were born and
buried in Truro but of whom little else is known or
remembered'.

In this more difficult task he has succeeded more than
one would have thought possible. He has the excuse that
the history of Cathedral and City, schools, churches and
hospital, corporation and Parliamentary representation,
are partly dealt with elsewhere. He prefers to consider
Truro as a rural borough, leaving out the grander aspects
of our little cathedral city and its most interesting
personalities. Even from the point of view of social life,

2. *Barracuda Books.*

however, some of the eighteenth-century gentry had a town-house there; the exquisite front of the old Assembly Rooms – the hall behind it, alas, demolished – still testifies to their assemblies, something of a capital socially even then. Someone wrote of 'the attractions of the Theatre, Assembly Rooms, the County Library, the Literary Society and the Cockpit'; another described it as 'that town of dissipation, notorious for its worldliness and frivolity', and compared its amenities to Bath, though in 'West Barbary'.

Truro was one of the original five Cornish boroughs to send members up to Edward I's 'model' Parliament, and was earlier made a 'coinage town' for stamping and collecting dues on tin – till coinage day it lay stacked in the streets – for the earldom and subsequent duchy of Cornwall.

The topographical situation of town and neighbourhood could not be more vividly set out. Mr Douch considers that the name of Truro refers to the three streams running down there; the site a triangle jutting out between two main anchorages, roads from across the county converging upon it, water-power for fulling mills, the town equipped with *open fields* – historians may care to note. At the highest point – now the cattle market – was the small castle of the Norman family, to whose patronage and protection (not 'despotism') the settlement owed its borough status, its subsequent charter giving it rights and privileges.

A populist approach hardly appreciates the give-and-take in these relations. During the eighteenth century the leading landlords nearby, the Boscawens, dominated the Parliamentary representation and the political colouring of the Corporation – mayor and his twenty-four colleagues – who returned the MPs. The famous fighting Admiral Boscawen was one, but in return he was expected to find places at sea for likely Truro lads. When it came to building a market-house, the always mendicant Corporation raised a loan from Lord Falmouth, who was expected to put his hand in his pocket on such occasions. When his lordship revolted, the Corporation turned down his candidates, two of his sons, with unkind remarks about his 'avarice', and returned his opponents to Parliament.

True, the Boscawens got their peerage for their political influence, but it may be doubted whether in cash it was not more expense than profit. However, the Corporation rebelled only that once, in 1780, from a tutelage that was profitable to them. It was usually with Truro and the Boscawens as Gibbon wrote of Liskeard, 'the electors of Liskeard are commonly of the same opinion as Mr Eliot'.

The Parliamentary representation of Truro illustrates clearly a development of general historical significance. Throughout the middle ages the borough sends up its own Truro men, with a few other locals. In Elizabeth's reign the gentry dominate, though still mainly Cornish; from the Restoration to the Regency, the Boscawens, who thus enter the peerage.

Mr Douch gives us a living picture of the economic life of the town from its small beginnings: oysters galore in the river, and until 1662, when Falmouth grew of age, Truro's jurisdiction extended all down the river Fal to its mouth at Black Rock – and we have happy accounts of the Corporation's junketings and river-feasts. A main import was timber, for charcoal for the mines earlier; there were smelting houses for tin, while the river was continually silting up from mine detritus. A rather unexpected feature is the amount of manufacturing in later times, worsted, blanketing, carpets, paper. Another centenary must be approaching, that of Furniss's well-known gingerbreads and 'Cornish Wafers', which I have been touched to meet as far afield as California.

Mr Douch is strong on demotic life: a whole chapter is devoted to 'The Deserving Poor', from which we learn that about 1840 'there were no less than 106 houses for the sale and manufacture of intoxicating drinks'. Perhaps this had something to do with the differential death-rate I observed years ago in the Report of 1844 on the Health and Conditions of the Working Classes. It is true that the low-lying quarters of the town were unhealthy, only the higher ground salubrious. Still, the eighteenth-century grandees lived low down by the river; so did the Robertses, who made an immense fortune by their tin-dealing and money-lending in Elizabeth's reign – to emerge as Puritanical members of the peerage as the Lords Robartes.

The most interesting aspect of the treatment of the poor – for sanitation we have always with us – is medical. Sir Francis Basset was a real county leader in the Industrial Revolution and the Napoleonic war, during which the population of Truro increased notably. On the whole, Mr Douch eschews the gentry; but it was owing to Basset and a St. Aubyn that the Royal Cornwall Infirmary was founded – intended for the miners and poor folk – before ever Plymouth possessed such an institution.

The Infirmary at Truro developed into a central hospital for the county, and again has an admirable history of it.[3] From it one learns of the work of a number of distinguished doctors, two of them Fellows of the Royal Society, another who made original contributions to optics, yet others who gave leadership to the civic life of Truro.

Further evidence of the centricity of Truro is provided by its educational institutions. Its ancient Grammar School, now combined with the Cathedral School, has had its history written by R.E. Davidson. Going back to the Reformation, it has had a more interesting history than any other school in the county and a far more

3. *The First Cornish Hospital.* By C.T. Andrews.

distinguished roll of alumni. They include Sir Humphry Davy, most brilliant of scientists, the effective creator of the Royal Institution in London; Henry Martyn, missionary to India, translator of the Bible into Persian and Hindustani; Samuel Foote, actor and dramatist; Hussey Vivian, right-hand man of Wellington in his campaigns; Admiral Pellew, Lord Exmouth, of various naval exploits; Richard Polwhele, historian of Cornwall and Devon – his history of Devonshire just reissued after some 160 years.

Truro Grammar School had three remarkable Headmasters in the Georgian period: Conon, Cornelius Cardew (or whom there is a biography), and Thomas Hogg. The first of these set going an Evangelical revival, which culminated in the career of Samuel Walker, vicar of St. Mary's, and friend of the Wesleys. He founded the Clerical Club and a number of religious societies, to offset the gay dissipation noted above. Of the gaiety, fun and frolics – and also the disputatiousness – of the town we have a sample in Dr Wolcot, the notorious Regency satirist, 'Peter Pindar', who made Truro too hot for him and departed for a wider career in London, where he launched the young painter, Opie, to fame.

Of the strong Methodist influence in the town we have ocular evidence in the largest of Wesleyan churches in the county, and also the biggest Public School – which now calls itself Truro School – dominating the skyline to the east. The skyline to the west is marked by a vast new County Hall, characteristic feature of contemporary society with its inflated bureaucracy.

Architecturally, Truro had a touch of distinction, a recognizable character imposed upon it by the Georgian families, whose standards and taste expressed themselves in admirable houses and streets. Lemon Street – which appears as Orange Street in the novels of Hugh Walpole (grandson of a leading Truro doctor) – retains its

Georgian distinction, climbing the hill to the column commemorating Richard Lander, African explorer, who traced the source and outlet of the Niger. The Red Lion, home of the Foote family, dating from 1671, with splendid staircase and fine assembly room, has recently been wantonly destroyed; while a large Regency area on the eastern approaches has been laid waste by the combined efforts of road-making and a metropolitan insurance society with no feeling for the character of Truro.

I commend these amenities so typical of our demotic society to the author of the admirable *Book of Truro*.

The Temples

The last bishop of Exeter to have Cornwall included in his diocese was Frederick William Temple, later archbishop of Canterbury. He always thought of himself as a Cornishman, and it is partly owing to this that he was so keen to advance the project for a Cornish diocese, even though it meant cutting off his own tail. On his mother's side he was pure Cornish. On his father's, the Temples came into Cornwall with his grandfather, William Johnston Temple, well known in his day – and now to students of literature – as the friend of Boswell and Dr. Johnson. This first of our Temples, a North Countryman, had been at Edinburgh university with Boswell, and thereafter maintained their friendship for the rest of their lives.

Temple can never have realised the full extent of Boswell's genius and, understandably, had no very exalted opinion of his character. But he did his duty faithfully as Boswell's confidant, and tried (in vain) to admonish him in his all too errant ways. What bound them together was that each had literary ambitions. The world knows Boswell's, when Temple's have been forgotten. Yet he was a sensitive scholar of considerable promise. In addition to the ancient classics he was exceptionally well read in modern literatures, French, Italian, Spanish. He published a volume of *Moral and Historical Memoirs,* which was well thought of. What was to have been his *magnum opus*, a book on 'The Rise and Decline of Rome, or Rome under the Papacy', (think of it alongside of Gibbon!), was never finished. So Temple failed to achieve fame.

He was in fact a disappointed man; he lived too far away from the metropolis. When he went to London he kept company with literary folk like Dr. Johnson, for whom he provided the character of Gray in his *Lives of the Poets*. Then, back he had to come to Cornwall, where he felt lonely and neglected in his vicaraage of St. Gluvias at Penryn, where Boswell once visited him in 1792. How much I wish that Temple's letters might be published by the Boswell industry at Yale! Temple had an idea of writing Boswell's life; though he was Boswell's oldest and most intimate friend, I do not think that that would have worked out. He was just not the man for it, and few of his plans ever did work out. His Diary tells us why.

Temple did not enjoy good health; he was low-spirited and much of a hypochondriac. The abounding vitality of his son Octavius and his archiepiscopal offspring must have come from another side of the family. Then, too, Temple was a discontented man, frustrated of his literary ambitions and perpetually complaining of the lack of books and conversation in Cornwall. But, when he got to London, where he knew a number of grand people, Dr. Johnson and, somewhat improbably, the unbelieving Hume, he found company fatiguing and longed for home. He was happiest alone with his books and papers. Even here he seems to have frittered his time away with much miscellaneous reading, never bringing anything to point. After all, Polwhele and Whitaker, his clerical *confrères* in even more sequestered situations at Ruanlanihorne and Manaccan-in-Meneague, 'contrived better' than he, as the Diary confesses.

Actually Temple had as contemporaries in Cornwall, besides Polwhele and Whitaker, Sir Francis Basset (whom he did not much like), the intellectual Francis Gregor and Christopher Hawkins nearby whose conversation he did find 'very pleasing'; and Davies Giddy, on his way to becoming Davies Gilbert on marrying an heiress, and President of the Royal Society. Temple found the conversation of the local squires uninteresting, confined largely to their own acres and fields. He detested their drinking and blood-sports and was shocked by a bull-baiting in his parish at Penryn. He was a man of refined taste and sensibility; even the delicate and sensitive poet Gray had warned him against giving way to his sensibilities.

In fact he had quite an agreeable social life, and there was always company coming and going at Falmouth and Penryn. He dines with the Duke and Duchess of Leeds on their way back from the Scilly Islands, to the historic lease of which the Duke had succeeded as heir to the Godolphins (and allowed Godolphin to lapse into decay!) Amongst many callers at the vicarage of St. Gluvias – to which Temple added an upstairs library with a fine view – we find Polwhele, characteristically too busy to await the vicar out for a ride.

In April 1796 Temple returns the visit. 'At half-past eleven Anne, Robert and myself got on horseback to go to dine at Manaccan with Mr. and Mrs. Polwhele. (He wrote the History of Devonshire, translated Theocritus, etc.). We crossed Helford passage and they met us on the other side. We walked to the vicarage up very hilly and steep ground: not ugly, and the river running up the valley with some wood on its banks is pleasing enough. The day passed very agreeably . . .' But what did they talk about? We should like to know.

Temple was more taken with mid-Cornwall, where August 1782 finds him stopping in the parsonage house of beautiful Boconnoc, riding in the park and rowing up and down the Lerryn and Fowey rivers. 'This row of five miles terminated all of a sudden by a noble view of the sea and the town of Fowey. Tor walk, though made in Elizabeth's time, pleasingly irregular. Rowed back again to St. Winnow, the vicarage of Mr. Walker, where we all dined.' O *sancta simplicitas!* the simple pleasures, the quietude of the Georgian countryside unspoiled; that exquisite situation of St. Winnow church above the river-bank, churchyard running down to the edge of the water, the grey vicarage above with its view down-river to the turning towards Fowey, we still have with us.

We see Temple's tastes as shaped by Gray, a connoisseur, sensitive to regular beauty of house and grounds, but also responsive to the picturesque, like Luxulyan Valley. 'The country around wild and savage, the Valley scattered over with immense stones or rather rocks, a rapid stream at bottom. The banks boldly advancing or retiring, sometimes thickly wooded, sometimes bare. The same day Prideaux wood, consisting of lofty and richly wooded banks, our ride was terminated by a beautiful range of sweetly swelling hills ending in the sea. All this neighbourhood is the Arcadia of Cornwall, abounding in finely broken grounds, wood, water and all the materials of Landskip, infinitely diversified.

There is much intercourse among the Gentry, they are liberal and sociable.' (Temple, like his famous descendants, was liberal, a pro-American over the War of Independence – like his Bishop, Keppel, in the chapel of whose Palace at Exeter Temple was ordained. His grandson was to reign there as bishop, his great-grandson born there.)

Temple was not really made for family life: he would have been happier as a celibate Fellow of a Cambridge college – but, then, we should not have had those archiepiscopal descendants. Of his family we are concerned only with their progenitor, Octavius. Temple finds him an affectionate boy, but stubborn and perverse; occasionally he has to 'correct' him. Most of the time Octavius is away at school at Liskeard; when he comes home he is usually out riding about the parish on his nag, or bringing back his friends from Falmouth for noisy junketings (which Father's nerves couldn't stand) at the vicarage.

When Octavius has to go back to school, he 'very reluctantly and with many tears set out in the gig with Mr. Rowe to go to Liskeard – but, when they had proceeded a little way, jumped out and obliged him to return, still crying and saying he should never see me again. Dear, affectionate creature. With much entreaty I prevailed on him to get in again. Nothing can be more amiable than his disposition; he is quick, but soon comes to himself again and has no sullenness or malice. They do not make sufficient allowance for his tender years: this often hurts me'.

At fifteen Octavius had had enough of school and insisted on joining the army, as an ensign. We see that he did not inherit his father's intellectual aptitudes, yet he passed them on to son and grandson. At twenty, in 1805 – Trafalgar year – he married a neighbour's daughter, Dorcas Carveth. There was opposition from both families; but the young officer was as strong-minded as he was manly, passionate in temperament, rather rough and imperious in his ways – characteristics which his son, the Archbishop, inherited. The Carveths were good old Cornish stock from Ladock and Probus. Dorcas got her name from her grandmother, Dorcas Gerrans. Her father, Richard Carveth, lived at Carvossa and also farmed Bartliver, both now part of the Trewithen estate. What could be more Cornish than these names?

Frederick was born, exotically, in Corfu, where his father had become administrator of the revenues; however, his mother had his birth and baptism faithfully recorded in the margin of the Probus parish register. The father died when only fifty, as Governor of Sierra Leone. Thereafter, Frederick took his mother to live with him in the School House at Rugby, when he became Headmaster. There is a charming photograph of this old lady on the arm of her stalwart son.

When he became bishop of Exeter in 1869, the first thing he did was to renew his ancestral associations. He took his summer holidays first at Nansladron, near St. Austell; the next at Glen Dorgal at Newquay; another in the vicarage at St. Breward. When he went back to his mother's old home at Bartliver, he noticed a cupboard in the dining room she hadn't told him about. She must have remembered everything that was in the old home; he took away a basketful of mosses and lichen and stonecrop from the garden wall.

From the first as bishop of Exeter he was careful to prepare the way for a Cornish diocese – holding ordinations in the county, one of them at St. Mary's, Truro, where the cathedral was to rise. Others have told the story of its founding – or re-founding; how it was made possible by the munificent Lady Rolle's foundation-grant of £40,000, Temple's sacrifice of one-fifth of his income, and the life's work for the cathedral of a St. Austell man, Edmund Carlyon. For a small county, with tin-mining declining and going out, it was all a tremendous and spirited undertaking.

The Cornish side to Frederick Temple's family may continue, for all I know. A Carveth uncle had been a surgeon at St. Austell, and he had descendants – Carveths and Carkeets. The archbishop's son, William Temple, also became archbishop of Canterbury; but, a philosopher, he was more interested in abstractions than in his Cornish inheritance or the concrete facts of life.

Charles Henderson, 1900–1933

It is hard for some of us to realise that it is half a century since Charles Henderson died – particularly for me, for the sense of his presence has accompanied me throughout my life. At every turn and corner, in churches and parishes, in Cornwall – and often at Oxford – I am reminded of him. However, many of you today may not have known him; so the best thing I can do is to recall him for you.[1]

He was indeed an unforgettable figure, who naturally stood out wherever he was, for he was six feet six inches tall. A red, rather rustic complexion, bright blue eyes under rather shaggy eyebrows, his face often lighting up with a smile, for he had a ready sense of humour. I recall the delighted mirth with which he would recount the humours of Cornish folk – when he told me, for instance, about the old Lizard fisherman who in his last illness asked the parson to read him the bit in the Bible about the Lizard lighthouse. 'The Lizard lighthouse?' puzzled the vicar. 'Iss, passon – the sun and the moon and all the Lezzard lights'.

In so many ways Charles was altogether exceptional – no one else quite like him. The most striking thing was his extraordinary precociousness. From the time he was a boy he was engaged in gathering all the information he could about everything that related to Cornwall. He could say, *Nihil Cornubiense alienum a me puto.*

1. An address at the unveiling of the memorial to him in Truro Cathedral, 25 October 1983.

First and most notably with regard to documentation. As still a youth he acquired an easy mastery of medieval handwritings and forms of documents, that many good scholars never achieve. What is more, he was so much at ease with rebarbative manuscripts that he saw through to the significance of what the document was saying – and that again was rare, almost unexampled in one so young. His knowledge of Cornish history then, and of history in general, was based on a solid knowledge of the Middle Ages – the best foundation for it. He was primarily a good medievalist.

From this secure base he launched out in every direction. He had a wonderful sense of topography; it was not only that the landscape came alive for him, but he could read it like a palimpsest, like a document, which it is – it told its own story to *him*. (Most people see nothing.)

For example, he notes that 'Tregear is naturally a common farm-name in Cornwall, and in nearly every case traces of the earthwork which gave rise to it will be seen close to the homestead'. Or again, 'St. Enoder land has always been esteemed very good for corn-growing; and in consequence the parish (especially around Arallas) contains more village earthworks than any other in central Cornwall, except Probus'. And somewhere he tells us that he had spotted several entrenchments around St. Enoder that had been overlooked and forgotten; while at Coombe near Fowey he had been led to detect a destroyed earthwork from the convergence of field-names.

The very detail of his knowledge is again so striking. 'There are fifteen places called Penquite east of Par, and at least eleven to the west of it called Pencoose.' I remember the way he recounted the names of the railway stations coming into Cornwall – the significance of Doublebois, for example, from the two old manors thereby – and his boyish chuckle: 'Then you wake up and find yourself below Par.'

He was really illustrating the linguistic distinction in place-names between East and West Cornwall – he always used to insist, by the way, that we should never underestimate the Cornishry of East Cornwall (even though some of us may think of West Cornwall as a kind of *Bretagne bretonnante*, a fastness of Celtic purity, as Caernarvon is for Wales).

His work throws a good deal of light on the meaning of our place-names, and his collection of their early forms is indispensable for their interpretation. A Guide to Cornish Place Names – and subsidiarily to our Surnames – is the prime necessity today, and it is high time that that came out. Peter Pool's admirable *Place Names of West Penwith* showed us the way: I only wish he could have come up the whole length of the county.

Charles was not a linguist, and I think it is only just to say that we in mid-Cornwall rather under-estimated the good work being done on the Cornish language in the far West, by Morton Nance especially: we were more interested in the historical, Quiller Couch in the literary, I in both. And archaeological knowledge has advanced extraordinarily since Henderson and Hencken's time: it has become so excruciatingly technical that the ordinary scholar has difficulty in knowing what it is all about. I think that that is a pity, and it is contrary to Henderson's inflexion, for he was keen above all to *communicate* his findings to readers – in any form, West Country papers, Diocesan gazettes, pamphlets, brochures, eventually books (alas, too few).

And also, we must remember, to hearers. For, on going down from Oxford, under the aegis of Exeter University, Charles was enabled to undertake a campaign, stimulating interest in the Cornish past by lecturing up and down the length of the county. This gathered in to him many friendships, notably that of dear Q., first of our Cornish writers. Charles himself had been stimulated when young by the encouragement of the old patriarch, Henry Jenner – *doyen* of Cornish studies in his time – and Canon Thomas Taylor of St. Just.

In return Charles encouraged some others – not all. It was curious that he did not care for the *stimmung* of the Tudor period – perhaps that was the medievalist in him. Anyway, he was very ready to encourage my interest in Tudor Cornwall, which really began with the Reformation (it destroyed so much of the Middle Ages – even I didn't like that!) and went on to the excitements of the Elizabethan age, historical and literary, which have occupied me ever since.

So we may say that, though not precisely an initiator, for there were others before him, Charles was our leader: his work in various fields has inspired a lot of work in others, not only by his published work but by his collections. To think of the hopes and promise of the Twenties, when we were young, and the tragedy of today – heart-breaking!

In addition to everything else, he was a great collector, with a passion for documents, thank goodness. For he happened upon a propitious time, in one way: after the first German war, a number of country houses came to an end and cleared out their documents. Charles himself told me that in one or two places he came to, 'Oh, we have just put that old rubbish down a disused well.' (At Stratford on Avon, Shakespeare's heir, Sir John Barnard, consigned all the lumber in the old house, books and papers, to be destroyed. Think of it!) Charles was very good at winkling out of solicitors' offices old papers they did not value. Other houses with historic families were friendly, welcoming and generous to the young scholar: notably the Carew-Poles at Antony, the Eliots at Port Eliot, the Edgcumbes at Mount Edgcumbe, the Rashleighs of Menabilly. Some others not – and that was a loss to us all. For Charles would have put their papers in order for them, and calendared them. As for his collections, they are invaluable to all scholars coming after.

Shortly before his death he made them all over to the Royal Institution of Cornwall. Can he have had some premonition that he would not live long? He was an extraordinarily rapid worker – he could write an article from his notes in a room with other people chatting around him. He had so many gifts: that beautiful handwriting for one, so many of us know. He would write in a railway train, carrying his bottle of purple ink with him, and – instead of a watch – a small Victorian travelling-clock. He was delightfully old-fashioned – modelled on the old country gentry of his family connections; and himself a great gentleman.

Moreover, an excellent map-maker and draughtsman. When he came back to Oxford as tutor in modern history at Corpus, he was so concentrated on Cornish medieval history, so overweighted on Cornwall, that he was behindhand with modern history – in this field amusingly amateur. It fell to me to take him under my wing in modern history and literature – introduce him to the ordinary text books and the creative writing going on in the late twenties, D.H. Lawrence, Virginia Woolf, T.S. Eliot and such.

And Charles responded. In those last years at Oxford he was developing, flowering, restless, catching up on life, racing against time, and moving out into wider fields. As his widow says in her Memoir, he was taking an interest in Italy and Spain, and would talk to me about a book on Charles III of Spain.

I suppose he would have come back to Cornish history eventually. He had begun by thinking of a history of the four hundreds of West Cornwall, from which he went on to think of a Parochial History of all Cornwall – like Polsue's or Gilbert's – though it would have been so much better. It is sad to think that he could have written the history of any parish in Cornwall – for in some ways it is more testing to write the history of a parish than it is to write the history of England (just as it is more difficult to write the biography of a cat than it is the biography of a queen).

This is not the place for a lecture on Charles's work, and all that he did accomplish, notably in his parish histories, in his short life. We must come back to the man, the dear man that he was, one of the two or three best, unflawed, men that I have ever known, along with Q. He lies buried in the famous Protestant cemetery at Rome, along with Keats (of Cornish stock), Shelley's ashes, and the faithful Edward John Trelawny.

When he died, Isobel – so good a classical scholar – wrote to me the beautiful line from Horace:

Quis desiderio sit pudor aut modus
Tam cari capitis?

I could have wished that to be inscribed on his stone; just as I could also have wished – since this cathedral is our Westminster Abbey in which to remember notable Cornishmen who have done honour to Cornwall, the sailors and soldiers, politicians and public figures, neighbour each other on the walls – so too our writers should be together, those friends Charles Henderson and Q., who had such affection for him, and such a high opinion of him.

However, we are all grateful to have him commemorated in the cathedral he regularly attended, at last, after half a century – though for me in all that time his memory has walked along with me in life, and never died.

Dr. Johnson and Cornish Nationalism

A feature of the twentieth century has been the resurgence of the Celtic peoples, now that the unifying influence of the old governing class has broken down: one sees it in Ireland and Gaelic Scotland, Wales and Brittany, and even in my own 'little land' of Cornwall. There is a residual feeling of Cornishry which pops up from time to time in the newspapers, with appeals to revive the old Stannary courts or 'parliaments', attempts to float a currency, what not. And why not, indeed, our own stamps?

In Elizabethan days, Richard Carew tells us, the Cornish feeling that they had been conquered by the Saxons was still very much alive. And English people coming into our little land would find their questions answered, '*Meea navidna cawsa sawznack*' (I can't speak English).

I must say I feel much like that, marooned on my headland, with trippers flooding down the lane asking me the way to it, when there is (or was) a perfectly good signpost to direct them. Sometimes I pretend I speak only Cornish; sometimes that I am deaf and don't reply (in the churlish fashion of Carew's Cornish folk); sometimes I point to the signpost with, 'Can't read, I suppose?' – All exhibitions of Celtic humour, with a good deal in inverted commas which the English never *hear*. After all, one must amuse oneself, marooned on a headland – though I sometimes suspect that some clever folk come down my lane just to observe the tantrums.

I haven't a drop of English blood myself, but I do not go so far as an inter-war pupil of mine, half-Welsh, half-Cornish, at the time when Professor Saunders Lewis was trying to blow up the aerodrome on the Lleyn Peninsula. My pupil wanted to blow up Saltash Bridge, Brunel's masterpiece, which was then our chief link with the mainland. However, the young man married, and that settled his hash.

I have enough atavistic sympathy with Cornish nationalism to wish that we could loosen our subjection to the mainland sufficiently to enjoy a reasonable system of taxation. An historian knows that the English have always been the most taxable of nations, far too submissive to predatory incursions upon their freedom, the shocking extravagances of bureaucratic expenditure, central and local. California set up the standard of revolt from such lunacy.

Wouldn't it be nice if Cornwall could stop penal English taxation at the frontier, with a sensible five-bob in the pound, quite sufficient for all rational purposes? – Only I fear we should have to mount machine-guns along the frontier to prevent the hordes of English, only too submissive (as Celts are not), fleeing from the flaming injustice they put up with, in such numbers as to submerge us.

So my sympathies have to remain in the realm of fantasy – as when I used to assure the famous friend of Proust, Princess Bibesco, who had a cult of Cornwall and a pretty place near Truro, that she would make a splendid *Madame la Présidente de la République Cornouaillaise*.

However, was it all fantasy, I wondered, when only the other day I came upon a passage in Dr. Johnson putting the case of a measure of Cornish independence.

I do not know that that inveterate Englishman got as

far as visiting Cornwall – though he penetrated into the Celtic highlands and the Western Isles. He would have known about Cornwall through Boswell, who visited his friend Temple (ancestor of the archbishops Temple) at Penryn.

The passage occurs in the most famous of Johnson's political tracts, which happens to be on the subject of taxation, which had goaded the American colonies into claiming – and winning – their independence. Dr. Johnson obviously thought that he was reducing the Americans to the absurd, a *reductio ad absurdum*, when he put to them the case of Cornwall.

'As political diseases are naturally contagious', the doctor said, 'let it be supposed for a moment that Cornwall, seized with the Philadelphian frenzy may resolve to separate itself and judge of its own rights in its own parliament. A congress then might meet at Truro, and address the other counties [we are *not* a mere English county but a Little Land on our own] in a style not unlike the language of the American patriots:

'We the delegates of the several towns and parishes of Cornwall hold it necessary to declare the resolutions which we think ourselves entitled to form by the unalienable rights of reasonable beings [in the manner of the American Declaration of Rights], and into which we have been compelled by grievances and oppressions [Penal Taxation for absurd purposes and to support English Bureaucracy], long endured by us in patient silence, because we hoped that others would in time find like ourselves their true interest and their original powers, and all cooperate to proper happiness . . . .

'Know then that you are no longer to consider Cornwall as an *English* county, visited by *English* judges, receiving law from an *English* Parliament, *or included in any general taxation of the kingdom*, but as a state distinct and independent, governed by its own institutions, administered by its own magistrates, and *exempt from any tax or tribute, but such as we shall impose upon ourselves.*

'We are the acknowledged descendants of the earliest inhabitants of *Britain*, of men who before the time of history took possession of the island desolate and waste. Of this descent our language is a sufficient proof, which, not quite a century ago, was different from yours. [Today it is being revived, taught and learnt.]

'Such are the true Cornishmen. But who are you? Who but the unauthorized and lawless children of intruders, invaders and oppressors? [True enough: the incoming English, from the mud-swamps of North Germany and Teutonic forests pushed us into the recesses of *our* land.] In claiming independence we claim but little. We might require you to depart from a land which you possess by usurpation, and to restore all that you have taken from us.

'Independence is the gift of nature. No man is born the master of another. Every *Cornishman* is a free man, for we have never resigned the rights of humanity; and he only can be thought free who is not governed but by his own consent.

'We look to the original of things. Our union with the *English* counties was either compelled by force, or settled by compact . . .

'Against our present form of government it shall stand in the place of all argument that we do not like it. While we are governed as we do not like, where is our liberty? We do not like taxes, we will therefore not be taxed. [Once before, in 1497, the Cornish raised a rebellion against English Taxation.] We do not like your laws, and will not obey them . . .

'We shall form a Senate of our own, under a President whom the King [or Queen] shall nominate, but whose authority we will limit by adjusting his salary to his merit. We will not withhold a proper share of contribution to the necessary expense of lawful government, but we will decide for ourselves what share is proper, what expense is necessary, and what government is lawful . . . .

'If any *Cornishman* shall refuse his name to this just and laudable association, he shall be tumbled from St Michael's Mount, or buried alive in a tin-mine. And if any emissary shall be found seducing *Cornishmen* to their former state, he shall be smeared with tar and rolled in feathers, and chased with dogs out of our dominions.

'From the *Cornish* Congress at Truro.'

Dr. Johnson thought all this was a joke, and that he had demonstrated that the argument of the American colonies was absurd – as he thought that he had demonstrated the absurdity of Bishop Berkeley's philosophical idealism and the reality of matter, by kicking a stone.

But in human affairs, historians know, the absurd sometimes becomes the real. The Americans turned the joke against the Doctor by winning their independence. An old American fan of mine was in college with De Valera in New York: they all thought his Irish nationalism a joke, but the joke came true at last. And the funny thing here is that the English Doctor, without meaning to do so, wrote a very reasonable Declaration of Independence for the Cornish, who share the odd Celtic sense of humour about the English.

The World In Your Pocket

Handy pocket-sized editions of works by classic authors. Many of the titles are not otherwise available in paperback. The series now incorporates Continental and Travel Classics in the same format.

A PASSION IN THE DESERT
Honoré de Balzac

The tales in this volume are among Balzac's best. Written before his long novels and stylistically different, they deal with the romantic, the strange, the bizarre and even the fanciful incidents of life.

ISBN 0 86299 249 4 £2.50

THE JOURNAL OF A DISAPPOINTED MAN
W.N.P. Barbellion

An inspired and expressive masterpiece 'by a scientist with an artist's sensitivity; a literary man with scientific training', who, knowing he was dying of an incurable disease, crammed a lifetime of intensity into his few short years.

ISBN 0 86299 098 X £2.95

ELSIE AND THE CHILD AND OTHER STORIES
Arnold Bennett

A tale of Riceyman Steps, a Five Towns story, and eleven stories set in the London of the 1920s make up this collection.

ISBN 0 86299 210 9 £2.95

HELEN WITH THE HIGH HAND
Arnold Bennett

A splendid domestic comedy set in Bennett's beloved Potteries.

ISBN 0 86299 076 9 £1.95

WHOM GOD HATH JOINED
Arnold Bennett

Bennett on his home ground of the Five Towns. With great sympathy and realism he tells the story of two domestic tragedies which, in their different ways, lead to the divorce court.

ISBN 0 86299 207 9 £2.95

MY FATHER'S LIFE
Rétif De La Bretonne

A brilliant, vivid and noble picture of peasant life in 18th-century France.

ISBN 0 86299 176 5 £2.95

THE BLACK MONK AND OTHER STORIES
Anton Chekhov

Twelve stories characteristic of the Russian master at his best.

ISBN 0 86299 230 3 £2.95

THE BITER BIT AND OTHER STORIES
Wilkie Collins

Tales of detection, mystery and suspense.

ISBN 0 86299 070 X £2.50

THE DEAD SECRET
Wilkie Collins

A story set in a dark mansion in remote Cornwall.

ISBN 0 86299 2524 £3.95

WITHIN THE TIDES
Joseph Conrad

Four tales from this modern master; two set in the East, one in Spain during the Peninsular War and one, telling of the effect of greed, set in home waters.

ISBN 0 86299 099 8 £1.95

CAPTAIN SINGLETON
Daniel Defoe

The fictionalized journal of a maritime adventurer.

ISBN 0 86299 073 4 £2.95

THE HAUNTED MAN AND THE HAUNTED HOUSE
Charles Dickens

Two of the best from the master of the ghost story.

ISBN 0 86299 214 1 £1.95

THE SIGNALMAN AND OTHER GHOST STORIES
Charles Dickens

Stories to be read at dusk in front of a blazing fire.

ISBN 0 86299 152 8 £1.95

THE EXPLOITS OF BRIGADIER GERARD
Sir Arthur Conan Doyle

In Gerard, Conan Doyle created a really memorable and living character, a vain, brave French brigadier with an amusing touch of stupidity, during the Napoleonic Wars.

ISBN 0 86299 148 X £1.95

THE LOST WORLD
Sir Arthur Conan Doyle

The discovery of a nightmare world beyond civilization. A Professor Challenger story.

ISBN 0 86299 072 6 £1.95

THE LADY OF THE CAMELLIAS
Alexandre Dumas

The translation by Edmund Gosse of Dumas' second novel, the tragic story of a doomed affair between a Second Empire courtesan and the son of a respectable family.

ISBN 0 86299 264 8 £2.95

WAY OF REVELATION
Wilfrid Ewart

One of the finest novels to come out of the terrible years 1914–19. Highly praised for its authenticity.

ISBN 0 86299 288 5 £3.95

THE MANCHESTER MARRIAGE
Mrs Gaskell

Six stories representative of Mrs Gaskell at her best, set in the remote mountain valleys of Wales and Lancashire and in the green seclusion of rural England.

ISBN 0 86299 247 8 £3.95

MY LADY LUDLOW
Mrs Gaskell

The doings of 'My Lady Ludlow', her tenants and acquaintances
are revealed with all Mrs Gaskell's skill and not a little humour
and sympathy.

ISBN 0 86299 248 6 £2.95

FATHER AND SON
Edmund Gosse

A beautiful portrait of Victorian life mingling merriment and
humour with discussion of the most solemn subjects and a feeling
for natural history.

ISBN 0 86299 094 7 £1.95

A GROUP OF NOBLE DAMES
Thomas Hardy

Splendidly forged character studies to provide a revealing critique
of Wessex social customs and conventions.

ISBN 0 86299 093 9 £2.50

LIFE'S LITTLE IRONIES
Thomas Hardy

Strongly characterized stories in the Wessex countryside which
Hardy made his own.

ISBN 0 86299 069 6 £1.95

THE STAR ROVER
Jack London

Darrell Standing spent five years of a life sentence for murder in
the 'living death' of solitary confinement. By a series of
self-induced trances he transports himself from the horrors of the
strait-jacket, into other times and places.

ISBN 0 86299 209 5 £3.95

PETER SIMPLE
Captain Marryat

The old sailing navy portrayed with the realism and attention to
detail at which Marryat excelled.

ISBN 0 86299 096 3 £2.95

GRYLL GRANGE
Thomas Love Peacock

Set in the New Forest, full of gentle satire and wit, looking back
to an earlier age before enclosure changed the face of the
landscape forever. A happy book full of memorable characters.

ISBN 0 86299 095 5 £1.95

ANECDOTES OF SAMUEL JOHNSON
Hester Lynch Piozzi (Mrs Thrale)

For nearly twenty years the intimate friend and confidante of
Samuel Johnson recorded a colourful and lively picture of her
lodger, hero and counsellor.

ISBN 0 86299 123 4 £1.95

ASK MAMMA
R.S. Surtees

The life and adventures of the Pringle family.

ISBN 0 86299 165 X £3.95

MR FACEY ROMFORD'S HOUNDS
R.S. Surtees

The triumph of Lucy Glitters, first seen in Mr Sponge, occurs in
this, Surtees' last and probably best novel.

ISBN 0 86299 154 4 £3.95

MR SPONGE'S SPORTING TOUR
R.S. Surtees

Full-blooded character and dialogue, comedy and satire told with
great zest.

ISBN 0 86299 153 6 £3.95

**SAMUEL TITMARSH AND THE GREAT
HOGGARTY DIAMOND**
William Thackeray

One of the most charming of all Thackeray's works, containing
many details of his own married happiness and tribulation and
lot of humour. One of his own favourites.

ISBN 0 86299 182 X £1.95

THE BERTRAMS
Anthony Trollope

A dark comedy from Trollope's early period, covering both
familiar and unfamiliar territory.

ISBN 0 86299 245 1 £3.95

LADY ANNA
Anthony Trollope

A tale of high drama and a struggle for an inheritance, set on th
wild borders of Cumberland and Westmorland.

ISBN 0 86299 181 1 £3.95

AN OLD MAN'S LOVE
Anthony Trollope

Mary Lawrie was twenty five, William Whittlestaff was fifty an
young John Gordon had newly returned from South Africa.
Sparks were bound to fly . . .

ISBN 0 86299 184 6 £2.95

THE THREE CLERKS
Anthony Trollope

The plot moves from Hampton to Cornish tin mines, from
London pubs to Westminster Hall and is certain to keep the
reader engrossed from beginning to end.

ISBN 0 86299 188 9 £3.95

**AN UNPROTECTED FEMALE
AT THE PYRAMIDS AND
OTHER STORIES**
Anthony Trollope

A varied collection of tales ranging from Egypt to the hunting
country of County Mayo, by way of Cumberland, Dartmoor a
Saratoga Springs.

ISBN 0 86299 129 3 £1.95

THE VICAR OF BULLHAMPTON
Anthony Trollope

A perceptive portrait of domestic life and manners in the typic
Trollopian setting of a small Wiltshire town.

ISBN 0 86299 075 0 £3.95

**DOMESTIC MANNERS
OF THE AMERICANS**
Fanny Trollope

Candid and sometimes critical observations of the new Unite
States. An authentic account of a novel society where moment
change and expansion had already begun.

ISBN 0 86299 086 6 £2.95

SMOKE
Ivan Turgenev

Set in Baden where many expatriates from all circles of soc
are working for 'the Cause' – reform in Russia.

ISBN 0 86299 199 4 £2.95

THE FORTUNE OF THE ROUGONS
Émile Zola

The first volume of the Rougon Macquart series which inclu
Nana, Earth and *Doctor Pascal*.

ISBN 0 86299 216 8 £3.95

HIS MASTERPIECE
Émile Zola

Part of the Rougon Macquart series, complete in itself, centring on the art world of Paris in the final years of the Second Empire.

ISBN 0 86299 293 1 £3.95

TRAVEL CLASSICS

ON HORSEBACK THROUGH ASIA MINOR
Colonel Frederick Burnaby

An adventurous ride of 2,000 miles across wild, inhospitable country in the winter of 1876 7 by the author of *A Ride To Khiva*.

ISBN 0 86299 231 1 £3.95

THE BIRDS OF SIBERIA: TO THE PETCHORA VALLEY
Henry Seebohm

In *The Birds of Siberia* Seebohm's narrative skill is put to good use in describing the birds he and Harvie-Brown found, together with vivid descriptions of their exciting experiences in this remote and hostile territory.

ISBN 0 86299 259 1 £2.95

THE BIRDS OF SIBERIA: THE YENESEI
Henry Seebohm

Seebohm was anxious to carry his ornithological and ethnological researches further eastward than those described in *To the Petchora Valley*. In this he was entirely successful but it was a long and adventurous journey. Truly a classic of travel.

ISBN 0 86299 260 5 £2.95

THE WEST INDIES AND THE SPANISH MAIN
Anthony Trollope

Trollope's journey through the West Indies, Central America and British Guiana in 1858/9 is full of personal anecdote told with all the detail and colour of which he was a master.

ISBN 0 86299 220 6 £3.95

PARIS AND THE PARISIANS
Fanny Trollope

The Paris of Chateaubriand, George Sand and Franz Liszt brought vividly to life by the author of *Domestic Manners of the Americans*.

ISBN 0 86299 219 2 £3.95

Prices subject to change

Available from your bookshop. If you wish to be kept up to date with forthcoming titles please write to:

The Sales Department, Alan Sutton Publishing,
30 Brunswick Road, Gloucester GL1 1JJ
England.

ALAN SUTTON PUBLISHING, 30 BRUNSWICK ROAD, GLOUCESTER GL1 1JJ